A Note From the Author

T elling my story is a scary, nerve-wracking proposition, especially to my local community who I betrayed and disappointed. The idea of people in North Dakota or New Mexico reading my book gives me hope the message of porn addiction can happen to anyone will be heard.

In Maine, I know that there are a lot of people who remember the kind of person I was in the couple of years leading up to my arrest. I wouldn't have wanted to do business or be around me either. I know that the personality of the guy I was, coupled with my horrendous crime, will cause many people to refuse to let themselves give my story the time of day.

For a very long time, I wondered what the magic bullet statement I had to say that would get the people who felt most betrayed, or were the most disgusted, to give me a chance. I told myself I wanted the chance to say sorry and not be immediately castigated like Hester Prynne from *The Scarlet Letter*, but I think what I actually wanted was to hear that I wasn't a monster.

This desire was a remnant of the person I once was who needed the approval of others. Back then, I couldn't even pretend to be cool enough to say, "I don't care what other people think." I did. It was one of the only things I cared about.

I have no right to expect anything from anybody. Nobody owes me the time to hear my apology and those willing to listen don't have to accept it. Like I said, I betrayed and disappointed many. They have the right to believe I am incapable of change, and for many, there is nothing I can say or do to change their opinion.

It's hard, but I've accepted this. All I can do is put myself out there and hope that I can do some good creating awareness of this addiction moving forward. As a professional writer, I've told stories about myself for more than two decades. I hope readers can find something to take away from this story, no matter who wrote it.

I'm at a place now where I'm not looking for the public's forgiveness. Only my victims can offer that, and only I can forgive myself. I don't think I deserve it from them, and I'm still working on forgiving myself. I think sharing my story is part of that process. I'm not looking for pity or anyone to rationalize their way to understanding what I did. Feel sympathy and empathy for those I violated, lied to, and treated as less than human—but don't waste those emotions on me.

What you're going to read is, to the best of my recollection, how things happened during my descent into mental illness and addiction that helped create conditions I didn't manage the way I should have.

If I got a date wrong, or tell a story out of order, it is unintentional. This is not a story that needs fiction. I want the average person to know if this can happen to me, it can happen to anyone they know. That may be hard to believe, but if I can get people to understand the realities of porn addiction and its potential ramifications, I'll feel like something was accomplished.

This story isn't graphic because it doesn't have to be. Addictions often lead to illegal behavior. Hopefully my specific illegal behavior doesn't taint the message I'm trying to share.

I very publicly ran a company into the ground while I plummeted toward rock bottom. I could change the names of everybody in the book, but anybody with the slightest ability to use Google could figure out who I'm talking about at every turn. I only changed the names of a couple people. If your name is in here, you were part of my story. Nothing deeper should be assumed than that.

There is nothing I can write that changes what I did because if I could, it would have been written long ago.

The Addiction Nobody Will Talk About

How I Let My Pornography Addiction
Hurt People and Destroy Relationships

Joshua Shea

Joshua Tree
Publishing

• Chicago •

The Addiction Nobody Will Talk About

How I Let My Pornography Addiction Hurt People and Destroy Relationships

Joshua Shea

Published by

Joshua Tree Publishing
• Chicago •

JoshuaTreePublishing.com

Disclaimer:
This book is designed to provide information about the subject matter covered. The opinions and information expressed in this book are those of the author, not the publisher. Every effort has been made to make this book as complete and as accurate as possible. However, there may be mistakes both typographical and in content. Therefore, this text should be used only as a general guide and not as the ultimate source of information. The author and publisher of this book shall have neither liability nor responsibility to any person or entity with respect to any loss or damage caused or alleged to be caused directly or indirectly by the information contained in this book.

Printed in the United States of America

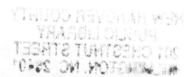

Dedication

To the most important person in my life,
My wife, Melissa
I am lucky to have somebody so loving
and so strong to help anchor my world

Introduction

The ironic part of our exchange was that in real life, I was in a position to help her. Jackie was trying to sell her artwork, mostly large ethereal watercolors and nature photography—both above average in composition and quality—to help pay for a stem cell operation her father's insurance wouldn't cover. I didn't really care though. I just wanted to see her breasts.

If she knew who she was really talking to, I would have asked for jpegs of her artwork, brought it to the people I ran the art gallery with at the back of the office from which I helmed a monthly lifestyle magazine. I would have suggested to them we could help a deserving person raise some money for a potentially lifesaving operation and spin the whole thing to the public and any media who would pay attention so we'd look like good people in the process.

However, in this virtual world, she didn't know she was talking to a 37-year-old part-time art gallery curator, film festival founder, burnt-out magazine publisher, aimless city councilor, neglectful husband and father, and a powder keg with a short fuse.

She thought I was Antony, a 21-year-old personal trainer from Boston, slaving away at his modeling dream in Miami. Why would she think otherwise? That's what was on her screen emanating from my end as we casually chatted on the peer-to-peer cam site Omegle in the wee hours of the morning in October 2013.

My pornography addiction had morphed into even something more sinister, like an X-rated version of the MTV show, *Catfish*. My eyes saw a pretty girl I knew was broadcasting from her bedroom, but she was on the receiving end of a very sick man's game. I'd recently learned how to use certain software and find specific videos that would make it appear she was talking to somebody else. Jackie was talking to a figment of my imagination, played out by a video of somebody I'd never met.

Her story checked out. Jackie was 21 years old and lived with her family in a New Jersey suburb. Her dad was a big deal research scientist at Princeton University who discovered something special about carbon isotopes.

She was your typical chatroom woman who thought they were good at protecting their identity. Her "anonymous" GoFundMe or whatever crowdsourcing page she was using to sell artwork to raise money for her operation, along with the few details she shared about her father were enough for me to start figuring out who she was on half of the computer screen while the Omegle con took place on the other half.

Princeton was forthcoming with information about her father, including plenty about his family in his faculty bio. I found Jackie's name, which led me to her Facebook account, which led me to other social media. Within five minutes of reading the sentence, "He does something with carbon isotopes at Princeton" I could tell you where her mother graduated high school in 1972.

Seeing her breasts was the secondary goal. I mean, sure, I wanted to see her breasts. I like breasts. I have enjoyed them as long as I can remember. She was wearing a T-shirt and shorts and didn't look sick. What I wanted was to figure out a way to convince her to show me her breasts because I knew from experience she was the kind of girl who wouldn't do such a thing in her everyday life. That's what the information gathering and research was about. Could I manipulate her into showing me without her knowing it?

The power to make her do what I wanted despite the fact she didn't realize it was happening was when the real rush happened. That's what my broken mind was after.

There was an article in one of her local newspapers I found online confirming she was trying to raise $40,000 to visit Mexico to try to get the stem cell operation. The story she told me twenty minutes earlier of getting sick her freshman year in college was all true. She didn't lie to me about anything, but beyond her first name, she was smart enough not to share too much, or so she thought. The average person may not have been able to figure out so much about her, but I was more average predator than average person at that point.

The idea I was special, "something more" than the average person, was part of what drove me from my earliest days. Plenty of people could sleuth their way to her life story in under ten minutes, but few could get this complete stranger to bend to their will in another ten. That was my goal. I was going to convince Jackie to show her breasts by whatever means, and once I accomplished my goal, the need to prove to myself I was "something more" was satiated for another night. No matter what horrible thing happened in real life that day, if I could get her to do this, I wouldn't be a total failure.

On her Facebook page, I was able to discern she was a dancer, having taken a lot of ballet over the years based on the number of photos. When she complained about her artwork not having hit $3,000 in sales, I saw an opening.

"Jackie, you don't seem like the kind of girl who would do this, but have you thought about maybe dancing online nude for tips?" I asked. Neither of us spoke, typing our responses. Based on the ambient noise in my headphones, I could tell she was really there. I simply told her that it was 2 a.m. and I had roommates sleeping, so I couldn't respond out loud.

"I could never do that," she said.

"Well, it was just an idea. You're a beautiful woman, and you seem like you don't have those kind of hang-ups and seem like you're open minded and artistic," I said.

"I think the human body is beautiful," she said. "I couldn't just like whip it off for people."

"I guess. You never know until you try. You could do something artistic. Make it your own thing like you do with your paintings and photos. Go at your own pace or your own style. I don't know. Just an idea. Never mind," I said, recognizing I was overplaying my hand too early. "So, tell me more about this place you want to get the operation done in Mexico."

As she began to tell me about a clinic she found, I continued digging for information, discovering a blog she maintained. A month earlier, she wrote about taking belly dancing lessons and how it got her in tune with her "goddess side." The question immediately became: How do I introduce the topic of belly dancing to this conversation?

"I went to Mexico once for a night in Tijuana and hated it," I claimed when she finished telling me about the town where she was hoping the operation would happen. "The only thing I learned while I was there was that belly dancing isn't stripping. It's much classier. It's about so much more."

Her eyes lit up. We'd been talking for about forty minutes at that point, so a rapport had been built. She told me she'd taken lessons and that she was getting pretty good at it.

"Next thing you're going to tell me is that you're also a ballerina," I offered, feeling inside like I was reeling in that night's catch.

"I am! Since I was a little girl!" Jackie said.

"That's your ticket to your lifesaving operation, if you ask me. The artwork is great, but if you're as free with your body as you said earlier, you should at least consider belly dancing for tips," I said.

"I could belly dance and not take my clothes off?" she asked.

"You'd make ten times more if you did. Why don't you show me one of your belly dances? See if you can even dance in your costume for a single person before you start getting any ideas," I suggested.

Within twenty minutes, I had her giving me a topless belly dance in a long, flowing skirt and admitting she thought she might be able to do it for money online. Within forty-five minutes, she was laying on her bedroom floor masturbating. I took a few screen captures of my success, called it a night, and dragged myself to bed for a few hours of sleep.

I wonder if she ever raised enough money for that operation. I hope so.

* * *

I've gone back and forth about telling the story of my fall because it brings me so much shame. It's not only because my pornography addiction eventually led to my arrest on child pornography charges. I was simply a bad person for a long time leading up to the arrest. Anything that appeared altruistic had a secondary motive usually designed to build myself up, or at least protect myself from close scrutiny.

I'll say this a few times in this book, because it needs repeating:

I don't consider myself a victim.

Despite sometimes fumbling my words, I neither minimize, nor rationalize my crimes. I am wholly responsible, have accepted and live with the punishment and sanctions that will follow me for the rest of my life.

Had I been an assistant manager at 7-11 and not a regional celebrity, I would not have had my case played out so publicly in the media. It's the trade-off for so many people knowing who I was in Central Maine. I get it. It took me a long time to realize that being a local celebrity may have been a blessing when it came to my arrest. I don't have closets for my skeletons because the contents of the police reports and investigations were all over the newspapers and evening news. Resenting the fact I couldn't skulk out the side door of the court after a hearing as just another anonymous offender, may have been the wrong reaction at the time. I recognize now it was an opportunity to hopefully do some good. Maybe I can raise awareness the 7-11 assistant manager isn't in a position to create.

* * *

The twenty-two months between my arrest in March 2014 for child pornography possession and my first day in jail in January 2016 were a time of great personal awakening. I learned that while I thought I had been pulling an elaborate con on the rest of the world—making them believe I was a capable, decent, contributing member of society—the ultimate con was the one I was playing on myself. I knew very well that I wasn't the person I presented to the world, but I discovered I also wasn't the Machiavellian prodigy I saw in the mirror.

devoted those twenty-two months to my mental, physical,
spiritual health. I spent ten weeks at an inpatient rehab facility
for alcohol in California and another seven weeks at a facility
for sex addiction in Texas. I also attended 12-Step meetings of
Alcoholics Anonymous and Sex Addicts Anonymous, and I had
hundreds of hours of counseling in Maine. Most importantly, I
spent a lot of time in quiet reflection. When you've lied to yourself
for so long, it takes time to figure out when you've finally reached
the truth. It's not lost on me that in a big way, I was lucky to get
those twenty-two months. Most people never get two months to
work on themselves full-time, much less twenty-two months. I
went to jail a healthier person than I'd ever been. I exited feeling
even better and the improvement continues to this day.

I met so many people in rehab who for reasons I couldn't
fathom more than luck, never got in trouble with the law. I met
a similar amount of people in jail who seemed to be cursed by
life, always in legal trouble and with the kind of background,
addictions, and coping skills that were tragic at best. But whether
it was the disgraced dentist at rehab who fondled his patients
while they were under sedation, leading to him losing his license,
or the guy who stole copper to feed his crack addiction who slept
in the bed next to mine for months in jail, I've met so many people
who have spent most of their lives hurting inside. I met people
with alcohol issues who had been to rehab a dozen times, and I
met people with alcohol issues who had been to jail a dozen times.
They're not very different at the core, and alcohol was never the
only problem.

I didn't develop a pornography addiction overnight, nor did
it veer into illegal territory on a whim. These were both symptoms
of much larger issues, just as my alcoholism, workaholism, lack of
empathy, and overall horrible way I treated people were. Shortly
after my arrest, the porn, alcohol, and work all disappeared from
my life cold turkey. Surprising me at first, the rehabs were where
I began to fix my people skills. I re-learned how to care about
people and treat them the right way with no ulterior motives—
something I hadn't been doing for a long time.

One of the other surprising things about my time in rehab and
jail was seeing how many people don't recognize, or are willing
to admit, they have multiple addictions and multiple obsessive

behaviors in their personality. I had to be shown whatever it was that drove me to collect over 150,000 baseball cards in the 1980s, or made me push away all of my friends in the 1990s, were probably the same things that led me to being an alcoholic with few real friends as an adult. What caused me to play Super Mario Bros. to the point my fingers were cracking, and left me dateless on prom night, might have been some of the same things that led to a porn addiction and turned me into somebody who almost nobody checked in on after he was arrested.

I look back on the way I was and the person I see reminds me of the bad guy characters in professional wrestling. The heel, as they are called in wrestling jargon, is most effective when he doesn't recognize that he's the bad guy in the situation. He believes everything he's doing is right and justified because he has a giant blind spot to the reality of the situation. For many years, I had blind spots, and they just kept growing.

I didn't see, nor understood, why so many people thought I was, for lack of a better term, an asshole. Factor in a life I built where people needed me for certain things, and it's easy to mistreat others as you fall blindly toward rock bottom. Facebook was filled less with good wishes and more with the kind of vitriol the person I was deserved upon my arrest. My specific charge stunned people, but for those who believed that bad people get what's coming to them, it was probably a vindication that the universe knows how to maintain order and not let the kind of person I was get away with things.

* * *

In rehab and jail, I met some of the most real people on earth, once they were willing to let down their guard and accept who they really were. They were never just an alcoholic or just a porn addict. There was always a suitcase full of other issues happening, and addictions are just coping mechanisms to deal with sadness, anger, self-loathing, and fear. Toss in pre-existing mental health conditions, and you've lit a fuse that will eventually go off. Mine was thankfully snuffed out when the police showed up at my door. Had they not, I think my story would have eventually resulted in death, as unfortunately too many stories I know ended.

I decided to finally start putting pencil to paper after many long conversations with a thirty-year-old guy I met in jail named Tom. He was busted on a probation violation for a dirty urine test. Life got the better of him, and he succumbed to heroin again. He was awaiting a hearing to find out if he'd have to go serve the rest of the armed robbery sentence he was released early from only six months prior.

He had done three of the five years he was given for robbing a McDonald's after hours. His ex-girlfriend was a manager, and he knew they transferred a giant amount of money from the time-locked safe to the bank on Tuesday nights between 11 and midnight. He jimmied open the drive-thru window, made his way to the manager's office, and took over $5,000. Tom wore a mask, and if not for the unique handle on the gun he used being captured on security camera footage, he never would have been apprehended months later.

Tom needed the money to pay some very, very scary people off from whom he had purchased heroin. Despite being a good-looking guy who probably could have been a model before the drugs and one of the smartest, most-well rounded people I've met, heroin had Tom in its grips and even three years away from dope while in prison wasn't enough to stop.

With many long, personal conversations about his shitty upbringing and lack of parental guidance, I saw in Tom what I saw in myself at the time of my arrest: a scared little boy who didn't know how to make his way in the world and just wanted to be loved. I tried not to make connections with anyone in jail, but despite our many differences, we were very much the same.

The day I started writing this book was the day Tom asked me about sex addiction. He wondered if he was a sex addict. He liked porn, but since his first consensual sexual experience at twelve (his first non-consensual was around the time he entered kindergarten), he'd been with over eight hundred women. He knew the answer, and I think it was the first time he ever really admitted to himself that his addictions went further than drugs.

When I asked why he never mentioned it to me, he said he was more embarrassed by the sex than the heroin. I knew what he meant. It's easy to talk about my alcoholism openly. I'm seen a hero by some for trying to conquer that beast and people congratulate me for going to rehab and being sober for over three years at the time I write this. Those same people who want to pat me on the back and shake my hand for dealing with alcohol addiction don't want to touch me and go searching for hand sanitizer when I mention porn addiction or sex addiction rehab.

Tom's admission made me reflect on the people I met who entered rehab for a drug or alcohol problem, but after spending time with admitted sex and porn addicts, they came to realize their sexual behavior was often negative and many times an unhealthy coping mechanism. Tom was just recognizing this. I've seen a lot of these "a-ha!" moments when people first connect-the-dots and realize their sexual behavior may be an addiction. It's powerful, and sad.

I never hit the town late at night needing to find a random stranger to satisfy my sexual needs . . . the pages of a magazine or a computer screen had been enough for me, but I understood every one of their stories. I understood the story Tom was finally brave enough to share. I don't know how many people are out there like us, but the few statistics that do exist make me think it's staggering.

According to the National Coalition for the Protection of Children & Families, 47% of families in the United States reported that pornography was a problem in their home in a 2010 survey. Keep in mind, this statistic comes from a time *before* the public was able to stream adult content into homes with services like Netflix or Hulu. It comes before social media like Instagram or Snapchat were being used by so many people. I haven't seen a more recent statistic, but there is no way that 47% figure has dropped since that survey was released.

If that's not disturbing enough, every second of the day an average of 29,000 people are watching pornography on the Internet. They're part of the 40 million who say they use the Internet for pornography and likely contribute to the 68 million searches for pornographic material every day, 116,000 of which are for underage material.

I wrote the first draft of this book sitting at the desk next to my bed in jail into four composition notebooks with around fifty of those pencils you use to score miniature golf. The commissary didn't sell pens or real pencils for fear the bad boys and girls in

Androscoggin County Jail would stab each other or make tattoo guns. It seems like an unfounded fear to me, but as a resident of a minimum-security pod under protective custody, I never saw anything more physical than a couple of guys take defensive postures with each other. I think they kept the dangerous criminals downstairs.

The first draft of this book was between 180,000 and 200,000 handwritten words. The version you hold is about 91,000 words. Despite nobody ever seeing the discarded half, it was cathartic getting those years of turmoil out of my head and onto the pages while I was sitting in jail. It allowed me to get lost for 6-10 hours every day while others played cards, slept, watched TV and paced the pod.

The bulk of this book is told in the last couple of years leading to my arrest because it was a time when my various addictions and different coping mechanisms I used to deal with people intersected at their worst points. The trail of people negatively affected in my wake is long. While I can't go back and fix the wrongs my addictions and boorish behavior caused, I can let people know what was going on in my head and behind closed doors at the time.

I was a sick, but functional person for a lot of my life—and then I was a very sick and very dysfunctional person for a small stretch leading to the super-public collapse of my professional life. I hope that my memories and feelings regarding the events recalled on the coming pages don't hurt anybody mentioned too deeply. For anybody I wronged, you're always welcome to come and talk things out with me. I think you'll find a much different person than the one you knew before. You might actually like me this time around.

For the vast majority reading this who have never heard of me prior to picking up this book and have no connection to anybody mentioned within, I simply ask you to recognize there are a lot of people like me out there who can't tell their story, and even more who would never dream of it because they haven't been confronted with their addiction or crime.

This addiction goes far beyond perverts hiding in the bushes or living in their mother's basements. It's hidden by doctors and lawyers and school teachers who don't want anybody to know their worst secrets. Hopefully, by sharing my story, they feel a little less alone and those who don't have an addiction recognize you shouldn't stereotype those coping with it.

I ask every time you think to yourself, "Why didn't he ask for help?" use that same judgment in your own life when things get difficult. And once you're done, file this book under "Cautionary Tale."

Chapter 1

I hadn't seen Paul Roy in a dozen years. I barely recognized the younger brother of my best-but-rarely seen friend Marc. I was only 70% sure it was him. The full head of whitish-gray hair and natural aging process forced me to carefully examine the man.

It was him. Paul was sitting next to his wife, Kate, at one of the many long tables crammed into the restaurant's function room in Alexandria, Virginia. We'd both come down from Maine to attend my brother Patrick's first wedding. Since his bride, Valerie, was from Virginia, attendance was tipped heavily in her favor against my brother's New England contingent.

Later that night, my wife, Melissa, would point out to me I ignored her and the kids at dinner, choosing to spend it locked in conversation with Paul. Neither of us saw it for the omen it was.

Paul took a few days off from his job selling cars in Southern Maine for the wedding. He was good at the job, though it was thoroughly uncreative. I was barely making a dime, yet enjoying my time as an editor and publisher for a weekly newspaper, *The Independent*, located in Windham, about 30 minutes south of my home in Auburn. I told Paul that ever since George Bush let the world know of the banking and housing crisis eight or nine months earlier, our revenue had plummeted. Cuts were made, but I knew eventually I'd have to create a second, successful publication.

A day later, as Patrick's reception was coming to an end, Paul approached me.

"I'd love to try to do something for your newspaper," he said.

I gave him my business card.

After a few days of back and forth through email once home, we settled on the idea he'd try writing a slice-of-life column with few boundaries. We both knew Paul had something inside that just wasn't bubbling up to the surface.

This something, however, was not writing. It was surprising how off-the-mark the submitted columns turned out. I broke the bad news but suggested we brainstorm. Paul and I met regularly during the summer of 2009 at Applebee's in Westbrook, just outside of Portland.

We'd drink beer, shoot the shit, and try to figure out how he could best fit into the mix. He just had that something. I needed to figure out what it was and exploit it.

* * *

Working with Paul on a daily basis would have stirred things up in my life. While the newspaper had freelance writers who were never in the office and several ad sales people I almost never saw, I worked directly with only one other person every day. Corey Gilding was the shy and gruff page designer at *The Independent* who became a fast friend when I first started in 2006. The large, multi-pierced 30-year-old bought a piece of the company a few years earlier when the newspaper was launched. Corey was a minority owner while it's founder was a cool, stereotypical Italian guy of about fifty-five years old, Donato Corsetti.

For years, neither Corey nor Donato knew how to run a newspaper business from top-to-bottom. When I came in as editor, four years after *The Independent* was born, it blew my mind they didn't follow a few tenants to newspaper publishing I'd seen everywhere else. They never changed the layout of the front page, never published unhappy, real news, and didn't determine how many pages an issue was based on the number of ads sold. I changed these things, along with adding special advertising sections to generate revenue and giving Corey design lessons.

After five months as the editor, Donato came into my office on a Thursday afternoon, the day after the newspaper came out and offered me the job of Publisher.

I made the mistake of telling Corey I had bipolar disorder early in my employment. He either was ignorant to the condition or had somebody in his life prior who must have suffered from it worse than me because when he disagreed with an idea I had that seemed too radical, he'd often ask if I was feeling manic.

Telling him stories of my mania didn't help either because I saw them as awesome war stories, not the tragic tales I see today. He had a fairly steady, risk-averse life from what I could tell. His parents divorced when he was young, and he had a brother in prison out-of-state. When I told tales of hanging out with professional baseball players in Japan, blowing $1,000 a night on strippers and champagne, or jumping in my car and just driving with no plan—all things I did in my early 20s—he seemed more horrified than amused.

Doing anything that deviated from the norm at the office at first freaked him out. While he never came around to embracing new things, I think he realized after a while that trying to grow the company was not connected to my bipolar disorder.

Before I took over as publisher, Donato sometimes kicked in a lot of money every week to print the newspaper. Despite the economy collapsing shortly after I took over, he didn't need to contribute a dime under my watch except in rare circumstances. The writing was on the wall, I told him and Corey. If we wanted to stay at least break even, the newspaper couldn't be our sole publication in 2010.

* * *

The idea for a magazine had lived in my mind for years. After seeing the glossy lifestyle magazines produced in Portland and Bangor, the two most populated cities in Maine, it seemed like there must be a market for a similar magazine in Lewiston, where I was born and grew up, and Auburn, where I'd made my home with my wife and two kids since 2004. Combining the number of people in Lewiston and Auburn produced a number larger than Bangor's population. The biggest hurdle I saw was that the Twin Cities were a cultural wasteland with no arts, dining, or entertainment scene.

The newspaper's ad sales team was still solid, and we usually eked out a tiny profit (always under $500) every week. This was a place where $100 meant something to the bottom line. Our coffers weren't brimming, but they had enough to launch a new project.

At what would be our last Applebee's meeting, I pitched the full idea of the magazine to Paul. We'd hopefully debut at forty-eight pages, although I knew that was optimistic. Since the idea had been floating around in my head in the abstract for years, I had some clue what the magazine would look like. I explained to Paul my broad goals of a high-quality product that would be read by the movers and shakers of Lewiston and Auburn. I wanted the content to be can't-miss and the people who created the magazine to be known by those who read it.

"This has to look better than anything in Lewiston-Auburn have ever seen. We want them to judge this book by its cover," I explained. "With what we're going to create, we have to be seen as an exclusive magazine for the people in that upper level of living. There are people with money in this community. These people are the most attractive customer base for our advertisers," I told Paul.

"It should sell itself, without a lot of pressure," recognized Paul. I could tell the wheels were turning in his head, contemplating a life not selling automobiles.

"After a few issues, we want people to pick up the magazine not because of what's on the cover, but because they know it will be great on the inside," I said, hoping he was buying most of the bullshit coming off the top of my head.

I told Paul that I didn't think there would be any opposition to launching a magazine, but we had to accept the friendship we had was going to have to change. He recognized it would never be the same; yet, this was a chance to build something from Day One in the place we grew up that had never been seen before.

We agreed on the title Director of Sales, but both knew our titles were only labels for our business cards. We'd do whatever we needed to make a great magazine. Something in my heart said that more than me, Paul was going to be the key to the magazine's success.

Upon pitching the idea, Corey said it was clear I was excited about a magazine and my heart would be in that project. Once decided, the next stop for Corey and I was a meeting with Donato. I don't remember if I made up any fake statistics or numbers showing how well we would succeed, but it seems like something I would have done at the time. I think Corey endorsed the idea because it meant designing a magazine from scratch. He'd evolved into a great designer and knew a magazine would let him flex his creative muscles in a way a newspaper didn't allow. Donato didn't seem to care either way. He just had a "This Better Not Cost Me A Dime" mentality.

I told them I was going to hire Paul as a full-time employee to help launch the magazine, and I would split my time between the magazine and *The Independent*, which I had running like a well-oiled, low-income producing machine.

* * *

Paul started as Director of Sales in mid-November of 2009, just as I created an outline for the magazine's content and how it should be organized, letting Paul and Corey help fine-tune the details. I started a relationship with a magazine printer in Hooksett, New Hampshire, after receiving the best pricing for what we needed.

I designed a rate card for ads and wrote up a one-page synopsis of what the magazine would mean to Central Maine and what could be expected in every issue. I asked Corey to mock-up a few fake covers to give businesses an idea where their money was going. We'd pull all of this together for our press kit to show prospective advertisers.

The only problem, Corey pointed out as he was creating these materials, was that we'd never settled on a name or a logo.

Paul and I gathered behind Corey at his computer at the last possible minute to figure it out.

"I always saw it being called *Lewiston-Auburn Magazine*," I said.

"That's it?" Corey asked.

"It's not inspired, but it's to the point," I offered.

We agreed on the direct route and decided style-wise there would be no hyphen between the words "Lewiston" and "Auburn." It would be Lewiston Auburn, not Lewiston-Auburn.

My only argument for going against the norm was that I thought a hyphen looked like shit on a magazine cover.

Corey mocked-up an accompanying "LA" logo in red, blue, and green variations that reminded me of the Los Angeles Dodgers, but I kept my mouth shut. We considered all three options, deciding red was the best.

We could have run focus groups, surveyed people, and tested mock covers on potential readers and advertisers. Instead, in the course of five minutes, our name, logo, and color scheme was complete. New business owners shouldn't waste valuable start-up money on "branding experts."

There is one important question: Will this logo look good on the outside of the building and on coffee mugs? That's it. Make it roughly a square and make sure it's only one color. If your business has a superior product or service, people will remember it. If you can't manage that, it's not the logo's fault.

We penciled in April 2010 as our official public launch, also deciding we'd publish every other month, for five total issues in 2010.

Once the promotional material was finished, Paul went back to the cold call grind. Corey began working on that week's newspaper, and I retired to my office to contemplate our next steps. The Monday after Thanksgiving 2009, Paul and I began the pre-launch of *Lewiston Auburn Magazine*.

Chapter 2

This was not the first magazine I'd launched. Six years earlier, in 2003, I published a newsprint-quality publication in Portland called *Metro*.

Brian Wallace, a friend of mine who I'd originally met through his ex-wife, was newly remarried and his bride, Heather Payson, loved my idea for a free, twice-monthly magazine catering to "socially active professionals." They decided to buy into ownership of the magazine, providing me with enough money to live while it got off the ground.

Heather came from a wealthy family, loved the creative end of the magazine, and regularly poured thousands of dollars into each issue. This behavior covered the cancerous flaws in our business model. I can create a magazine or newspaper all day long, but running a business is a different beast altogether. Sales, distribution, human resources, legal documentation—it was all an unknown blur I mostly ignored, choosing instead to drink the days away with Brian.

While the initial undoing was the amount of time Brian and I spent hanging out and boozing on Heather's dime, it became clear none of us were exactly the poster children for good mental health, especially Heather.

Brian, crazy in his own special way, saw Heather getting sicker as she poured more time and resources into the magazine. He got upset with me because while I saw it happening, I also saw her money as the only way *Metro* could stay afloat and didn't intervene to stop her. I chose business over friendship, leading to a tense crescendo where I couldn't tell if I was playing them off of each other or if they were playing me off one another. It was probably both: a triangle of sick people who had no business being in business together.

Although I had begun seeing a therapist at the time, I was still a few years away from being diagnosed with bipolar disorder and PTSD. I was on low levels of anxiety meds but didn't yet understand the extent to which I was mentally ill.

Shortly after Heather's predicted full-on breakdown, she and Brian pulled away from the magazine, retaining their ownership stake but never again contributing for the eight months *Metro* survived after their departure.

It was not the first time, nor the last, I'd exit a business with an acrimonious relationship with my partners.

Five years earlier, I briefly co-owned a professional wrestling company that produced shows in Northern New England. After one show, my partners—a couple of wrestlers who never made it to the big time—caught wind that I had not paid for liability insurance on that particular show. Had there been an accident, we would have been in major trouble. They asked me to walk away—and I reluctantly did. A few months earlier, they stopped letting me write the storylines, so all the fun was gone anyway. Not having the script was like not having any control.

And yes, I did actually wrestle a few times. Naturally, as a bad guy.

* * *

On the Monday after Thanksgiving, Paul and I met at my house in Auburn, ready to hit a couple meetings I had set up.

Both meetings were in the same building on Lisbon Street, the primary street running through Lewiston's downtown. It intersected with Main Street on one end, and about 10 miles in the other direction, it ended at the Lisbon town line. That last half-mile leading into Main Street was once a commerce Mecca in Maine. Lewiston was known worldwide for its manufacturing of both textiles and shoes from the start of the 20th Century up through the early 1970s. When Americans stopped caring about quality, the mills closed, laying off thousands. In turn, the department stores, restaurants, and specialty shops on Lisbon Street went out of business. By the mid-1980s, Lisbon Street was a ghost town.

Having been born in Lewiston in 1976, I have faint memories of a few of the department stores, but my memories of downtown are mainly as a drug-addled ghetto until the late 1990s. An influx of several thousand African immigrants, mostly Somali, changed the dynamic of downtown Lewiston. They filled the vast number of vacancies in the nearby low-income and subsidized housing neighborhoods once populated by millworkers' families. Without local stores offering the dietary or cultural needs of these new citizens, two blocks of empty storefronts came alive. Immigrants opened markets, restaurants, and clothing stores in an area some dubbed "Little Somalia."

I have no real perspective if Lewiston and Auburn are truly unique in terms of a mix of socioeconomic demographics, history, and prevailing attitudes. With the exception of six years in the super-diverse Portland, a year at college in Bristol, Rhode Island, and six months in Tokyo, I've never lived outside of Androscoggin County. Until the influx of Somali immigrants, everybody was either White, Catholic, and Irish or White, Catholic, and French.

I read Ira Levin's *The Stepford Wives* when I was in high school. Lewiston and Auburn reminded me of Stepford, except without the careful planning. It was a homogenous group that despite minor differences, largely acted, thought, and lived the same life. People weren't bad by any stretch. Most were very decent, but they didn't appear happy to my younger eyes. Most of my schoolmates were as down on Lewiston as I was at the time in the early 1990s.

It seemed like if you were born here, people went to church because they were supposed to, which is why you, too, went and it was just better not to question the routine. If you were a boy, you were going to play youth ice hockey for your church team. If you were a girl, you were going to be a cheerleader for that team. By the time high school came, it was pretty well established that a small group of kids would leave and go make something of themselves in the "real world" while everyone else cultivated lives locally. Eventually, it would be your turn to get married. You'd buy the same kind of ranch house you grew up in. Odds are your spouse, also from Lewiston or Auburn, grew up in a similar one. You'd have kids and raise them in the church because you were supposed to and knew not to question the routine. Rinse, wash, repeat.

It was a safe place to grow up, and people always said it was a nice place to raise a family, but being on the end of the raising side, I would have much preferred my parents moved us somewhere else. I never felt like I was part of the modern culture or life I saw on television, only happening in places we visited on summer vacation. Lewiston and Auburn was frozen in time and frozen in mindset.

We're not talking about Mayberry from *The Andy Griffith Show*. The combined population of Lewiston and Auburn has hovered around 60,000 my entire life with Androscoggin County just over 100,000. They aren't small numbers, especially by Maine standards. The sameness in everything and everybody was eerie but simultaneously provided a sense of security. Nothing out of the ordinary happened here.

I've been to plenty of communities of this size throughout the United States. Most seem to exist mainly as bedroom communities for larger cities. There are nearly two dozen cities in Massachusetts between 40,000 and 70,000 and almost all exist simply in service of Boston. People sleep there at night but live their lives elsewhere. That's not the case with Lewiston and Auburn. This place has a personality all its own.

The new millennium sparked a new interest in Lisbon Street. The courthouse, pawn shops, and Somali stores were joined by a smattering of new business ventures, most notably Fuel restaurant.

A native of Lewiston-Auburn, Eric Agren left a successful job in advertising in Chicago to—almost comically—open the fanciest restaurant downtown Lewiston had seen in decades. In the adjoining storefront he owned, he donated space to the local arts organization, L/A Arts, to curate a legitimate art gallery, called Gallery 5. The whole thing sounded like a ridiculous idea when I heard about it, but Agren proved the naysayers wrong with his French restaurant. He showed Lewiston could support high-end ideas and watching his success from a distance partly convinced me a glossy magazine could have legs.

Paul and I entered Key Bank Plaza, and I pointed out the Androscoggin County Chamber of Commerce on the first floor, where our second meeting was to be held. We were heading to the fourth floor, the offices of the Lewiston-Auburn Economic Growth Council (LAEGC). It was a quasi-governmental agency tasked with spurring the local economy by attracting new businesses. With a stagnant, under-skilled population and little movement in property value, the LAEGC mostly helped the region remain at a plateau. The biggest problem is most of the smart kids don't return after college, and despite being home to Bates College, Lewiston and Auburn never see an influx of young talent mainly due to the lack of high-paying specialized employment opportunities.

I wanted to meet with Paul Badeau, the LAEGC's marketing director. Badeau was a quiet, smart guy. What he lacked in outward enthusiasm he made up for in knowledge and execution.

After ushering us to a large conference room and making introductions and pleasantries, Badeau cut to the point.

"What is this magazine you talked about in your e-mail?" he asked.

"We're starting a high-end lifestyle magazine. If Bangor can have one and Portland can have one, why can't Lewiston and Auburn?" I asked, recognizing this was the first chance I had to develop my concept pitch on its target audience. It would be fine-tuned and repeated hundreds of times.

"You do know it's not exactly the greatest economy?" asked Badeau. "We're very different from Portland and even Bangor."

"Yes, but some publishing company from outside of Maine is going to come here and do it. The market is here. I want to be first. Paul and I both grew up here. I still live in the community, and we both have plenty of family and friends who call it home. If somebody is going to try this, it should be two guys from here," I said, far more passionately than I expected.

Badeau gave me a conciliatory nod and began to look at our press kit. He urged us to immediately get a website together if for no other reason than to reserve a domain name and provide a telephone number to contact.

He wished us luck at the end of the meeting, but his tone and body language were not suggesting belief in the magazine.

Our next meeting was with Chip Morrison, the big cheese at the Chamber of Commerce. Chip looked much older and thinner than I remembered, having written about him when I worked at the local daily newspaper, the *Sun Journal* years earlier. He appeared more like a kindly grandfather than I recalled. A mischievous grin I remembered from years earlier was still there, and it was a grin I would grow to love.

Chip couldn't have been more gracious or welcoming. We began a relationship that day lasting until the very end of the magazine. He became a professional sounding board, advisor, and the magazine's greatest cheerleader.

Unlike Badeau, Chip was immediately excited with our idea, telling us what a great thing *Lewiston Auburn Magazine* could be for the community. Spouting a handful of sound bites I stole for my future sales pitches, I approached the subject I knew to be the key to the magazine's success.

"I'd like to send the first issue to every member of the Chamber of Commerce and after that alternate issues between the top and bottom halves of your membership list, like A-M and then N-Z—or however it works out," I said holding my breath. I hoped the list wasn't as closely guarded a secret as the formula for Coca-Cola.

"That would be a terrific member benefit!" Chip exclaimed. "That's just terrific!"

"So, we can have the mailing list?"

"Absolutely! Just ask Maureen in the office for it when you're ready. What about becoming a member?"

"We have no money. We could trade for an ad," I suggested.

"Sure! Just contact Maureen with the specifics," he said.

Telling potential advertisers that Chamber of Commerce members would receive the magazine for free could deliver the exact consumer they craved. In retrospect, this was probably the most important meeting the magazine would ever have.

Day one went well, I mentioned to Paul as we left. Very, very well.

* * *

The Independent kept me busy the next few days. I knew I couldn't let the quality of our flagship product slip. Without making an extra dime, I doubled my workload overnight. Paul spent those days working from his home, trying to set up sales appointments.

I'd recently hired a new sales manager at the newspaper. Doug Grossett was a tall, smart guy around my age. We got each other's pop culture references, he sailed through his initial interview and was a supremely nice guy, but he had trouble out of the gate at the newspaper.

Doug was never going to be a major sales presence at the magazine by design, but I thought it was important he at least knew the sales pitch to cross-sell in case an advertiser in *The Independent* wanted to attract an audience from Lewiston and Auburn. I asked him to join Paul and I that Friday, the slowest day at the newspaper, to visit potential magazine advertising clients Paul lined up.

The first was Central Maine Medical Center, Lewiston's largest hospital and the second or third biggest in the state. They advertised everywhere. If we were ever walking into a slam-dunk, this was going to be it.

I don't recall the woman's name we met with, but it was immediately clear she wasn't the final decision maker. We met with her in the hospital's cafeteria, and I began improvising a speech about how we were going to bring something to the area never seen before, but her demeanor was the opposite of Chip's. It threw me off a little, especially when she quasi-insulted our veracity.

"There have been a lot of people to come through here over the years, tell us they were starting this or that, and we never see them again," she commented.

"We're not asking you to pay in advance," I said. "I've been in publishing long enough not expect anybody to pay for an ad up front."

"OK, let's see what kind of deals you've got," she said.

Before Paul – who was the magazine's director of sales – could speak, Doug jumped in.

"Oh boy, do we have deals for you! You're going to love these deals!" Doug exclaimed, pulling out a rate card. "Here's how to read this . . . "

"I've seen rate cards before," she interrupted. She looked it over, gathering together the other pieces of the press kit. "OK, give us a call closer to your publication date."

We shook hands and left.

After lunch, we headed over to one of the few advertising and marketing agencies in Lewiston or Auburn, Rinck Advertising.

The three of us waited in their lobby until a nearby door opened. Several people streamed out, and the receptionist brought us in.

Peter Rinck, an unassuming looking guy was at the head of the table. I couldn't tell if he was interested in what we had to say or if he was taking the meeting out of pity on a windy Friday afternoon. He appeared stern, but kind.

We introduced ourselves to Peter and his two co-workers. A woman, who introduced herself as Laura Davis, co-owner and Peter's wife, popped in to say hello. She had once been the "cool" sixth grade teacher at my elementary school almost twenty-five years earlier, but I never had her as a teacher.

I started pitching the concept of the magazine to the Rinck Advertising team.

"What you're doing is trying to make people proud of living here," Peter observed.

"That's exactly it!" I said, glad somebody came up with what I hadn't been able to put into words. From this point forward, I always referred to the magazine as "the chance for residents to the tell the rest of the state we're proud of where we came from, where we live now, and where we're heading."

"There's something going on around here now. There's an energy building," Peter said. I stole that line for my future pitches, too.

Nobody who lived in Lewiston or Auburn liked being mocked or hearing bad things about our cities, especially when they weren't true. It was like the brother or sister who annoyed you and you earned the right to pick on, but whose defense you'd come to if anybody else tried. *Lewiston Auburn Magazine* was going to be about pride, and it was about tapping into and highlighting the new energy, while also fondly recalling the area's better days.

"So, who's ready to see a terrific rate card?" said Doug out of the blue, completely killing the conversational flow. We recovered from Doug's abrupt interruption, and Peter nodded at the rate card.

"This is a good place to start. I think Mechanics Savings Bank is a good fit," Peter said.

"Well let's sign them up! Who else you got?" said Doug.

"We'll have to take a closer look at this first and talk to them," Peter explained.

"I'll be in touch soon," said Paul. He and I were both able to see Peter's body language was telling us the meeting was over. We shook hands with them and left.

Selling with Paul and Doug that day taught me that if the magazine was going to get off the ground, the people involved had to really care. This was a passion for Paul, it was a job for Doug. This couldn't be just another job. It was a start-up that needed passion more than timeclock punchers.

A few days later, without Doug's "help", Paul closed a three-issue back cover deal with Mechanics Savings Bank through Rinck Advertising. We had our first paying advertiser.

* * *

I never kept a chart, but I know the frequency of intimacy with my wife, Melissa, dropped when I started working on the magazine. I returned to the familiar crutch of pornography to take care of certain needs.

Much like the first time I had a glass of champagne or bottle of beer and knew I'd found something special, there was a sense of awe and wonder—as if the universe had just shared one of its great secrets with me—upon seeing my first pornographic magazine when I was seven or eight years old.

Uncle Bill, my dad's younger brother, had rented a small house at Old Orchard Beach for a week during the summer, and we visited a few times. Scott, my eleven-year-old cousin who never hid his love for the ladies while I've always felt a level of shame for my animalistic tendencies, called me up to his bedroom. He pulled three copies of *Penthouse* from under his bed.

He claimed to have stolen them from the store. It wasn't until years later that I realized most stores didn't carry three months worth of issues. It was more than likely my cousin simply discovered them at the summer house than pulled off what I thought was a brilliant heist.

I'd seen naked women on HBO. My mom would get flustered and tell my father to change the channel when that happened, likely adding to my fascination. It's probably a good thing she didn't care about me seeing scenes of violence, or I would have grown up wanting to collect guns. These women in *Penthouse*, though, were not like the ladies on HBO.

Now, I had an up-close-and-personal look at what was hiding beneath the underwear HBO kept on the ladies. I also saw what men with erections liked to do with these women. I knew how babies were made in theory, but what these tanned, sweaty people were doing on the pages of this magazine seemed far more recreational than simply for the sole purpose of creating another human.

There was a dangerous side to what Scott and I were doing. We knew our parents wouldn't want us seeing magazines like this. There's a reason they were dubbed "dirty magazines." I flipped through the pages looking at each pictorial like an archaeologist who just discovered a new fossil. An occasion like this deserved time to examine and reflect, but when Uncle Bill yelled up the stairs it was time to head to the beach, Scott just popped the magazines under the bed.

I got scared because I had an erection. Seeing these women who wanted to have their pictures taken with their clothes off while men—who had erections—fondled them was exciting. I managed to hide what was happening to me with a beach towel and was back to normal by the time we left the house.

Those images were seared into my brain. Over the next five or six years, I don't think I saw another pornographic magazine and had yet to see a real porno movie, but the memories of the five minutes with those magazines burned deep. I wanted more.

Lord knows what possessed me to try, but at thirteen-years-old, I walked into a convenience store and bought a *Playboy*. This was still when they weren't behind the counter, in plastic wrap. The little, independent convenience stores would probably have sold me beer and cigarettes if I put them on the counter back then, too. I don't think I missed an issue of *Playboy* for the next four years. I never had the nerve to buy *Penthouse*.

It didn't take long to discover I could also rent movies from an independent video store's pornographic section when I was fourteen. Keep in mind, 99.9% of us still weren't connected to the Internet even with the slowest of dial-up. I went from having no access to pornography outside of what HBO might show to whatever magazine or video I wanted. I knew I wasn't supposed to have them and that my parents wouldn't have wanted me to collect *Playboy* magazines or rent hardcore porn. That element of danger just made things even more exciting, just like wondering if someone was going to walk in on Scott and I looking at the magazines he allegedly stole all of those years earlier.

If Scott had shown me that *Penthouse* in 2004 instead of 1984, I could have gone home and found more on the Internet. There wouldn't have been any five-year waiting period to get my nerve up to try and buy a *Playboy* or rent a porno. But the danger that came with it—the fear that I was going to be found out—was a big part of that high. The next generation only had to click the tab that said "Clear Browser History" and the danger was gone. My experience came with that adrenaline rush of danger. It was as exciting as the porn itself.

* * *

I didn't share a lot of details about *Lewiston Auburn Magazine* with Melissa, but that was because I didn't want to build it up and have it fail. She saw *Metro* go down the tubes, and I didn't want to tell her just how much this was "my thing" to make or break until I could see it all play out a while. If I made it, I could surprise her. If I broke it, I could limit the embarrassment by hiding it meant much more than just another product the company was creating. I couldn't tell you exactly why—maybe it was because I wasn't rich, famous, successful, and was still living within five miles from my parents—but I felt like a failure in my early 30s. Staying quiet about *Lewiston Auburn Magazine* mitigated being seen as a failure in her eyes.

Melissa was two hours late to our first date in 2002. A couple weeks later she tried to break up with me, but I said no. Either it was a test on her end, or I cajoled my way back into her heart. One of us was a master manipulator that day. Some people would have seen that as a red flag, but I was going to fight for this one. I was able to do one thing with her that I never really could with another woman: be myself on the telephone.

It may seem minor, but talking on the telephone is tantamount to getting my toenails cut by very dull scissors from an elderly woman with shaky hands. I'll avoid it at all costs. I met Melissa shortly after I turned twenty-six, and in the prior decade or so I'd been dating, if I could last fifteen minutes on the phone, it was like a marathon. With her, four hours would breeze by. It was a sign something was different with this one.

She was pregnant within three months of us being together, and I proposed to her a month or so after we found out. While it scared the hell out of me, it never felt forced and never felt wrong. I'm very quick to shut people out, and she's been one of my worst victims when things used to go wrong in my life—but I've never run out of things to talk about with her. I think she's the only person I've ever met that I can say that about.

A spoiler to this story is that she stayed with me through it all. I am so lucky to have her, and she has such a giant heart I don't think I would have made it this far without her.

Chapter 3

I attended sales appointments with some of the larger potential clients while Paul flew solo on most. We were slowly inching toward the $5,000 first-issue sales goal. I started a Google Docs spreadsheet we could both access to track our progress.

There were moments, like Chip giving us the Chamber contact list, that made me believe destiny was working in our favor. A major one came in the form of an e-mail from Badeau at the LAEGC that first week of December 2009.

"I was thinking about your magazine over the weekend. We could work a deal to give you one of our office spaces on the fourth floor, alongside us. You'd get your name in the directory in the lobby and in the elevator. We have a shared receptionist, and our conference rooms would be available to you. Wi-Fi is also included. It would make you look more professional in many eyes, at least I think so."

It didn't take Paul and I long to work out a deal with Badeau. The LAEGC would get an ad in every issue as long as we rented space. In return, there would be no lease, and the magazine would only pay half the rent, a little under $200 per month. I saw our expenses would slightly increase, but to offset the cost of that kind of legitimacy meant we had to sell one additional quarter-page ad. Badeau's offer was yet another positive sign. The universe wanted us to succeed.

I use the word "universe" instead of God most of the time. Back when we were first putting *Lewiston Auburn Magazine* together, I would have claimed I was an atheist, although I know that was never the case. I have never liked the strict dogma that comes along with formalized religion. As a kid, neither my parents nor any of the teachers at Sunday school could answer many of my simplest questions, offering whatever the Catholic version of "Because I said so" came to them. That was not the way to win me over.

I don't have a list of rules I need to follow and don't pretend to have the vaguest of understanding how the universe works. I don't think the human mind is supposed to and I think it's this perfectly acceptable ignorance that forced many people to codify the idea of something larger than them into a religion. I'm not anti-religious by any means, and I think your opinion or practice of religion should not be seen as a litmus test for your quality of character, or what's going to happen to you after you die. Here's the absolute truth: we have no idea what happens to us after we die, and I'm perfectly OK with that.

I take comfort in believing that there is something—a form of stabilizing energy we can't measure—keeping things in line. I don't think it loves or hates, punishes or rewards, and is sentient in any way we could understand. It just is, and it makes me sleep easier to believe that. I don't call it God because so many people have preconceived notions of what God means, especially me. The universe makes sure what is supposed to happen does, and what isn't supposed to happen doesn't.

* * *

I had been internally sorting through ideas for stories since Donato gave us the thumbs-up. I wanted a public figure for our Q&A feature who would be quickly recognized by everyone and double as the focal point of our first cover. The name I kept returning to was John Jenkins.

Jenkins had quite a pedigree. A decade earlier, he became the first man to ever serve as mayors for both Lewiston and Auburn. Prior to the immigrant influx, the area was achingly non-diverse. As an African-American born in New Jersey, the mayoral accomplishment was all the more remarkable. A Bates College graduate and judo world champion, Jenkins parlayed his local popularity into a successful national motivational speaking career.

Here's the thing about me: I'm easily starstruck. I'm not just starstruck; I want those I've deemed a star to become friends with me and treat me as an equal. That meant I rose to their level, not that they fell to mine.

My awe of famous people was not fine-tuned. I probably had the most loosely defined sense of celebrity of anyone you'll meet. CEOs of large area businesses, the local TV news reporters, and regional politicians all got the starstruck treatment from me. It's kind of pathetic, but it was what it was. I craved the acceptance of people I viewed as well-known.

More pathetically, I craved the situation where someone was starstruck by me. I wanted people I've never met to know who I was and to draw positive conclusions based on my body of work. It was what drove me day-after-day. I wanted a wall full of plaques and the admiration of society ever since I won the Montello School Science Fair in fifth and sixth grades. They were the last trophies I had earned to that point . . . only a twenty-year drought.

John Jenkins was somebody I was starstruck by. I had been ever since elementary school when he gave a martial arts demonstration and motivational speech to a group of fourth graders and was the commencement speaker at my high school graduation.

All it took was a simple e-mail to an address I found on his motivational speaking business website. Within a day, he agreed to an interview after Christmas.

With that chunk of the content assigned space, I turned to a list of story ideas to determine which should be our first feature story. A target size of forty-eight pages meant there would be space for only one long story. I needed to produce something everyone could relate with and enjoy reading.

Lewiston Auburn Magazine wasn't competing with the *Sun Journal* or TV news. I knew we were recreational reading. If we didn't convince readers in 2010 that we were worth an hour or two of their time, there wasn't going to be a 2011.

The story needed to be something of value no other local source could provide. Readers unanimously needed to conclude,

"I've never seen anything like this. I want to see what they do next."

For several days, I struggled. I have an internal ability to not sweat things when an idea isn't coming to me. I just know it will, and it will be the correct one. Maybe everybody has this sense, but I've always felt alone with it. I stress about a lot, but coming up with good ideas has never been something that worries me. Solutions sort themselves out and up to that point, everything always worked out for me, or at least I'd convinced myself that was true. I had a mix of self-confidence but also trust the universe was always on my side.

As I drove by the building on a Saturday, a flash that "The History of the Lewiston Armory" was going to be our anchor story struck me. The Armory was more community center than military training hall. From middle school graduations, to rock concerts, to craft shows, I realized everybody had been inside that building dozens of times in their life. But, I had no idea what the history of it was. Maybe others would wonder, too.

In almost the same nanosecond, the universe told me the cover photo would be John Jenkins standing in front of the armory and the headline would read "Enduring Icons." How all of this happens in the span of driving three feet is beyond me, but I don't question it.

Neither Melissa at home, nor Paul at work, shared my enthusiasm for the story, but I was too set on what I thought was right to care. She didn't work for me, and Paul couldn't veto my ideas, just provide input. I was going to do exactly what I wanted because I was in a position where nobody could say no to me. That's never a good place for a leader to be.

* * *

You'd think an attention whore like myself would relish the idea of now getting to attend networking events, but there is something about the dynamic that had always frozen me in place. Such was the case when Paul and I attended our first Androscoggin Chamber of Commerce Business After Hours (BAH). Held the first or second Thursday of the month, our initiation was the annual holiday celebration held at Lost Valley Ski Area in Auburn.

Imagine your typical ski resort, then gut 90% of it. That's Lost Valley.

Paul and I were not natural conversation starters with strangers. While two hundred people ate, talked to each other, and represented their companies, Paul and I stood in the back, moving only to refresh the beer we were drinking. It was an awkward hour into the event when Peter Rinck and a few of his employees arrived. They came over to say hello, and Peter introduced us to his son, Calvin, who was newly returned from a stint in the Merchant Marines.

Peter asked about the progress of *Lewiston Auburn Magazine*. We gave the typical, "It's moving along, we're doing well, getting excited, people are responding" banter he likely expected. It was the first time I'd seen him since Mechanics Savings Bank came on board, and I thanked him for making that deal happen.

"We're excited to see what you come up with," he told us.

The Rinck crew spent fifteen more minutes there before leaving. As much as I wanted to leave, I didn't think it was smart for us to go. People needed to see our faces for future reference. We agreed we'd leave during the door prizes giveaway, but the second or third name pulled was mine.

"Joshua Shea!" Chip bellowed from the front over the microphone. "He's starting a great new magazine, *Lewiston Auburn Magazine*. You've got two tickets to The Public Theatre's next production."

I walked to the front of the room, the first time more than three sets of eyes were on me.

"At least we got to give you a plug," Chip said away from the microphone, handing me tickets which instantly became a prize on our Facebook page.

Paul and I left after I collected the tickets, sizing up the evening.

"On the positive side, plenty of people saw the name of the magazine on our name tags or at least heard the name when I won the prize," I offered.

"We also got to say hello to Peter," Paul said, trying to help me put hash marks in the positive column. "He saw we're out trying to market the magazine."

I went home that night, and once everyone was asleep, I renewed the alcohol buzz I had at the BAH. I was flipping around our premium cable channels, but as often happened, it led to me jumping on the computer to look for porn.

I had this habit where I'd see a beautiful—or even not-so-beautiful—actress on TV or in a movie and want to know what she looked like naked. "Celebrity Skin" is a massive porn genre online, so if the actress had ever done a nude scene I was usually able to find it quickly.

If I was flipping around channels and had not heard of a movie, I'd often put the title into one of the celebrity nudity website search engines to find out if there was anything sexy coming up worth watching. I just thought it made sense to do the research instead of waiting for a nude scene that may never come. It was the smart, time-saving choice, right? In reality, it was just one of the thousands of rationalizations I'd make, telling myself while I liked porn, it wasn't a problem.

* * *

I've always had a complicated relationship with the rest of the humans. Dating back to being a child, I've never felt like I've really belonged anywhere when I've acted like myself. The only way that I can get through a situation is by adapting to whatever the person who is the authority figure wants. Ideally, I'm able to become the authority figure and create my own reality.

Professionally, I was always able to detach from who I am as a person. It's a must when interviewing people. In real life, I'm shy. I don't want to talk to people because the idea of getting caught in a conversation causes great anxiety.

Old people and kids scare me the most. I feel like everybody else is playing by some social handbook I was never given so all I can do is fake my way along. The bitch of it is, I'm not very good at faking it. I look uncomfortable, and that's always been interpreted as snobbery. In reality, I'm awkward, scared, and usually don't know how to handle myself.

My way of being able to run a magazine or serve on the City Council or give any speech in front of a group of people was to simply detach. Another mental health professional theorized I had a detachment disorder. Like all the other mind maladies I've been diagnosed with, there's no blood test to prove or disprove it. I'm the same guy I was five minutes before I was diagnosed with "people phobia" or bipolar disorder or PTSD or anything else and I'm the same guy five minutes after you close this book. Detachment disorder? Maybe. Add it to the list.

One of the mental health professionals I saw post-arrest diagnosed me as literally having a fear of people, likely developed from the trauma of a babysitter when I was a kid. He's right.

My ability to adapt to the people around me began as a kid because of my response to the person who was my babysitter. She took care of me while my parents were at work before I started elementary school.

Looking back, it's very clear to me that she was not a healthy person, and not just because she was a morbidly obese woman in her early 50s. While I hate to use the word abuse because I've met people who have been severely abused, her obsessive-compulsive disorder led to what would best be called inappropriate situations or worst be called mild abuse: sexual, physical, and mental.

Much of the time, she was an emotionally unstable basket case who I learned to tip-toe around. Her quirks were many. On the very mild end of things, she vacuumed her entire house three or four times a day and not a single floor was without carpeting. The bathroom, the kitchen, the entryway—all carpeted. I was made to follow behind every time and pick up any crumb she missed. She would get fidgety if she was sitting in her chair and saw a piece of lint on the floor because she couldn't bend over to get it.

She liked to call me George and comb my hair. It's a wonder I'm not bald now given the fact she'd drag a plastic comb roughly across my scalp a dozen times per day, always calling me by the wrong name. I asked her once why she didn't call me Josh, and she just said she liked the name George better.

I was never allowed to sit on a piece of furniture and would often be left outside with my younger brother alone for three or four hours at a time. I was only allowed a drink after I ate my lunch. She never let us call her by her name, instead using the French word for "aunt."

If I broke rules or talked back, I might be sent to a dark room, sometimes for a few minutes, sometimes for a long time. I might be sent to the room if she simply had enough of me, but there was no way to tell when that was going to happen.

Those things sucked, but others went further. She watched every boy go pee, afraid we'd get some on the seat. Commanded to sit like a girl, she had to stay there and tell us how bad of a body part the penis was. When I was three or four, I recall her forcing me to touch a two-year-old's vagina, telling me it was to learn how girls were different. When my brother, Patrick, was two and had an accident while potty training, she made him stand there, naked from the waist down while the two or three other kids were forced to say, "Shame, shame." When I didn't join, she threatened to do the same thing to me.

I don't recall ever being struck, but I remember seeing other kids get it. One, who was special needs although I don't remember what he had, would get swatted a lot because he was just slow and it frustrated her to no end. Thankfully, he wasn't in her care very long.

Unlike my house, profanity flew all over the place. She taught me to swear in French. There were also R-rated movies regularly on television, and no topic was inappropriate to talk about in front of the kids, nor was any idle threat in their direction. While it seems funny in retrospect, scaring kids into believing you had a special key you'd put in their belly button that would make their ass fall off, is frightening to a four-year-old.

I've got dozens of other stories, but I've tried to move beyond dwelling about this experience. More than one mental health professional has told me that if I remember this much, it probably was worse, but there's no reason to go too deep into it.

The irony was, she'd tell anybody who would listen I was her favorite, and she did treat me better than the other children. I think I equated being singled-out as a good thing because it meant preferential treatment. Being liked by authority has always been a natural tendency for me because I like being treated special. I may still be treated like crap, but it's a special piece of crap.

These situations taught me to adapt and be who I needed to be at any given moment. They were the coping skills I adopted as a three-year-old that served me well, but never evolved. It was as much that three-year-old standing there awkwardly at the Business After Hours mixer as I was a guy pretending to be a magazine publisher.

* * *

Emails from writers and photographers who heard about a magazine starting began to arrive and the number of fans on our Facebook page jumped daily in the weeks leading up to Christmas. Most of these freelancers found out about us through Facebook, and I politely told them I'd keep their names on file as the magazine grew. It's what every potential employer has ever told me who was trying to brush me aside. Who am I to break the cycle?

When I took over as publisher at the newspaper a few years earlier, I spent $8,000 on software that did everything for a publication such as ours from tracking leads to scheduling future ads to creating bills.

Paul was working from home the day I installed the software on the computer at our new office. As I hauled the computer from the car to the elevator, I noticed a man installing the "Lewiston Auburn Magazine" sign under the "Fourth Floor" heading on the lobby directory.

An hour later, as I finished with the computer, the sign man from the lobby appeared at the opening of our jumbo cubicle. He was wearing a jacket with "Marquis Signs" embroidered over the heart.

"Hi, I'm Dan Marquis. I'm putting up your signs," he said.

"Josh Shea," I said. We shook hands.

I didn't know what to say next. Since my interest in lobby sign installation never developed as a child, silence enveloped us.

"You're starting a magazine?" he asked a few seconds later.

I knew he could potentially advertise so I suddenly made time to talk to him.

"Yes, glossy, full color. It'll cover dining, arts, entertainment. It'll have a good health section and a few longer stories," I said. "It's nothing like what's out there now."

"That sounds good," Dan said.

Silence. Another conversation break. As I waited to see which one of us would say something next, Dan reached into his pocket and gave me a business card. It wasn't for Marquis Signs.

"Daniel J. Marquis Photography" was written at the top, imposed over the card-sized photo of a duck. Fantastic. Just another freelancer looking for work. No ad was about to be sold, so I reverted to barely-interested mode.

"I take pictures. Not of people, but of nature. A lot of birds. Other things, too," he said as I put the card in the pocket of my shirt and patted it for him to see. It makes people think their card is special and will be protected, or at least that's what people like me who are full of shit try to communicate through the charade. It really just means that your card has a stronger chance of being lost in my washing machine than in my desk.

"Thanks. We're going to need people, especially for outside shots," I said.

"I've got a lot of good photos from the river and the balloon festival," said Dan. "Check out my site."

"I'll make sure to look at it soon. We're not quite at that point yet," I said.

After Dan left, I ran to the elevator to check out how our name looked on the sign.

* * *

The late-December holidays came and went. Paul was scoring some success with meetings, and I continued to gather content while still keeping a watchful eye at *The Independent*, probably working 50-60 hours per week between the newspaper office in Windham, the magazine office in Lewiston, and my home in Auburn. Still, I loved everything I was doing so it didn't feel like work. It felt like I was put on this earth to publish.

By mid-January, I was having a little trouble balancing everything and realized creating the content for the magazine was taking longer than I thought. I also started to think about the second issue. We had almost five months to put the first issue together. We'd have only two for Issue No. 2. I realized I couldn't write all the content for the first issue, much less the second. If we went up in page count on the second issue, we were already falling behind. Other people needed to start working on stories as soon as possible.

I knew I needed an editor for the arts and entertainment section and another for the dining section. It had to be people who wouldn't need to be babysat and could generate ideas that would fill three or four pages every issue, along with an occasional feature story.

I had an idea of who I wanted as the dining editor. Jennifer Boenig, a woman around my age who had two kids a little younger than mine, had worked for me at *The Independent* off and on. She was an above-average writer with no need for supervision. We met at the Dunkin Donuts in Auburn where she accepted the job upon hearing my pitch. She liked the magazine concept and was OK with the "Fill three pages for $150 per issue" salary I offered.

The Arts & Entertainment editor was more of a question mark. This needed to be someone very specific who had a passion for writing and for the arts and had a working knowledge of whatever current arts scene existed. There aren't many opportunities to write about the arts in Maine, which I knew might help the quality of candidate. I felt the position would be best served by someone under thirty-five years old who could cultivate that "hip" aura, but I didn't personally know anybody who fit the bill.

I threw a Help Wanted ad up on Craigslist and within a few hours had a dozen resumes and work samples. The best resume came from a woman in her mid-to-late 20s, Molly McGill. Like me, she had worked in Asia for an English-language publication. We also both had writing for the *Sun Journal* on our work histories. Her clips were the kind of feature writing the magazine required and the fact she went to college in artsy Burlington, Vermont, made me comfortable. As long as she carried herself well, the job was hers.

Molly and I planned to meet at Gritty's, a popular brewpub, in Auburn. I arrived fifteeen minutes early as I did for all hiring interviews. Once you pass my background check which is a quick Facebook and Google search, the next hurdle is the "15 Minutes Test" as I called it. It told me a lot about a job candidate. If I arrived fifteen minutes early and they were already there, it showed they were anxious. It's a good thing, especially in a deadline-driven business, but most business owners don't want you showing up fifteen minutes prior to an appointment because they are busy. If you're an ad salesperson and show up fifteen minutes early four times per day, you've lost an hour of productivity.

Molly wasn't there yet. I knew what she looked like because of the Internet, so I could watch her behavior from the moment she got there. If the job candidate sits down without looking for me, it's a bad sign. It means they expect people to come to them, including their potential boss. These are not the kind of employees who can self-manage. If they look around, but don't ask people who they are, then sit down, that means they give up too easily. Molly walked in, figured out who I was almost immediately, and sat down.

Some months later I told Molly about this little test she passed. Instead of seeing it as a measure of one's personality, she just thought it was stupid, bringing it up mockingly every now and then. I don't think she ever appreciated my ways of reading people. The way I see it, you're either a dominant or a submissive person. I only wanted dominant people on my team.

She treated the interview professionally, choosing to neither eat nor drink. She liked the concept and the idea of an editor title, but seemed to lack the passion Paul and I had. She was a little cold but could talk the talk. I was running out of time and either hired her on the spot or waited a couple of hours to look like I was considering other applicants and told her by e-mail.

* * *

As another mid-winter Friday came to an end, and we neared the halfway point to the $5,000 sales goal, Paul returned to the office around 5:15 p.m. after a sales appointment. I was kicking around, waiting to see if he wanted to get a beer.

"I was just at Gallery 5 talking to the girl who curates it, Jeanelle. She said there's an opening there tonight," Paul informed me.

"What time is it at?" I asked.

"Six-to-eight," he said.

"Seems like the kind of thing we should go to," I offered.

"Yeah, like every other non-profit around here, she doesn't have the money to advertise, but I think a lot of people will be there," he said.

I called home and told Melissa I'd be late because I had to an art gallery opening. She seemed mostly amused, never pegging me as a lover of art. I wasn't a lover but enjoyed looking at it more than she probably realized.

Paul and I left almost immediately, opting to grab a beer at Fuel, adjacent by a small hallway to the gallery next door. I'd only been inside Fuel once before. I admired it for what it tried to be, but I wasn't in the socioeconomic demographic it sought. Melissa and I enjoyed a dinner there a couple years earlier but weren't overwhelmed, especially when the check for half of our weekly grocery budget arrived.

Fuel was probably 25 feet wide, but 125 feet long, typical of a Lewiston downtown building. The first quarter had the hostess station and a small lounge with leather furniture and a well-stocked bar. The place was dark, but it fit the hip, sophisticated atmosphere. Low lighting and tea light candles bathed Fuel in a warm glow against brick and dark maroon walls. The rear 75% of the restaurant was its main seating area. On the walls hung framed French language advertising posters looking like they were from the middle 20th Century. The music was low and unobtrusive. It was as swanky as you were going to get in central Maine in early 2010.

"Hi Paul, here for a drink?" a beautiful woman said from the hostess station.

"Yeah, that then the art thing next door. This is Josh Shea. He's the magazine's editor and publisher," Paul told her.

The woman extended her hand, saying, "I'm Katie. A magazine is exciting stuff."

"We hope so," I said.

"Just go ahead and sit anywhere at the bar," she instructed, tending the reservation list at her station. The place was empty save for one guy at the bar. Fuel had been open only a few minutes, but since it was a Friday night with a gallery opening, it was going to be busy.

Instead of beer, I opted for a Red Bull and tequila, my cocktail of choice for the last several years. While I was mainly a beer man,

95% of the time I drank this nameless concoction in a hard-plastic cup at my house late in the evening. Now I was having one in the fanciest restaurant in Androscoggin County. I felt a little like Don Draper from *Mad Men*.

We each ordered a Stella Artois from the pretentious beers on tap for our second drink. It came in a snifter-like glass with the beer's logo on the side. We quickly drank these and ordered another when Paul noticed it was just past 6 p.m. He led me down the small hallway where Fuel and Gallery 5 shared the same set of bathrooms.

Few people had arrived by 6:15 p.m. at the small gallery with local art on three walls, buttressed by a large window looking out onto Lisbon Street. Paul and I scouted the walls, commenting loudly on what we liked and whispering when something didn't meet our approval.

The gallery slowly filled with artists, their family members, art lovers, and people who wanted to be seen. A convenient reality was that fifty people made the place look packed. It didn't take long before I felt like I was at an "event."

As I nursed my beer and growing buzz, a shorter woman with long salt and pepper hair came up alongside me as I was looking at a beautiful photograph of a flower.

"My husband Dan did that," she said, clearly proud of his efforts. "He tells me you're starting a magazine. I just saw your Facebook page."

"It's good to know word is getting out," I told the lady.

A third person approached us. It took a few seconds before realizing he was the guy who installed the signs at the office. I never looked at his website. I didn't know what happened to his card. I quickly gazed at the description of the photo on the wall to refresh myself on his name.

"Hi Dan, good to see you," I said, holding my hand out. He was enjoying a tall glass of beer garnished with lemon. He shook my hand like an old friend.

"Josh, right?" he asked.

"Good memory," I said.

"I'm Sandy," his wife said. "I run the sign business with Dan. He's the creative one, I'm the business one."

"Did you get a chance to look at my website?" Dan asked me.

"Yes, I did. I thought the birds were beautiful," I lied, hoping there wouldn't be a quiz. I just remembered the duck from his card and assumed there were more.

"Is there anything there worthy of a magazine?" he asked.

"Technique-wise it's great. I just don't know how often we'll need pictures of birds. You said you didn't take pictures of people, right?"

"No, I never have," said Dan.

"That doesn't mean you couldn't try," urged Sandy.

"I guess so," Dan said sheepishly.

"As you can imagine," I said, spotting my out, "we don't have money now. I really can't pay anyone at this point."

"I'm in business, I can understand that," said Sandy.

My need to make people happy always heightened with alcohol. It was clear the shy Dan Marquis would take no for an answer, but I didn't think he should. If I was going to be a first-time magazine publisher, why couldn't I have a first-time magazine photographer? He'd probably be easier to work with than a veteran.

"Would you guys consider a trade for either the sign business or to sell your photos?" I asked.

The looked at each other in agreement.

"We could do something," she said.

"OK, we'll figure it out when we get a little closer. I've got about two months before the first issue goes to the printer," I explained.

Paul came over, and I made introductions as he hadn't met Dan or Sandy yet. Dan quickly excused himself to mingle.

"I'm so excited. I'm so glad we're going to have a magazine," she said, genuine in every word.

We learned Sandy was the chair on the Board of Directors for L/A Arts and introduced us to a few of its other board members. I found it easier to talk to these people than the faces of business at the BAH.

I was coming out of a period in my life where I had my bipolar disorder in check with daily medication and wasn't drinking much alcohol regularly, leaving my tolerance low. Somebody bought me another beer, which I think made four drinks. I wasn't going to let it go to waste, but I knew it meant a call home to at least let Melissa know I'd be delayed.

Once that beer was finished, I decided to come down off my buzz out of the gallery, in the Fuel bar area, where I could nurse water and maybe strike up another conversation.

I saw Paul off to the side, talking to a man around our age with a beard. On the other side of them were Dan and Sandy, returning their empty glasses to the bar. They offered to buy me a drink on their way out, but I politely declined.

Paul introduced me to the bearded guy, whose name was Kerry Landry. He had worked with Paul at The Ground Round as a bartender in the past.

With the clock nearing 8 p.m. and Paul facing a forty-five-minute drive home, he decided to take off, but I stayed and spoke with Kerry for a while. He and his brother, Jason, had formed an artists' collective called Captive Elements. He'd turned the basement of his family's home into an art gallery/studio where he and a core group of about ten local artists regularly worked and displayed. It was fascinating . . . or maybe I was drunk.

The water extinguished much of the buzz and once confident I could drive, I closed the tab. With tip, it came to around $60. Thankfully, the newspaper paid.

I left, saying goodbye to Katie on my way out. Always make sure the gatekeepers like you was a mantra of mine. You never know when you're going to need a favor.

* * *

I apologized to Melissa when I arrived home for being late and claimed to have had one Red Bull and tequila and one beer. She probably couldn't tell I was lying this first time, but as more events happened and I came home in the evening with a bit of a slur in my voice, I'm sure she caught on that my tallies were less than half the actual totals.

I wish I could drink only what I claimed, but if a drink was available, it was in my hand. With each sip came more confidence, less anxiety, and a sense that I was worthy of being in the exciting, impressive position of the first-ever magazine publisher in the area. The drinking wasn't recreational by any means. Addictive drinking never is.

Trying to explain the feeling of addiction to someone who doesn't suffer from it is like trying to explain what it's like to be a parent to someone who has no children. No matter how well you paint a picture, you know that unless they experience it, your description falls short.

I didn't believe addiction was a disease until it was explained in medical terms to me at the second rehab I attended in Texas. I just thought all of us who overindulged with porn, or alcohol, or gambling, or whatever just had no will power. I thought about addiction the way that most non-addicts do: It's the crutch of weak people.

It wasn't until sincerely looking closely at my relationships with my vices—especially how early experiences were burned into my mind—that I understood what it meant in the Alcoholics Anonymous "Big Book" when it says, " . . . there is no such thing of making a normal drinker out of an alcoholic." I was never a normal drinker from the first sip, nor was I normal user of pornography from the moment my eyes fell upon it for the first time.

I've never been addicted to hard drugs, gambling, food, or plenty of other substances that feature 12-step self-help groups; yet, I completely understand how easy it would be to fall into any of those addictions. Each offer a moment of relief from the harshness of real life. When I've played a slot machine, I enjoy the quick hit of adrenaline that comes in that moment when you see the bars line up on the first two reels, but the third has not stopped yet. I like chocolate cake more than most foods and know that eating it makes me happy. But for some reason, I don't spend very much time gambling or eating dessert.

While the damage to your body can vary depending on the addiction, science has shown that the addictive process itself is very similar person-to-person regardless of the specific addiction. What's happening in my head with porn is what happens with the crack addict or the cigarette smoker. We all need that little hit of dopamine that comes with satisfying the urge.

The sinister thing about addiction is that the addict never realizes what has happened until it's too late, and it's too late almost immediately. In the very beginning, the conscious mind makes the decision to try something, but then the subconscious takes over. This is the part that non-addicts don't experience. They can put down the bottle or walk away from the poker table with no thought, but they don't understand that when the addict puts down the bottle or walks away from the poker table, it comes with the subconscious mind screaming to return.

No, they aren't real voices. Addiction isn't schizophrenia, but for me, it sometimes felt like my body was inhabited, or at least controlled by something else. It sometimes felt like I was on the outside, watching myself succumb to the drinking and porn. My conscious voice said no, but my body was listening only to subconscious voices.

Addictions are beyond cravings, beyond basic desires. They feel like a fundamental need, like oxygen. Hold your breath as long as you can. Eventually, you let go and have to take in a gulp of oxygen. If you don't, you'll experience great pain and eventually die. I'm sure that sounds dramatic to a non-addict, but I'm sure the addicts reading this are nodding their heads. It's just something that unless you experience it, I don't think it can be truly appreciated or understood. Just be grateful you don't experience it but understand it's not a personality flaw of weakness. It's a disease of the mind.

Chapter 4

We saw a healthy burst of sales in late January 2011, passing $4,000 with six weeks left to go. Surely we would hit the goal.

I knew Paul kept bumping up against the, "Well, let's see it first" mentality. Businesses like FX Marcotte, the best furniture store in Lewiston, took a wait-and-see approach. I remember I was particularly offended because one of the owners, Mike Bonneau, was my across-the-street neighbor growing up in Lewiston. I was still friendly with him when we'd bump into each other. But, this was another lesson in business. People will not throw money at me just because it's me.

An interesting conundrum developed when an advertiser decided to pay for their add up-front. It was only $200, but I didn't want to deposit it into the newspaper's bank account. Donato, Corey, and I met at TD Bank in Windham to open a new account.

Donato preached not only having accounts at different banks but separating business entities as much as possible. He suggested we make the magazine its own company, registering the name LA Publishing with the State of Maine and getting a tax ID number. It was one of those things that caused a surge of unexpected adrenaline. This wasn't the newspaper's scrappy kid brother. This was now its own company.

Traction with the public was being visibly achieved when Paul and I went to our second Chamber BAH event at a new Urgent Care branch of St. Mary's Hospital. While it was a smaller healthcare operation than Central Maine Medical Center, it was where both of my kids were born and I always preferred its emergency room over CMMC. More importantly for the magazine, though, was that St. Mary's committed to a full-page, multi-issue deal, which put us not only a few dollars from the goal for the first issue, but just as importantly, we had already sold over $2,000 for Issue No. 2.

There was no longer any need to fear approaching strangers in the room. They started to approach us. Paul had met a few in his travels, but most simply saw the "Lewiston Auburn Magazine" on our nametags and wanted to know more about this "thing" they'd heard about. Paul tried to line up meetings while I excitedly talked about our first issue coming together, giving what had evolved into my stump speech about pride, history, the future, and not positioning ourselves as second-tier cities in Maine to be looked down upon. The delivery was getting strong with conviction because I believed every word. If I was going to get the others to drink the Kool-Aid, I needed to already be drunk on the stuff.

Ad sales grew at a steady rate, passing the $5,000 goal on Groundhog Day. Most of the time I went on one of the sales meetings Paul arranged, I'd sport three days' worth of scruff and dress like I was working around the house on a Saturday morning. I wanted to look like the eccentric artist who had more to worry about than money while Paul would still put their business sense at rest with the way he carried himself. Bipolar disorder worked to my advantage as I'd manically describe the magazine, with Paul sitting by patiently waiting his turn in a suit and tie. He'd methodically explain the rate card structure and often negotiate a deal on the spot.

I will take 15% of the credit for our advertising sales. It was almost all about Paul. He was shattering my expectations as Director of Sales, hitting home run after home run. I was giddy wondering where we'd end up, knowing the newspaper wasn't going to take as much of a financial hit as I expected getting the magazine off the ground.

* * *

Fuel and Gallery 5 played host to our third Business After Hours in early February. I think it was that night they unofficially became like the magazine's second home in those early years. I recognized a few people, including Dan and Sandy, but I was the mystery to most people that they still were to me. I forced myself to speak with a few people whose names I recognized on their tags as people Paul had sold ads to. I thanked them all for the vote of confidence and knew I had to get them to like me if they were going to consider being repeat customers.

Sandy introduced me to a bald friend of hers, Tammie Grieshaber. Trying to avoid looking at her head was like trying to avoid looking at a stripper's boobs. The brain could not fight the magnetic force of the eyes.

"I'm not sick, I just wanted to try something new," she said. Sandy later explained Tammie had recently separated from her husband. It seemed like an interesting way for a woman in her 50s to rebel.

As the event was ending around 7 p.m., Paul introduced me to Fuel owner Eric Agren, who was starting to clean up a large beer and wine station. He, like most restaurateurs we approached, said they couldn't afford ads so Paul and I agreed to sell one to him at a fraction of the rate card. Eric purchased a large ad for the price of the smallest. Since Fuel was the gold standard of local restaurants, I needed them to have the largest restaurant presence in the magazine. I figured others would follow. Paul introduced us.

"I'm sure you're hearing that you're crazy," Eric said. "I heard it a lot."

Eric was right. We'd been told we were "crazy," "brave," "fighting an uphill battle," "nuts for doing this in the worst economy ever" and so on since the first time we mentioned the magazine in public.

"We get a bit of that," I said as Paul nodded.

* * *

I never, ever planned on making a life for myself in Lewiston once I graduated from high school. I was going to leave and get some kind of amazing job by which I would define myself. I was going to stay single, become a movie director or an actor or novelist or something else where I would be famous, hopefully rich—although it was never a prerequisite—and never return. Spending my adult life in the Twin Cities of Lewiston and Auburn with a family was unthinkable.

The first wrinkle came early when I landed a job as a sports clerk at the *Sun Journal* the summer before my senior year of high school. The duties were to take calls from local coaches whose games we didn't cover and get enough information from them to create the box score and a three-paragraph capsule story. Within three months I was covering high school sports as a staff writer, and a few months later the City Desk editor asked if I'd like to move out of sports and cover traditional news. I was a high school senior who had bylines on the front page of the third-largest circulated daily newspaper in Maine.

More importantly, I was treated like an equal among smart adults. That didn't happen when I worked at the Athletic Attic shoe store at the Auburn Mall or Burger King on the Maine Turnpike. Most of my senior year of high school wasn't spent with friends attending school events. It was in the newspaper office or out chasing down stories.

When I left the following autumn to attend Emerson College in Boston, anxiety and depression struck hard and fast. In a weird good news/bad news twist-of-fate, my roommate turned out to be a drug dealer. I made a stink about it and then told my parents I hated it there and was scared for my safety and returned home, a college dropout, by Halloween. I immediately returned to the *Sun Journal*, and the anxiety and depression disappeared. I tried college two more times in the next few years but the fear that I would never find anything as professionally satisfying, along with the fact I was paying for an education to get the job I already had made school seem pointless. Anyway, I did manage to leave Lewiston, technically. My first apartment was in Portland, which is the biggest move you can make in Maine. It didn't matter that I still worked in my hometown. I made it out.

The only thing that coaxed me to leave the *Sun Journal* was the only thing that could: a job offer fell in my lap. A former executive editor at the newspaper had left after I'd been there for about four years to take a job with *Stars and Stripes*, a daily newspaper operated by the Department of Defense for our military service members in Europe and Asia. Within four months of leaving, he started poaching the best the *Sun Journal* had to offer. I was the fourth person he asked to come work for him. I said yes, barely thinking about it and was told I could work in Darmstadt, Germany or Tokyo, Japan. For a twenty-two-year-old white guy who occasionally enjoyed Asian-themed porn sites and Japanese pro wrestling, the answer was obvious.

In a searing red-hot warning of things to come, I was fired just before I reached the six-month point with them for either showing up to work drunk, or not calling out because I was too drunk to work. Both happened a few times, and the discussion about my dismissal wasn't long.

I couldn't handle the freedom of having more than enough money and being completely on my own for the first time in my life, much less the fact I was doing it in Tokyo. Once I stopped hanging out with Americans I worked with, my nights were filled with bars and strip clubs. I partied with famous athletes and musicians, able to get close enough to them because of the connections I could make as a *Stars and Stripes* writer. My body had trouble keeping up with the schedule, and my mind scrambled its priorities.

I was given a plane ticket and told I was going home the day after I was fired because my special Status of Forces Agreement standing as a Department of Defense employee that allowed me to be there without a work visa was going to be revoked in forty-eight hours. I was kicked out of Japan for drinking; yet, it would still take me another fifteen years to recognize I was an alcoholic.

I went back with my tail between my legs to the *Sun Journal*, telling them working for the government wasn't a good fit with my personality. I think they felt burned by my departure, or somebody at *Stars and Stripes* told them what happened, and I never got the hours I needed. I moved back to Portland and found a small publishing company that was trying its hand at regional business-to-business newspapers. I was hired and was the only one in the company with real newspaper experience. Within a year, I was named managing editor of *Interface Business News*. It was the most professionally satisfying thing I'd done up to that point, and I regularly worked 60 hours weeks, loving every second. I neither worked nor lived in Lewiston for the next four years.

Rarely did I ever look to improve my job situation. I didn't make much money, but I was basically my own boss, and the guy who was technically my boss trusted me and didn't get too involved. A professionally satisfied Josh is one that doesn't need to be in Hollywood or writing the Great American Novel. Let me take pride in my work and have a handful of people consistently tell me that I'm doing a good job, and there's little need for change.

I had met Melissa during this time and, at twenty-six, was thinking about the next phase of my personal life. When she became pregnant, moving in with her made the most sense since I could work from anywhere there was an Internet connection, and she had a job in Lewiston. I returned to the city I said I never would.

As you get older, you make deals with yourself, come to certain conclusions, and realize that when they make a movie of your life, there is a lot about the script you didn't have complete control over. It's not necessarily bad, it just wasn't the plan. It really made the most sense to stay where both of our families were who could help with the kids and where we could more easily afford to live. It's not like we would have been taking advantage of Portland's nightlife if we lived there. This was around the time I created *METRO* magazine with my friend Brian and his ex-wife, Heather. It kept me in Portland during the day, was another step forward professionally, and satisfied that need to define myself based on my job.

We lived in Lewiston about two years before buying a home in Auburn. Why pay rent when you can pay a mortgage? The answer is because a mortgage is an anchor, attaching you to a place with little hope of escaping. We set small goals for leaving. Melissa didn't want to leave before her elderly grandmother passed away. When *METRO* was happening, I didn't want to abandon it. Before I could realize it, the kids were in school, and I was in my early 30s. Thankfully, a newspaper company in Windham came calling.

By that point, though, I understood what I saw on many of the adults' faces when I was a kid walking around in Lewiston and Auburn: the resignation of not being one of the few who makes it out, reluctantly trying to make a go of it because your destiny was here all along.

I thought that conclusion sucked. This area wasn't so big that one person couldn't make a difference. Eric Agren brought fancy dining here. Why couldn't I bring the belief we lived in an area worthy of a lifestyle magazine? Sometimes, all you need is a different mirror, or a different lens, to look through. I knew I had the talent to provide that lens, or at least have fun trying.

Change doesn't happen shuttling the kids around to hockey or cheerleading practice. It's doesn't come by going to a non-descript job from 9-to-5 and falling asleep to *Friends* reruns five nights a week. If Lewiston and Auburn were ever going to be places where I was excited to live, I'd need to start doing some heavy lifting, and encourage others to join.

* * *

Coming into the home stretch of building the first issue of *Lewiston Auburn Magazine* was an exciting time. Dan Marquis shot the cover photo of John Jenkins in front of the Lewiston Armory on a frigid day a few weeks before we went to press. All of the little things were falling into place and the lack of drama putting together a first-time publication was surprising.

Paul continued his months-long reign as company VIP when the floodgates opened just prior to our deadline. Even in the last few days of Corey designing the final product, I was constantly refiguring things as Paul closed deals with many of the fence-sitters. When the final PDF was sent off to the printer in New Hampshire, the magazine featured over 30 advertisements representing trades, sponsorships, and over $9,900 in billable ads.

I couldn't believe how much the bottom line exceeded my expectations. It was not lost on me that we might be financially independent from the newspaper by the third issue, important considering we still drew our salaries out of the newspaper's Independent Publishing Group company.

The printer needed their money when we picked up the magazines. Traveling to Hooksett, New Hampshire, meant we lost five or six hours of a day, but saved about $300 in delivery fees. We'd amassed $5,500 by the day we went to pick up the first issue. Unfortunately, the printing bill was $7,000—and neither the magazine nor the newspaper had an extra $1,500 laying around.

"Donato," I started on a phone call to the boss a day before we were heading to N.H., "this is a one-time thing. We're $1,500 short on paying the printer. I don't want to take it out of the newspaper since they are different accounts. I will if you absolutely want me to, but it's a different company. Regardless, I have to give the printer $7,000. If you can front us the $1,500, we'll be able to pay it back to you within the week."

I hadn't asked him for money in a long time. It made me feel like a failure even though we were technically successful beyond expectations.

"I'm proud of you boys. I can give you $1,500. I don't have a problem with that," he said.

"I promise you this will be the only time," I said.

"I lost so much money on that newspaper. You stopped it. We haven't made any money yet, but maybe the money is in the magazine," he said.

That gift meant $1,500 more to our bottom line, although I tried not to think of it that way.

The next day, Paul, Corey, and I met at Donato's convenience store. He and his wife, Belinda, took their Suburban, and I brought the guys in my car. While more than half of the 5,000 issues were being mailed to Chamber of Commerce members, a list of VIPs, and about 300 waiting rooms in central Maine, we still needed to pick up more than forty bundles. I had no idea how much that meant in terms of actual space.

The first time it felt like we really were creating a magazine was when Dave, our rep, took the check and told us to drive our vehicles to the loading dock. Barely half of the back section of the Suburban was needed. So much for being worried about running out of room in two vehicles.

While Dave and Donato loaded the magazines, Paul, Corey, and I started tearing through the issue. In terms of quality, it was so much more impressive than anything I had ever created.

The five of us enjoyed a meal at the Hookset Applebee's. I thought we had a fine product in our hands and something the people of Lewiston and Auburn would go nuts for, but I also knew it was a rough draft for better things to come.

Belinda took a photo of Corey, Paul, and me holding up copies of Issue No. 1. She titled it "Three Proud Papas" on Facebook. Looking back at that photo it's like I'm looking at a trio of strangers I never knew. After all, who could predict within five years of that photo being taken one of us would move out of state, one would serve six months in jail, and another would be dead?

Chapter 5

If you ever have the opportunity to launch a magazine, I urge you to do so. If you're a glory hound who gets high on the adoration of strangers the way a feline gets high on catnip, starting a magazine is a must.

Once we reached Windham with our magazines, we left two bundles behind with Donato. Paul took twenty-five bundles out of the back of the Suburban so he could hit the hotels and a few distribution spots on his list when he got into Lewiston the next morning, but at that point, he headed home for the day. The magazine wasn't going to be in mailboxes for a few days, so there wasn't a rush to get them into stores that night.

Driving back toward Lewiston and Auburn with a dozen bundles, I felt like I had precious cargo in the car, far more delicate than a baby. Ninety-nine percent of the population didn't know about it yet, but there I was, heading home feeling like I was about to release my own special anthrax into the area. They'd never see it coming.

My then 10-year-old daughter Katrielle seemed more impressed with the magazine than anyone else in the house. Melissa caught me leafing through the magazine several times that night.

"Admiring your work or finding your mistakes?" she asked, knowing I often simultaneously patted myself on the back and kicked myself in the gut when it came to my work.

"Something isn't right, but I don't know what it is," I mentioned.

I would have liked to spend the next several days running around getting pats on the head. Instead, I was working on issues No. 2 and 3. The only pat on the head came shortly after lunch the day after we picked up the issues.

"This is outstanding. This is just incredible," said Chip Morrison, sticking his head into our space, having made the trip from the first floor, where I left a bundle.

"Thank you. If you like it, maybe we'll make a few more," I joked.

"I hope so! This may be the single best piece of marketing for Lewiston and Auburn I've ever seen," he said excitedly.

"Anything to make your job easier, Chip."

"I mean it. I'm proud of you and let Paul know I'm proud of him," he said.

"Thank you," I said, genuinely touched.

"Thank you for having the guts to do it. Good work, Josh."

Chip retreated to the first floor. A couple of hours later, I checked the mail. Ironically, there was just over $1,500 in ad payments.

* * *

I've always compartmentalized my life more than most people I know. There is the me my wife and kids know, the me my parents know, the me my few friends know, the me my professional colleagues know, and then the one that only I know. Those worlds sometimes intersect, revealing parts of myself that I may not have wanted to share.

The early success of the magazine meant a new part was going to emerge, a public figure. It's a part I always knew was there and wanted the world to adore. I knew I had to do something impressive for the world to ever see this person. For the first time in my life, I nailed it. Paul knew the me that my close friends knew, but he also got to know the publisher guy who was full of shit from day one.

The kind of adoration and attention I craved for decades might just be satiated by the magazine, I realized in the first few days of it being released. I'd never been so unanimously praised for anything I'd done in my life by so many people who I both knew and had never met. Facebook was a fun place to visit.

You could say I was finally a big fish in a small pond, but I don't know if that's accurate. It was never calculated on a conscious level. I didn't have career goals and didn't yet recognize or appreciate my need for acceptance. I just went with the flow and tried to take advantage of opportunities that seemed fun and would get me attention. I didn't mind hard work as long as I saw an achievable goal.

Paul asked for more money, and I gave it to him, while also moving his salary over to LA Publishing's books as our first legal employee. I was giving him at least $20 per week in petty cash to fill his gas tank so he could make it back and forth to his home. Making it official with a raise wasn't going to hit the bottom line hard, and it was a gesture that rewarded him for the stellar work he did on that first issue.

* * *

Always looking for the opportunity to share our area's shiny new magazine, Badeau pitched us on taking a two-booth spot at the Androscoggin Business-to-Business Trade show about a month away at the Central Maine Civic Center.

I did the math and realized if we moved up the deadline of issue No. 2 by a week, we could pick it up in New Hampshire on a Wednesday afternoon and have it ready to debut the following day at the trade show. Our first issue would be two months old by that point and a fresh issue was going to show we weren't a one-shot deal.

On top of the deadline push, we needed to get a cover made for the second issue before I appeared on a local news show, *207*. This was a popular talk/variety program immediately following the *NBC Nightly News*. I was able to get on the Fox affiliate's morning news show *Good Day Maine* with the first issue, but as far as local media outlets went, *207* was the gold standard. We needed the cover of issue No. 2 done quickly, two weeks ahead of our already early deadline.

I like concept covers, whether it is something needing closer inspection or simply visually intriguing. I wanted *Lewiston Auburn*

Magazine to take risks. The cover of our second issue was dipping our toe into that water for the first time. Molly was writing about the high-end guitar company, Bourgeois Guitars, which was to be the cover story. On all of their models, at the top of the guitar neck, where the tuning knobs are, it said "Bourgeois" in an interesting script. I thought a white background with nothing but the end of the neck near the top of the guitar would be interesting.

The neck of the guitar was mostly brown, and the background was blazing white. I knew we'd need some color in the flag and teasers. In one of those "the universe talks to the mind in mysterious ways" moments, I remembered the cover of a *Playboy* magazine from when I was a teenager. Instead of the guitar, that cover had a girl sitting on a basketball in front of a bright white background. I found a copy of that cover on Google Images and sent it along to Corey. He used the exact same color scheme on our magazine as it appeared on the *Playboy* cover.

"We probably shouldn't tell people the second cover was inspired by an old *Playboy* cover," Corey noted as he designed the cover in advance of my *207* appearance.

"No shit, Sherlock," I responded.

* * *

Appearing on *207* was a huge boost to my ego because moments after the eight-minute segment aired, people were giving favorable reviews on Facebook and congratulating me through email for a great appearance. A few days later, when I dropped my son, Kaden, off at my parents for his weekly Saturday visit, my mom mentioned many of her friends had told her that they'd seen me.

I knew things were going to change as I started to become a public figure, and maybe if I had been a single guy, I would have thought about the opportunity to start hooking up with a lot of women, but even if I weren't married, I'm not wired that way.

There is something about sex that has scared me on both a conscious and subconscious level since I was a kid and despite the counseling and therapy I've had, it still remains mostly a mystery. This is part of the reason why pornography has been part of my life whether I have been in a solid relationship or single, going all the way back to being a child. It's a surrogate. If I didn't have a girlfriend in a given moment, I could still have a beautiful woman. If a girlfriend or my wife was not interested in sex that night—or more likely, I just didn't want to put in the effort to satisfy them—the woman on the magazine page, TV or computer screen didn't need satisfying. With porn, the other person never says no. If you want her to be a cheerleader, or African American, or you want three blonde women that day for whatever reason, you can have it. Porn gives the user all the control.

I don't think my teenage or young adult sex life was abnormal. There were plenty of peers who had no sex and many who were over-active. I tended to form relationships with females before attempting sexual physical scenarios. When the very rare spontaneous make-out session with a stranger or one-night stand happened, I usually felt a responsibility to at least attempt a relationship.

I always wanted to be one of those more sexually active people. In an adjacent apartment I had in Portland when I was twenty-two-years old, there were people my age who would come back from the bars at 1 a.m. and play Spin the Bottle or Strip Poker. I had two very unique, separate circles of friends but neither did stuff like that, much to my chagrin. I'd seen my neighbors, and they were good looking girls. It killed me to think of what was going on next door with guys who just sounded like giant dumb-fucks. I couldn't understand why guys like that got girls, and I was sitting by myself drinking and looking at porn.

I never went skinny dipping. I never had a girl perform a striptease for me that I didn't pay for at a club. I never had a threesome. I never had a girlfriend who was sexually "free." I never went to a nude beach and took it all off.

The only time I've ever vicariously done any of these things was when I was sitting watching pornography. When I was younger and saw those scenarios in pornography, I couldn't wait until they happened to me, but for the most part, they didn't.

I tried to tell myself that most guys never hung out in Red Light Districts in Amsterdam, Montreal, or Tokyo. Some of the things I saw and experienced there were certainly beyond what you're going to ever find in Lewiston, Maine. I've seen women doing things with bananas and men dressed in gorilla suits doing things to those women. I've seen women perform sex acts on other women three feet from my face. But nothing I've paid money to see in real life was the kind of spontaneous thing that happened in the kind of pornography I liked to watch. I was never one for the movies with cheesy acting or ones that tried to be "art" and have a budget. People being themselves was far more interesting. I wanted to find these people. I wanted to be with the people next door. I wanted to be myself, whoever that was sexually, and not be afraid.

"Hey, who wants to play strip poker?"

"What are you? Some kind of fucking perv?"

That's the way it would have gone had I suggested anything like what the people did on the other side of my wall to any of my friends.

If a friend suggested strip poker to the group and they went for it, I don't know if I could have handled it. Had I befriended the girls next door and they invited me over, I suspect I may have made an excuse for bailing before any clothes hit the floor. The small adrenaline rush of the danger that came from looking at porn would have been at such a maximum height, my fight-or-flight response would have carried me right out of there.

When I was at rehab in Texas, I was sitting on a chair in a common area talking to someone sitting across from me. A girl from the eating disorder program came in and threw herself down on the couch to the side of the chairs we occupied. She was wearing very tiny shorts and no underwear. I could see directly up her leg and had a perfect view of her vagina.

Instead of playing it cool and enjoying the view, which you think somebody who was seeking help for porn addiction would do, I jumped up and ran out of there. I had a surge of excitement that went straight to nausea, feeling like I was going to get in trouble. Suddenly I was five years old seeing something that I shouldn't.

Yes, I feel like I missed out on a part of life that I was looking forward to and thought was important. At some point you recognize it's just not going to happen and that ship has sailed. There are more important things in life. I'll also never pitch for the Boston Red Sox or be an astronaut. Once you get married, have kids and settle into a life, you trade in the potential of sexual adventure. Those people and couples who don't trade it in end up at those weird swingers campgrounds profiled on HBO's *Real Sex* and that was never a hope of mine.

* * *

I worried a little bit about filling the 20-foot by 8-foot space at the trade show. I asked Corey to be there to see people's reactions to the magazine so he'd know he was working on something people were reacting to positively. I'd describe him as intensely shy and reluctant in most social situations. Working from the newspaper office in Windham kept him isolated from the community we were creating the magazine for. I asked Molly to attend since she wrote the guitar cover story for issue No. 2 and could answer potential questions. It was also a good chance to get her face seen as our arts and entertainment editor.

Paul continued his hot streak, bringing the second issue total to over $14,000 in ad revenue and getting Issue No. 3 to a place where it stood at over $10,000 before selling it as an individual issue began. Adding Paul to the magazine's payroll was easily offset by the higher-than-predicted sales, still leaving us with profit.

I loved pressing the flesh and answering questions during the trade show. Many knew me only as the guy from the front of the magazine where my photo appeared with the "Editor's Letter" although I was also recognized as the person they saw on *207* a week earlier.

This was the first opportunity I had to spend a day with Molly. She presented herself as rigidly professional, but you could tell she really enjoyed herself. My guess is that she saw how casual Paul, Corey, and I interacted with each other and let her guard down a bit. She was a terrific representative of the magazine, and there was something to be said for having female energy in the booth.

I knew she was capable of putting a good article together, but I was introduced that day to a smart, funny woman who had enough of a twisted, snarky side that she fit right in with us. Her stock skyrocketed in all of our eyes that day.

Sandy and Dan were there with Marquis Signs but spent time visiting our booth. I felt like I was forming a nice professional bond with them that could turn into a friendship.

Business After Hours was held at the conclusion of the trade show near the front of the Civic Center. During it, Molly expressed her desire to be part of more networking events.

"Let me know when more of these things happen," she said.

"Absolutely," I responded. I knew we had something special with her the way I knew we had something special with Paul.

* * *

Looking at the second issue, something was still aesthetically wrong. It didn't click for me. I couldn't say, "This is nice."

Paul had been working on a local bank as a customer since the first week. Banks purchased large ads, provided us additional prestige, usually designed their own ads and paid their bills quickly. It was all upside. As a large local bank, it seemed natural they'd come on board for issue No. 3 as several of their competitors already were in the magazine.

I don't remember if Paul asked me to go or if I thought my presence would help seal the deal when it came time to meet with this bank. I was wrong. So very, very wrong.

We met with a woman named Carmen who seemed angry from the outset. We followed her to a small conference room where she sat across from us, flipping through the magazine, touching the pages as if they were covered in dog shit.

"Why would I want to advertise in this?" she said in a pissed-off tone.

"Because we're the magazine of Androscoggin County, and you're a bank in Androscoggin County?" I responded.

"No," she said.

"Branding?"

"What I'm asking is why would I want to advertise in a magazine that looks like this?" I'd not heard that question before.

"I don't understand what you mean," I said, looking nervously at Paul.

"I used to work in design," she said, putting down the magazine on the table. "This is messy."

She picked it up again and stopped on a page in the arts and entertainment section.

"What's this? The header?"

"Yeah . . ." I responded.

Corey designed the section header as a strip of color across the top of the page with the words "Arts & Entertainment" in a cursive font on the upper right-hand part of the page.

"It's too blocky. You don't need this color, and the font is ugly," she said, tearing through the magazine at a torrid pace.

She stopped on another page and looked up at us. Then another. Then another.

"What's going on here? Why is this ad in the back? Why does everything look so crammed together?" she asked flipping through.

I reached a point of silently seething, and I could see Paul scrambling to think of something to say. Once she finished telling us why we sucked, Paul spoke.

"If we considered some of the things you've suggested, do you think you'd advertise?" he asked.

"I don't know," said Carmen. "Most of our marketing is aimed toward Portland. We see the most growth there."

"OK, we'll keep sending you the magazine, and I'll be in touch," Paul said.

I still couldn't speak. I was angry, gritting my teeth when shaking her hand as we were leaving. I have no idea what my face said because I simply had no words. We walked out the lobby door and onto the Lisbon Street sidewalk. I looked at Paul.

"I know," he said.

"How . . . I mean . . . wow!" I said, still dumbfounded after being told for twenty minutes how everything we were doing was wrong.

"That was bad. I think I'll wait a while before we bother them again," he said.

"I don't even want them in the fucking magazine," I said tersely, feeling twenty minutes of pent up anger about to spew forth. "I mean, how fucking rude is it just to shit all over us like that. Fuck her. I mean . . . fuck her! She doesn't like our fonts? Fuck her. Fuck her. We don't need them."

"That meeting was rough," said Paul, taking the harsh rejection better than me.

"It was a fucking massacre!" I said incredulously.

"I don't know," Paul said calmly. "It's just one bank, and we're almost up to $16,000 for the next issue. Don't sweat it."

"I can take rejection. That wasn't rejection," I said.

Paul let me have my tantrum on our walk back to the office, keeping his cool the entire time. I wondered if he heard this every day and shielded me from it.

Once calm, I asked myself the rhetorical question, "Is she bitter she's not in Portland doing creative work or was that just an inappropriate way to give us quality constructive criticism?"

On my way home that day, I picked up several magazines at a newsstand. After dinner, I sat down and highlighted what I thought was hip and well designed, putting Post-It Notes on those pages. Once finished, I went back to those pages to figure out if there were any subconscious patterns I hadn't noticed. Things became clear. I didn't think *Lewiston Auburn Magazine* looked like a magazine because Corey and I designed the ad/content blocks as if it were a newspaper. Ads and content didn't belong on the same page in a magazine.

The next time I was in Windham, I walked Corey through changes I wanted to see starting with issue No. 3. I tried to frame it as if we hadn't known any better, but I think he took it personally.

Chapter 6

My email box was starting to fill daily. As a person who thought it was a big day if he had three messages, suddenly dealing with 20 or 25 felt a little overwhelming, in a good way. My favorite emails were automatically generated by our website telling me another person had subscribed. They trickled in through regular mail from a coupon in the magazine, but we'd get two or three a day online. We were offering the last three issues of 2010 for $5.95, which barely covered production and mailing, but it was an e-mail address captured and a little pat on the back and bit of adoration every few hours from a stranger.

Once in a while, a subscriber would call or email saying they missed an issue. If we put it into a manila envelope, it cost over $2 to send in the mail, so we often just drove them to people's homes. The time and gas money was nothing compared to the ego boost it gave me.

"I couldn't believe I saw Joshua Shea getting out of his car," a nice elderly lady said once in that first year. "Your magazine is the best thing to come in the mailbox."

"Thank you. We'll keep trying to do a good job," I said.

"I'm going to tell my friends Joshua Shea from *Lewiston Auburn Magazine* was here," she gushed.

"My friends call me Josh, so please call me Josh. If you ever need anything, just give me a call. That's my direct line," I said, giving her my business card.

"I'm going to show this around. I had a celebrity come to my house," she said, in a tone of voice denoting bragging.

I left her, floating my way to the car. Whatever thrill I gave this elderly lady, she returned to me tenfold.

* * *

After issue No. 3 went to the printer, but shortly before it was delivered, Paul and I decided to take a much-needed breather for a week—or at least I tried. I knew I'd have to work a day-and-a-half at the newspaper, but figured I could be home most of the week with the kids, relaxing by the pool.

Not a chance.

I was on my computer at least three hours every day, checking and responding to email and plotting the future. I dropped by the office every day to see if checks came in the mail.

Going to the mailbox became a daily ritual for me during the life of *Lewiston Auburn Magazine*. I didn't want anybody else doing it. Turning the key and hoping for as many envelopes as possible was a way of life. Envelopes usually meant money and money meant I wouldn't have to work at a call center ever again. Two envelopes didn't necessarily mean a small amount of money, and many envelopes weren't always a jackpot. By the start of the cycle for issue No. 4, I estimated with all our expenses, we needed to take in around $450 every day except Sunday to break even.

When a check for $3,000 or more would come in covering a client's last two or three ads, it was a happy day. It meant a week of expenses paid from a single rectangular piece of paper. There were days I deposited more than $5,000, and those were days I could feel the stress melt off me like pounds off a fat guy in a sauna. The bank account balance was directly tied to my stress level. On the flip side, there were weeks only about $400 came in the mail. Those weeks felt like I was wearing a big, wet fur coat. I tried to always keep a minimum of two-to-three weeks' worth of expense money in the bank as a cushion.

Those who knew about the magazine were loving it, but the number aware overall was still low. We got over this hump when Nick Knowlton invited us to hand out copies at a giant concert— by Lewiston standards—he was promoting, reuniting popular local bands of the late 1950s through early 1970s. That period was a huge time for music in the area with boy bands popping up in every other garage or basement, hoping to be the next Beatles. There was a weekly concert, called The PAL Hop, hosted by the Police Athletic League at City Hall on Friday nights in the 1960s featuring these bands that turned them into local legends. Now, around forty years later, Knowlton, who sang with Terry and the Telstars, thought a reunion show at the Central Maine Civic Center would be well received.

When the crowd, probably about 1,500 people, filed out at the end of the night, we handed everyone a copy of one of the first three issues of *Lewiston Auburn Magazine*. The surprise of getting a magazine given to them about their hometown was palpable. I realized we couldn't only be a magazine for the elite. Our stories were relevant to everyone leaving that concert, and our advertisers wanted their money as much as anybody else's.

The week after we handed out copies at the concert, subscription forms poured in. We hit the $20,000 mark for ad sales well before the deadline for issue No. 4 approached. It would be years before we'd drop below that amount again.

* * *

"But can we afford it?" Paul asked me as we walked back to our cars following August's BAH mixer at a small manufacturing company in Auburn.

"I think so. If she works cheap. You know the *Sun Journal* will hire her if a writing job comes along just to fuck with us . . . and she'll take it," I said.

Molly wanted to come to more events so we invited her. She continued to be a well-received ambassador of the magazine, especially among women. By the time BAH was over, she had several story ideas and a couple new advertising leads. Paul and I had decent Corona buzzes.

One thing poking me in the side like a thorn over the last few months were the terrific freelance stories Molly had been writing for the *Sun Journal*. Even when I gave her a little paying work at the Windham newspaper to supplement the magazine, it wasn't enough to live on. I understood why she worked for the *Sun Journal*. I just didn't like it. I wanted exclusivity over her talent.

The debate to hire Molly full time became a bit clearer when Jennifer Boenig, the dining section editor, left the magazine. She couldn't juggle her other projects and family life with the magazine, so we parted amicably.

"Jennifer left which frees up a tiny amount of money," I told Paul. "Once we start doing magazines every month, we're going to need at least one other full-time person. That's not many months away, and we're doing better than expected."

"I just worry about the money right now," he said as we leaned against his car, a few minutes after having said goodbye to the person's fate we were now deciding. I knew I could—and would—make the decision without him, but wanted him to sign off on it.

"I'll keep myself on the newspaper payroll longer. It's not like anybody keeps track of any of these books very closely. It also shows everybody we're growing. Eighty pages is going to be our norm soon. If the *Sun Journal* hires her to its staff, they won't let her write for us," I said.

"Yeah, I'd like to wait, but we can't," he said. "Figure it out and make the offer," he commanded as we parted ways for the evening.

The next day, I met with Molly in the small conference room. She agreed to less money than I thought it would take. She also asked to work from home most of the time and wanted me to know she'd need time to travel, a passion we both shared. She sounded like a younger version of me who hadn't yet learned the reality of children and a mortgage. I told her as long as the magazine came out on time, looking as good as it could, I didn't care what she did with her life, just check email twice a day in case I was trying to reach her.

The Internet had technically allowed people the freedom to work from home for nearly twenty years, but it was only now that people like me were becoming bosses that it was happening. There was ample opportunity to telecommute in our company, and I'd never understood rigid hours or attendance policies. Someday I figured I'd need to formalize a policy, but it wasn't then. The loose policy was that there were no specific sick or vacation days, just let me know. Don't miss meetings and check messages enough so I can find you within a couple of hours. Other than that, whatever.

Take a three-day weekend. Take a four-day weekend. As long as it doesn't hurt the quality of the magazine or the bottom line, go see your niece's school play or meet your friend in Portland for lunch. Spend the day sleeping or getting drunk. If it didn't deter from the magazine, it didn't matter. Be a responsible grownup. If you couldn't, get off my team. Molly wanted on.

I also wanted people on my team who would be passionate to the point of being obsessed with our product. I wanted them to be as addicted to the job as I was getting. There are plenty of opinions on when a vice crosses the line into addiction. I like the idea that it has less to do about the behavior and more to do about the consequences of the behavior on your life.

With porn, drinking, drugs, gambling, and most addictions, it's not hard to gauge when things have gone off the rails, but with certain addictions, like work, the line of demarcation isn't as clear.

I've always defined myself on my work and tried to overachieve. It took seventeen years to work my way from sports clerk at the *Sun Journal* in high school to a regional magazine publisher. There were many stops along the way, picking up different skills, but I always seemed to excel in the fields of journalism and publishing. My mother tells stories of me asking her to write down the news as it was dictated by Walter Cronkite when I was a child. I would copy what she wrote and, at five years old, ride around the neighborhood the next morning passing out my "newspaper." If that story is true, I was destined for my job at a young age.

Operating *Lewiston Auburn Magazine* was never a concrete goal, but rising to the top of my profession where I had to answer to nobody and could run things the way I wanted was. I worked for half my life to get to that point, and once I did, it became my life.

I never saw the high-quality life I was unintentionally building with Melissa and the kids as a goal. I never planned on being married or a father. Those were just things happening while I focused on the real plan. It makes me angry at myself to think about how many years I wasted on the wrong priorities. There are people who want nothing more than a normal, stable family life, and I stumbled into it, not appreciating what a lucky person I was when the kids were young.

I told myself I was dedicated, had an outstanding work ethic and the payoff would come when I got rich and my family didn't need to worry about anything down the road, but those were never real goals. I didn't have real goals, just a need to continue moving forward to dull my pain. I thought everybody loving the magazine would stop the pain. Eventually, the work itself became the pain. Like a detoxing addict, I would writhe during holidays, knowing nobody was doing business and I couldn't go to work.

It wasn't long into the life of the magazine that I started to stress every detail, finding diminishing joy in something that first gave me more than I imagined. I was a workaholic and the way to ease that pain, just like for an alcoholic, drug, or porn addict was to push myself even further into it. My diseased mind said if working 12 hours per day, seven days a week wasn't making things better, the solution was clearly to work longer.

* * *

Despite our liberal attendance policy and lip service to working at home, we all wanted to be in the office. We felt the energy and enjoyed being around each other, but one desk and a small table designed to fit one person could not comfortably sustain three. I asked Badeau about a bigger space on the fourth floor. He told me the Androscoggin Land Trust was moving out of a space housing three desks. They'd be gone in a week, and it would only be about $150 more per month.

"I hear you're taking over our space," said Jonathan LaBonte, sticking his head into our cubicle at the end of day after we told Badeau we'd take the bigger spot.

It was the first time he said a word to me, despite sharing office space fifty feet apart for nine months. LaBonte, five or six years younger than me, was an interesting character in my life from that point forward. He had a standoffish demeanor I found fascinating before he ever talked to me and even more fascinating once I broke through. I think it came from a genuine shyness and social awkwardness but also knowing he was the smartest guy in the room ninety-nine percent of the time. Unfortunately, this smart guy had trouble smiling and nodding when imbeciles were talking. I shared these traits with LaBonte, although not to his extreme.

"Yeah, where are you headed?" I asked.

"We're moving to a space above Gritty's in Auburn. It's bigger and overlooks the river. It makes sense for us, and I'll be able to kayak the river to work in the summer," he said of the building they were headed to, directly next to the Androscoggin River.

It was an interesting priority but seemed to match the non-profit's mission statement to acquire, preserve, and protect land along the Androscoggin River, keeping it safe from reckless development.

"That sounds miserable, but if it makes you happy, that's good," I joked. He looked neither amused nor offended. I signed him up to write a nature article in every issue of the magazine and began a valuable friendship that day.

* * *

I wanted to create an event that had never been seen before in Androscoggin County with the magazine's name in the title that would forever link the two entities, similar to the way the NBC affiliate had an art festival in Portland. To the best of my knowledge, neither Lewiston and Auburn had ever played host to a film festival.

I sat with Sandy Marquis and explained my vision for the Lewiston Auburn Film Festival. She thought it was a terrific idea and couldn't see why L/A Arts wouldn't want to be associated. Creating a small film festival wasn't a hard sell to Molly or Paul, who both loved movies. Had we known what the whole thing would eventually turn into, I don't think any of us would have signed off on the idea.

By September, my calendar began to saturate with unique opportunities and public speaking engagements. Creating a magazine was turning me into the kind of minor celebrity I had always fawned over. Now I could put myself on a pedestal in an egotistically masturbatory way I never thought possible, but always wanted.

I appeared on a couple of public access cable shows, talked to classes of students ranging from sixth grade through college level, regularly appeared on the Fox Network affiliate's *Good Day Maine*, and spoke to organizations like the Rotary Club at least once a week. I reached a point I'd always wanted. There was always something coming in my schedule that put me in front of a group of people who somehow deemed me special. In prior years, I would have prepared for weeks for an appearance, but when I was doing two or three in a week, they became normal and just part of my routine.

Most of the time, I just gave a version of the same twenty-minute speech along with a Q&A session. I was doing so many of these appearances I'd joke to audience members they'd probably heard my ramblings elsewhere and I wouldn't take it personally if they put their head down on a table and rested. I did it for a laugh, but as much to passive aggressively say, "I'm so in demand, the odds dictate you've seen me before."

I wish I could go back and read the minds of those audiences. I'm sure plenty were thinking I was a narcissistic asshole, but I was blind to receiving that opinion at the time.

A benefit of creating the magazine and being the main face of it was the positive feedback my parents started getting. I knew my life hadn't gone exactly as the script they created had called for, especially the passages where I take their advice and always tell them the truth.

My mother was my biggest fan, but now she was regularly hearing from others how great the magazine was, what a great speaker I was, and how she must be so proud of me. I think it may have happened with my father, but only she shared it with me.

In getting my wish to be an in-demand regional celebrity, it didn't take long for me to start taking it for granted. The next classroom or speaking engagement was just another day at the office, sometimes even a nuisance. It took something over-the-top unique for me to even notice the amazing opportunities coming my way. It was self-centered and immature of me not to be more grateful during this time of my life. I think part of me thought if I could be annoyed by people who wanted to hear me speak, that made me super-duper extra special.

* * *

Corey, Paul, and I talked about the future of the magazine often. Corey and I had been busting our asses pulling double duty at the same salary for nine or ten months, and Paul was still woefully underpaid for all of the work he did. The magazine was making decent money, and it was being reinvested, but to what end? When should everybody's salaries go up? Should we just give bonus checks? What if someone came along and wanted to buy the magazine for $1 million? Where did that leave the three of us?

After a short meeting with Corey and Paul, we sat down with Donato in Windham just before the fourth issue of the magazine came out. I knew I'd have to do the talking.

"The magazine has been doing well, much better than I expected, than we expected," I told Donato. "We look like we're going to be eighty pages for a while. It's going great, but we've been killing ourselves to make it a success. If someone came and offered you good money for the company, you'd be stupid not to take it. I guess . . . we all feel like we're owed something more. Paul, Corey, and I would each like 15% of the company. It leaves you the majority owner, but we also get a piece of the action if it gets sold."

Donato looked at us for a minute. He didn't appear happy. I had a counter argument for what he was about to say. We could do the magazine without him and none of the names or logos were trademarked. If he fought that, *Great Falls Magazine* would be born within twenty-four hours.

"This is something," he said in his slow, low, slight Italian accent that reminded me of Paul Sorvino in *Goodfellas*. "I'm proud of you guys. I was hoping this would happen. You do deserve a piece. I feel very happy about this. Fifteen percent each? I'll have Neil do the paperwork."

Neil was Donato's, and the company's, lawyer. A couple of weeks later, the three of us legally owned part of LA Publishing, creators of *Lewiston Auburn Magazine*.

Chapter 7

Things chugged along into autumn, and we finally reached the plateau in sales we expected would arrive eventually, although it wasn't obvious for a few more issues that it happened at issue No. 5. For the next two years, a low month hovered around $23,000 and a good month was $28,000.

Melissa and I, married for more than seven years at this point, always had an unspoken pact: "I won't make you come to my stupid work shit if you don't make me go to your stupid work shit." It was a system that we liked, but I was taking for granted she didn't want to be part of the magazine social life and realized I missed any cues when she asked one day, "How come I'm never invited to these things?" when I mentioned some event I had to go to.

The next time there was an art exhibit opening at Gallery 5, I invited her while Molly asked her husband Erik to join us. Paul invited his wife Kate, but it was inconvenient for her to join us after a day of work in Southern Maine.

I introduced Melissa to everyone, although she already knew Paul. Sandy mentioned she, Dan, and Tammie had reservations at Fuel. Tammie had taken over as curator at the gallery and was debating changing the name to Lyceum Gallery.

Molly said she and Erik were thinking about eating there after the opening. I suggested we all eat there together courtesy of the magazine.

"Katie, my dear friend," I said, moments later, approaching the hostess station. We'd become casual acquaintances over the last several months.

"We're booked solid."

"Nothing?" I said in a mocking tone of disbelief. "What if Dan, Sandy, and Tammie release their table and we swallow it up?"

"You're going to be waiting until like 10." said Katie.

"That's like two hours. Come on, Katie . . ." I said, almost begging, yet egging her on to figure out a solution she couldn't deny me.

She looked down at her seating chart and reservation list.

"How many?"

"Seven. Maybe eight."

"Can you wait half an hour?" she asked.

"Of course we can" I said.

As the last few minutes of the exhibition wound down, I let the group know we were all set.

"Katie said they were all full tonight," Sandy remarked.

"They were for the general public," I said, starting in on my fourth or fifth beer. Since we'd be there a while longer, it seemed OK to keep going. Melissa was going to drive us home anyway.

"Ooh, I guess it's nice to be a big shot," Sandy said mockingly.

"Yes, it is." I said back to her, without a hint of sarcasm.

I don't know if Katie did that for everyone. I don't know if Katie did that because I was in Fuel regularly and spent too much on booze there. I don't know if it's because the magazine was always mentioning the restaurant. I don't know if it was because I was cultivating a status as a local celebrity. All I know is that I just pulled off the move where I was the guy who got the hostess of the best restaurant in town to juggle things even though the place was booked. Things had really come a long way in a year.

As we waited, Melissa and I strolled through the now almost empty gallery again.

"I really do like this one. You should buy it. It would make the little girl happy," she said.

It was a photograph of a piece of denim that had been stamped with white paint from a door handle. The background was a rich orange. It was visually compelling and nicely matted and framed. The 12-year-old who created it was in attendance with her parents, and Tammie made a big deal she was the youngest artist ever to hang in the gallery. Compared to some of the crap we'd seen, she was one of the better ones, too.

"You should make that little girl's day and buy it for your office," Melissa said.

The price tag was only $200. In my increasingly buzzing state, it sounded like a nice gesture. Katrielle was around this girl's age, and I knew what it would have meant to her.

So the drunk magazine publisher walked over to the little girl looking ready to leave while her parents were talking to Tammie.

"Come here," I said. "I want to ask you something about this."

We walked over to the photo.

"You know that of the fifty or sixty pieces in here, only five or six may get sold, right?" I asked.

"That lady Tammie told me," she said.

"Lucky for you, yours is one of the five or six. I'd like to buy it," I said.

The girl went squealing back to her parents. The fifteen or so people still in the gallery turned to see where the sound was emanating. Tammie looked at her then at me. I nodded. She gave me a wink and a wide smile, walked over and put a red dot on the tag.

"Did you just buy that?" Sandy asked me, smiling.

"Yup. Well, the magazine did."

"That's nice. That's really nice," she said.

"Now doesn't that make you feel good?" Melissa asked me. It did, but I know I did it mostly just to make me look like a nice guy.

I can't remember if Paul joined us for dinner or if it was his brother Marc, who had become part of the magazine's extended social circle. He was my only friend left from the Lewiston High School Class of 1994. After a decade of living in Alaska, Marc returned to Lewiston permanently shortly before the magazine launched. He didn't have half the gray hair of his younger brother, and it was great to have someone else around who knew me long before the magazine life began.

Katie showed the group to our table. I took the head because, damn it, I was the boss. I asked the waitress to settle our bar tab since we'd be buying at the table now. Melissa and Erik had a couple of drinks not normally on the tab, and I always bought a few drinks for other people. I'm not great at math, but I should have known what I was going to see. The tab was around $170. It impressed me I ran a company where we could run up that kind of a bill for liquor in just a few hours. I left a $30 tip, calling it $200 even.

I liked Erik from the second I met him. Molly was lucky to have such a good guy. He came from what seemed like a well-off family in New York. His mom received some level of prestige as a dancer and I think he knew a bit himself. He was a cabinetmaker, a handsome man and a genuinely decent human being. I always enjoyed his company and usually sought him out at events we were both attending.

When the check came, it was for around $525. The magazine could easily afford the cost and with the tip, it was rounded to $600. I appreciated Sandy reaching for her wallet, because it did feel like a bit of a punch in the gut, but I knew we had the money and dinner was my idea. I waved her off and knew that the bonding at that table was another one of those things that's hard to put a price tag on.

"You spent a lot tonight," Melissa observed on the ride home.

"Yep," I said.

"Do I want to know how much?" she asked.

"It's not our money," I said, worried she'd get mad.

"I know, I was just curious."

"Exactly $1,000."

"Holy!" she exclaimed.

"Yeah. We can afford it, but we can't afford it very often," I said.

"No kidding," she observed.

* * *

I got an email from the Chamber of Commerce in early October saying it's Young Professionals of the Lewiston Auburn Area (technically YPLAA, but everyone just called it "Y-Play") group had named me "Best New Entrepreneur in Androscoggin County for 2010."

Awards are a dime a dozen in the newspaper world. I've had boxes full of these kinds of things and usually threw them away when nobody was looking. If you're a journalist and get an award, it's rare you actually earned it. This young entrepreneur award was the first real award I earned since the sixth grade science fair.

News of getting the award would reach my mother quickly, so instead of the "Why didn't you tell us?" speech I'd get hours later, I preemptively called.

"Hi, it's me. Have dad get on the other line. I have good news," I said.

"I'm here," he said a moment later.

"So there is a group at the Chamber of Commerce called Y-Play. It's the young professionals version of the Chamber, and I found out today they are giving me the new entrepreneur of the year award," I said.

My mom let out one of her happy squeals, and my dad said his standard, "Terrific."

"Do you guys want to come to the award ceremony later this month?" I asked, assuming they'd say yes but prepared for a not-so-surprising no.

"Of course!" said my mother, deciding for both of them.

I knew that I couldn't get drunk at the awards ceremony because I had to make a speech and would say something stupid. Over the years I'd had too many voice-mails, texts, instant messages, professions of love, professions of hate, deep conversations, babblings and ramblings while under the influence to know I should never be put in a situation where I am on the spot and am expected to deliver something of value. I usually crumble, get emotional, and start blurting what is deep inside of me.

Unfortunately, what is deep inside of me are uncharted abysses of anxiety, self-doubt, intense self-loathing, insecurity, and fear. As a kid, I was usually just able to ignore it. I found alcohol in my mid-teens and it helped dull all of those feelings. In my late-teens, marijuana helped as well. The other thing that helped was engrossing myself with work at the *Sun Journal* because it made me forget who I was. If I wasn't working, drinking, smoking, or enjoying porn, I wasn't happy. Thankfully, in my early 20s, I was finally diagnosed as mentally ill. Though the correct bipolar diagnosis took a few years to establish, medication made me believe I was finally starting to feel like the rest of the people around me.

Mixing prescription meds and alcohol was almost always stupid, and the magazine was reminding me of this again. Until starting the magazine, I'd kept my drinking under control for quite a while, thinking that part of my life was over. My drinking exponentially grew once the magazine started. It was an elixir for anxiety and made me forget just how much stress I was under, but I wasn't always able to predict the results of imbibing. After going many vomit-free years, I was now throwing up once or twice a month.

My emotions rush to the surface when I drink. Whatever I may be trying to hide comes out. With alcohol, it was an involuntary reaction to get loud, or angry, or sad. But I could also get happier and friendlier. I became more attentive. I was drinking for the same reasons that I drank before the bipolar pills began helping years earlier. The magazine stress caused the pills to not be enough.

The first time this ever got downright embarrassing was the night before the awards ceremony. I convinced Dan, Sandy, Molly, and, I think, Paul that we should go to the grand opening of a new Mexican restaurant in Lewiston. I heard they were doing real mariachi music and Jell-O shots and I liked tacos. We went after a BAH and everybody seemed tired at first, but I knew we couldn't really party the next night because we had to be in business mode. I called Melissa and let her know we were checking the place out and invited her despite the fact I knew she'd say no.

I drove drunk from the BAH to the restaurant, and there was a lot of us at the Mexican place. I think the magazine paid for most of it, and I did a lot of Jell-O shots.

Melissa called a few times, and after ignoring my phone, I finally answered. She could tell that I was plastered. She made me promise I'd have Dan drive me home.

About halfway back to my place I started crying, telling him that I was scared to run a company because I didn't know what I was doing. I didn't know how to balance books or make sure employees were taken care of. I saw no growth potential. I didn't know if it made me happy. After a few minutes of sitting in his car in the driveway, I gathered myself and went into the house.

Melissa was sitting in the chair, angry that "checking out" the restaurant took almost five hours, but before she could say much, I laid on the couch and started sobbing. I tried to explain some of the things I said to Dan but couldn't. It was loud, wracking, full-body sobs unlike I'd had since a close friend died fifteen years earlier. I know she was mad that I was hours late and gallons drunker than expected, but I think that anger probably turned into fear because this was not the person she suspected was coming home that night.

I never talked about that night in the car with Dan, Sandy, or Melissa. I don't know if any of them kept it in their "red flag" bank, but if they did, it had to be one of the first major deposits.

People who brag about their drinking exploits have always annoyed me. Usually it was because I thought they were an asshole sober, a bigger asshole drunk, and a colossal asshole recounting their tales of being "totally wasted." Most of the time, it's also because my top anecdotes throttled theirs.

Your buddy once threw up in the front seat and back seat of your car because he drank so much? I threw up in five states in one day after a night of drinking at seventeen-years-old in New York City.

You once got so blackout drunk you woke up in a strange woman's bed? I once woke up on the floor of my bathroom naked, seven hours and three miles from where I last remembered being and never found the clothes or the reason I lost them.

You once had to puke into your drawer at work because you were hungover? I once stormed off the set of a live public access TV show where I was promoting an upcoming wrestling show and started profusely vomiting because I showed up drunk and they still put me on air.

I've been rushed to the hospital, almost got kicked out of college, and was forced to leave the entire fucking country of Japan because of my drinking.

I don't brag about these exploits to people because they are embarrassing. They cause great shame because they illustrate times I've been out of control and made major judgment errors. They are a laundry list of clues that I never put together proving

I had issues with alcohol from the very beginning. Whatever "totally awesome" thing happened to you while you were drunk is not totally awesome and should not be celebrated. I think that's the difference between recreational drinkers and problem drinkers. My stories were not something I wanted to recount. I ran from my history of drinking.

The company bought ten tickets in addition to the free pair Melissa and I were given to the awards dinner. Along with my parents, there was Molly, Erik, Paul, and Marc at my table. Donato, Belinda, Corey, and his date were at the table next to us.

I would have purchased tickets for Dan and Sandy, but they went with Tammie, who was the first person to nominate me, so she gave my introductory speech.

It was surreal, touching and embarrassing to hear such a positive speech about myself. As Tammie spoke, it was like she was talking about someone else. She wasn't saying anything untrue, but my feat of publishing a magazine was not special in my own eyes the way it was in others. People did it all over the world. The only thing she should have said is: "He was smart to do this first, work hard, and put together an amazing team."

During my acceptance, I said whatever I said, then threw attention to the table so I could highlight Paul and Molly. As I was talking, I asked myself internally how to end the speech, but the universe was too busy to assist that Friday night. "This is very special" I said, held up the engraved picture frame, and walked back to the seat.

* * *

A couple of random things happened the first week of November in 2010, including the initial meeting for the Lewiston Auburn Film Festival, held just days after getting my award.

The core team for the film festival was Sandy, Molly, Paul, and I. We agreed since we would wait until April for the festival, we would make the event a little larger than I first planned, showing films at multiple venues on a Saturday afternoon, hopefully feature some kind of spotlight movie, and then hold an awards dinner that night. We all took on little tasks for research and agreed to meet back before Thanksgiving to share what we learned.

One night later that week, after an event at Martindale Golf Course, Molly got bad news about her father's health. Since the death of her mother was still fresh in her mind, she understandably jumped to worst case scenarios such as being parentless before thirty and her future children never knowing a grandparent on her side of the family. Paul and I listened for a half hour and said our goodbyes.

When I got in the car, I saw Melissa had tried to call a couple of times. I figured I'd get the typical "How many beers did you really have?" speech that was becoming more frequent and well-deserved because I was always later than I said and usually more intoxicated than I planned. There was something satisfying about this instance because there was altruism, not alcohol behind it. What I didn't know was that Melissa was carting our newly sick children around town because I wasn't there to watch them when I said I'd be.

I should have taken Melissa's calls, and if I had, I would have left Molly, but instead, I chose the crisis in front of me because I tied it to the magazine, which was without question becoming my top priority. The takeaway Melissa wanted me to leave our heated conversation with was that I was getting too close to my employees and they were becoming close friends, but not only that, they were becoming closer than my family.

* * *

I allowed advertising barter deals with two types of businesses: arts organizations and restaurants. The arts groups traded for sponsorships and tickets to events. Despite my attitude the magazine was for everybody, arts supporters were still the pretentious people with money who would keep the magazine alive in the long run. We needed them to see arts were important to us. Like them, I firmly believed if Lewiston and Auburn was ever going to pull itself out of the gutter it wallowed in for decades, it was going to be through the arts.

When it came to restaurants, we would offer steep discounts on ads and allow them to pay in gift cards. My desk drawer was regularly full of over $1,000 of gift cards for places to eat all over Lewiston and Auburn.

Some restaurants were still hesitant to give us gift cards since they were scraping by to stay alive and saw any deal as giving away free food, no matter what they got in return. One such place was Holly's Own Deli in Downtown Auburn.

I decided in November we should hold a Christmas party and invite all of the magazine's friends and advertisers. Being in the center of the storm, it's hard to know for sure, but it seemed like we had quite a buzz going about us and it seemed like it could be a fun, popular party to be at. We worked a deal with Holly where she gave us private use of her upstairs dining room, a wide selection of appetizers and a drink tab of $200 for people closely connected to the magazine in exchange for a nice advertising package. I traded an ad with a local DJ to give us music and karaoke for the night.

The party was a success. At one point, I surveyed the packed room and felt proud at the assemblage. There was Lewiston Mayor Larry Gilbert. There were some of the people from Rinck Advertising. There was Kerry Landry and some of the other artists from Captive Elements. There were some advertisers and other random people from the BAH events. I couldn't identify a lot of the people.

I was shocked to see Eric Agren there and not at his own restaurant on a Friday night.

"Wow, you showed up!" I said over the loud crowd.

"I can only stay a minute!" said Eric.

"I really appreciate it."

"I had to come and say congratulations."

"Thank you!" I said loudly, shaking his hand. "It means a lot!"

Hopefully my sincerity was present in my eyes because I doubt it was in my voice. Eric Agren showing up to my party was validation of success in my eyes.

Holly came up to me shortly thereafter with a potential problem.

"I think some of these people just walked off the street," she said.

I wasn't thrilled, but it gave the place more energy. I couldn't tell you who may be a potential advertiser Paul invited, a husband of a freelance writer we used, or someone nobody knew. I didn't think offending somebody of note would be smart. Plus, good for them for crashing our party. Enjoy the food. Have a drink. Sing a song. Tell everybody you had fun.

"Oh well," I told Holly. "I hope they buy lots of drinks from you."

She gave me a smile that said most business people would have let it get to them.

Melissa came a little later, and we hung out toward the back of the room where it was a little quieter. I was sobering up, and loud parties were never my drinking scene. She'd brought the kids for a sleepover at their grandparents so we had no curfew.

"How many people have you had?" she asked.

"At this point, I have no idea. Maybe 200? Maybe 250?"

"Wow. That's a lot more than I thought would be here," she said in one of the few times she seemed impressed by something I put together. Maybe that's not fair to her. She was probably impressed at more things I did than I realized, but she knew that it was often smarter not to let me know.

A couple, probably in their mid-40s came up to the table.

"We just wanted to thank you for the party," the woman said.

"No problem. Glad you had a good time. Thanks for coming," I said and shook both of their hands. "Be careful getting home."

They smiled and exchanged hellos with Melissa before taking off.

"Who were they?" asked Melissa.

"No idea."

"Really?"

"I've never seen them before in my life," I said.

"Who invited them?" she asked

"Maybe nobody. Not worth worrying about. At least they had fun."

As the party wound down a little before midnight, Molly and Erik invited a bunch of us to their place. Melissa was open to the idea since we hadn't stayed out that late in years. A few hours later, we ended up at Denny's. After dropping Paul off at his parents' house to sleep, Melissa and I got home around 4:30 a.m. I think it was the latest we'd ever stayed out.

Chapter 8

A few weeks into 2011, Calvin Rinck was hired as the LAEGC's new marketing guy, replacing Badeau. Around ten years younger than me, I'd met Calvin once briefly at the Christmas BAH a year earlier at Lost Valley. There was always a thin layer of awkwardness I felt with Calvin that didn't exist with his father, Peter. Over time, I believe Calvin grew to dislike the way I carried myself. He knew, while the magazine was the classiest portal to the community, we were not the classiest people. He was a professional through-and-through, even in the privacy of his office.

We were as non-professional as he was professional. Coming and going whenever we wanted, gorging ourselves with pretension, and seeing people falling over themselves to tell us how great we were probably rubbed him the wrong way. He sat on just the other side of our super-sized cubicle. I'm sure he heard every conversation from the hypothetical of where we'd bury a body locally to the disgustingness of pregnancy boudoir photos, each discussion always speckled with profanity. Maybe he'd dispute my hypothesis, but Lord knows if I was Calvin, I would have fucking hated us, especially me.

January brought yet another art exhibit opening. We were tapping the same well of people for the most part but being seen flitting between Fuel and the adjoining art gallery was never a bad thing. There were plenty of the "right" people to impress who never went to the gallery but were always on the Fuel side of things.

I arrived around the same time as Sandy, so I bought her a martini and something possessed me to get one. Melissa joined us about an hour later as I was buying my second one. I was proud to tell her it was only my second drink.

Sandy had always told me Fuel's martinis kick in a little later than most, but it was strong and one was her limit. Smart lady. Only three or four small sips into my second martini, the first one hit me quicker and harder than any alcohol ever had. I went from sober to drunk in a couple of seconds without any stops at toasty, buzzed, or reached my limit.

Toward the end of the exhibit, Melissa was at the bar with Molly, Sandy, and Dan while I remained in the gallery talking with Jonathan LaBonte and Kevin Morrissette, a good friend of his. He and his longtime girlfriend, Gabby Russell, were architects who had recently bought a building in downtown Lewiston next to L/A Arts on Lisbon Street, and he was excitedly telling me about it.

Kevin regurgitated my familiar pitch about Lewiston turning around, downtown being reborn, blah, blah, blah. It was hard to focus with the martini flowing through my veins where blood should have been. I don't know exactly where my next idea came from: either the universe or the good people at Absolut.

"I'd be interested in looking at it. The magazine should have a storefront on Lisbon Street. If it's any good, we'll rent the first floor," I said, or something to the effect of: "Yes, I'll move my company to a place I don't know anything about because I make grand gestures when I'm hammered."

LaBonte and Kevin went on their way, and I found Melissa at the bar. Instead of trying to parlay the evening into dinner or maybe a movie with Melissa, I just wanted to go home.

"You shouldn't have done that second martini," Sandy said as I told Melissa we needed to leave.

Much to my surprise, I didn't immediately vomit when we hit the crisp winter air. There was no debate about leaving my car behind. I was too plastered to know where it was. Hopefully I'd remember by the light of day.

"You're going to have to give Molly more money or something," Melissa mentioned on the ride home.

"Why do you say that?" I asked.

"Because I heard her telling Sandy she was going to need either more money or benefits," explained Melissa. "What do you pay her?"

"Four hundred per week," I said.

"Holy shit! That's horrible!" Melissa said, sounding shocked. "You need to give her more money. I don't think Erik gets benefits where he works and she's going to want to have kids eventually."

"Why do you say that?" I asked.

"She told Sandy that she and Erik were trying."

Melissa was right. Molly was woefully underpaid. The following Monday, I bumped her up to $500 a week. A few months later, Paul, Corey, and I voted her an equal minority partner in the business.

For those wondering, I was able to make it home and get my face into the toilet before the projectile vomiting began.

By the point Molly became an owner, I had signed a deal with Kevin and Gabby to take occupancy of the first floor of 223 Lisbon Street once a remodel was complete that would take four to six months. They agreed to do it at their own expense, so I didn't feel like I had the right to say much about what they were planning or when they'd get it done.

There are many times in the history of the magazine I made a game-changing decision like moving the office or starting a film festival. I look back and can't remember getting the support of anyone before jumping in with both feet. I utterly have no recall of telling Paul or Molly about our future office. I don't remember any pushback. When I get my heart and mind set on something, you're going to follow me into the light or you're going to get left behind.

I've been told that this Pied Piper act is one my greatest natural abilities, but also a personality trait that is among the most off-putting. I tell myself that I want something and then I go get it. If I want to start a magazine or film festival, I'm going to. If I want Italian for dinner, you're either having Italian with me or you're eating alone. You get on board or are left behind.

Ironically, the person who first wanted Chinese food is usually excited about getting Italian, once I've explained it's what I'm doing. While I never cared if people were happy about going along with my program, I was able to get them to follow me into whatever I was doing. I could get people excited about my plan often without realizing I was doing it.

People in life look for leadership. They don't want to make the decisions and deal with the consequences.

With faux confidence and a plan that's more developed than anybody else's plan around you, you're going to get to be the leader if you so desire. When you're the leader, you get your way because to challenge you would be someone saying they wanted to be the leader, and statistically, almost nobody wants that.

The leader of the magazine was getting a new office on Lisbon Street and I just saw my employees as along for the ride.

*   *   *

Capturing the Y-PLAY New Entrepreneur of the Year award was a kicking-off point of sorts. For the next year, either the magazine, or I as an individual, started racking up awards. Once four or five were given, they started to lose their meaning. In my first thirty-four years of life, I won two trophies. A wall full of plaques was something that I always wanted to prove my worth, but I lost sight of what it meant quickly when somebody would recognize my accomplishments.

I thought being called an overnight success by people when I'd pick up the latest award was insulting. It took several months, not one night, I thought without an ounce of hubris. I couldn't help it if it took other businesses years or decades to win the same awards I was getting only ten months after putting out our first issue. Instead of being thankful the community was putting me on a pedestal, I started to wonder why it took eight or nine issues to get there. I couldn't see the rapid evolution into a hyper-pretentious, entitled asshole.

Most of the awards I individually won, I had no idea existed. There was an award given out by the *Portland Press Herald* newspaper to forty people in the state under 40 years old who were having big impacts. The biweekly business newspaper, *MaineBiz*, named me one of the state's ten young business people who would be a difference maker on the state economy in the following year, or something like that. I just liked the fact the awards came with stories in those publications about how awesome I was.

The list of accolades was long. With perspective, I can see it's actually impressive, but they now are less about my accomplishments and more like little mile markers along my descent into madness.

* * *

My proudest achievement, aside from the fact I was simply able to keep a company afloat as many years as I did, was the Lewiston Auburn Film Festival. It took me a few years removed from the entire to situation to figure out why the film festival felt like such an accomplishment, far more than *Lewiston Auburn Magazine*. It's about discovering a new skillset. I knew we could make *Lewiston Auburn Magazine* with our eyes shut, but with LAFF, I thought we had a viable idea, yet no clue how to mechanically see it through. I didn't know if we had the ability to successfully run a film festival, just that we had a strong team for me to lead.

Molly, Paul, Sandy, and I met biweekly, then weekly, then almost every day leading up to the early-April 2011 festival. Never knowing when to stop adding, we arranged for nine locations in Lewiston and Auburn to show films. Why feature forty films in five locations when you can show eighty at nine?

The centerpiece film was *PAL Hop Days,* a documentary of the rise of the local music scene forty-five years earlier. The movie was created by filmmaker Bill Maroldo who wasn't living locally at the time of the weekly dances, but heard stories from many, including his neighbor, Nick Knowlton.

I liked Nick a lot. I think after our release of the magazine at the PAL Hop reunion concert and running into him at many events, he really grew on Molly and Paul, too. He was like a crazy, but loving uncle. He died while I was writing this book. I never got a chance to tell him how much he meant to the magazine, but more importantly, to me. The shame of my arrest and conviction severed so many relationships I didn't cherish like I should at the time.

Nick brought Bill and I together several months before the festival to talk about the movie. At first, Bill was hesitant. He had no timeline to complete the film, deciding he was going to take his time and get it right. I asked if he'd consider a rough director's cut, but that idea didn't grab him either.

Even the lure of the Franco American Heritage Center, a beautiful former Catholic church converted into an amazing arts center with a giant auditorium boasting around 550 seats, wouldn't budge him. I thought offering to show his film in this landmark with its stadium-style seating would seal the deal. Ever the artist, Bill left me scrambling . . . until the next day. He called and said he'd had a talk with his wife, and she'd sold him on the idea.

"She said that I'd be crazy to pass this up. It may be rough, but you'll have something," he said.

"You saved my ass," I told him.

The organizers decided an awards dinner at the end of the night would put a classy cap on the day. We spoke to Eric Agren about Fuel holding the dinner. He agreed, at $50 per head, to close for the evening and cater the event as long as we kept it to one hundred people.

Watching the movies during the judging period was the most satisfying part of the experience. Over 200 films were submitted and while there were painfully inept ones, it was a treat to get something from another country, knowing I was the first person in Maine, and potentially the entire United States, to see it.

My run of good luck continued when introduced to Colin Kelley, a guru in the video department at Bates College. We pitched him the idea of LAFF, and he agreed to come on as technical director. The little issue of having no idea how to show films was solved before we had to admit it was a problem. There was no Plan B, much less a Plan A. Colin, a genuinely shy guy with some of the expected personality quirks of a brilliant guy who worked in technology, reminded me a lot of Corey. I think Sandy intimidated him a bit. Molly and I seemed to speak his language.

My life to this point had been a series of no plans, just moving forward, expecting the right thing to happen—and it always did. I wasn't foolish enough to think this happened to everybody, but I wasn't gracious enough to be thankful how lucky I'd been either.

A few days before the festival, the *Sun Journal* (finally accepting there was a magazine in town operated by a former employee who wasn't trying to compete) ran a film festival story.

The photo that ran in the newspaper featured, in order, Sandy, me, then Molly. It was appropriate as the two women represented opposite priorities. Molly was artistic, creative, a people person. Sandy was logical, strategic, a realist. I was in the middle. I understood needing more money coming in than going out and appreciated being able to talk to Sandy about the business side of things with LAFF because she too was running a business.

I also understood money couldn't be made without a great product. Taking a loss our first year of the film festival could be acceptable if it was seen as an investment. Molly never let a lack of knowledge of the numbers stand between us and a great idea. I could relate as somebody who believes it is impossible to make money without terrific content. There needed to be a balance between the two sides, and I am nothing if not a reliable fulcrum.

Tickets sold well in advance. VIP tickets, which included a day pass and dinner were $75. We sold out of them two days before the festival began. Most of the VIP tickets were sold to filmmakers and their families, although a few dozen were simply film fans or local people who wanted to be part of the action like Chip Morrison and his wife, Jane. Enough day passes were sold at $22 each that, when coupled with the VIPs and sponsorships, we were almost at break-even the day of the festival.

I started my day as the host of films at the Lewiston Public Library, As a couple of volunteers and I we were setting everything up about thirty minutes prior to opening, my cell phone started vibrating, indicating I'd received an email. It was an alert there was a charge to our merchant credit card account. Paul at headquarters sold a pair of day passes for $44. At least two people bought tickets, I thought. We would be adding to the bottom line. With every few chairs I set up, the phone vibrated.

The first film kicked off at exactly 10 a.m., a documentary about a local non-profit. It wasn't well-attended in the beginning. Only twenty people were at the library when the lights went off, but more trickled in throughout and the steady vibration in my pocket continued. I texted Paul to see how things were going.

He only responded. "I'm Busy. Good."

By the time the director of the documentary and I were conducting the Q&A session, the room had more than doubled in attendance. The hall's large size and 60-70 empty chairs still made the crowd look sparse, but not embarrassing. Thankfully, it continued to grow through the next couple of films and probably held steady at 75.

I built a small lunch break before 1 p.m. into the library viewing schedule. The pinging on my phone died down considerably at that point. I called Paul who said sales had come to a standstill, but I could hear the smile in his voice.

"I don't know for sure how many people," he said. "Probably over 100 people. They were almost always buying more than one ticket. There were sometimes people waiting outside. A lot of people were disappointed they couldn't buy tickets to the dinner. We need a bigger place next year."

Once my shift at the library was done, I literally ran to the Franco Center to host the *PAL Hop Days* screening. A volunteer was manning the box office when I got there, out-of-breath.

"How we doing?" I asked

"A little over 100 plus the people who already had passes," she said.

Pal Hop Days was the only movie we allowed single tickets to be sold for. I knew many local people would spend $7 to see that movie, but not $22 for a festival pass. We did, however, allow people with passes to attend the film at no extra charge. The walk-up $7 tickets meant another $700 in revenue for LAFF off the film. I thought we'd draw 400 and was disappointed introducing the film to a crowd of about 175 people. A couple more people trickled in, but we never got to 200. I hoped Bill Maroldo was happy with the turnout. I never asked him because he would have been honest, and I didn't want to hear anything negative.

I texted Sandy and let her know we did $700 for *Pal Hop Days* which was less than I projected. She'd been collecting money from venues all day.

"It's going to be close to break-even," she said in a return text.

The audience seemed to enjoy *PAL Hop Days* and the Q&A afterward, but the whole "centerpiece" of the festival fell flat for me. The film was good, but it didn't feel like a special event. I fully blame myself. When it was over, I thanked Bill and made my way down to Fuel where the awards dinner cocktail hour was just getting into full swing.

It seemed like everyone was full of energy, but I just needed a few minutes to catch my breath, so I walked into the gallery and sat down on a couch that had been put in there to make more room for seating at Fuel. Paul brought me a beer and sat down.

"You OK?" he asked.

"Truthfully, I'm exhausted. My adrenaline was up and down all day. I must have walked and jogged three miles all over downtown. I'm physically and emotionally spent," I said.

"That makes sense. Good news is we probably took in around a couple thousand in ticket sales today," he said.

"Did you get that number from Sandy or are you guessing on your own experience?"

"What I saw," he said.

"With or without *Pal Hop Days*?"

"Without. You can sit here another minute, but you have to go mingle. A lot of the filmmakers want to meet you, and it never hurts to kiss people's asses who might want to be sponsors next year," Paul said.

"I suppose you're right," I said sucking on the Corona.

"You did this," Paul said, looking at me earnestly. "This was all your idea."

I soaked in his words for a minute after he returned to Fuel. The event was my idea, but the four of us built a machine. Paul was the one who brought me the beer and congratulated me when he could have been drinking with a lot of cool people. It's because at the core, we were still the two friends who started the crazy ball rolling.

Molly hosted the awards ceremony. Even I knew I shouldn't host the show, but rather represent the magazine as we had sponsors giving awards and the magazine was the lead media sponsor. The four of us sat at a table near the podium so Molly would have easy access. Colin, Erik, and Dan were there as was Donato and Belinda, who came down from Windham just for the dinner.

We gave the awards out between courses, two at a time, saving the Best in Festival for the big finale after dessert. I gave the penultimate award and didn't give Molly any instructions on how to introduce me.

"The next presenter will be giving our Producers' Award. It's decided upon by the festival organizers and given to someone who has contributed to film in a unique way. Representing *Lewiston Auburn Magazine* and let's be honest, this is the guy who thought Lewiston and Auburn should have a film festival: Joshua Shea."

I stood up and pivoted, since the podium was directly behind my seat at the head of the table. The audience graciously applauded. And it kept going. And then they stood. I was getting the first—and only—standing ovation of my life. I looked around and saw Paul, Molly, Sandy, and Dan. Further back near the bar were Eric Agren and Katie. There were Chip and Jane Morrison. A few other friends, both professional and personal dotted the crowd along with other people I'd meet for the first and last time that day. For many of these people, especially the filmmakers who got a submission into a legitimate film festival for the first time, this would be a day they would never forget. Here they were. With me. Standing. Clapping. I was too exhausted to comprehend it all.

As the applause subsided and people took their seats and grew quiet, the universe delivered a clever opening line through my mouth.

"That is the first time that has ever happened, so thank you. Just a note, especially to the locals. It would be deadly if I said yes to everybody who has so far offered to buy me a drink tonight, but I don't want to be rude. So, before you leave, see Eric Agren at the bar. He'll collect your money and record your name. During the year, I'll work through the list, and I'll send an email thanking you when I get to yours."

A genuine chuckle worked its way through the room, but the effects of the standing ovation was still overwhelming me. I couldn't take my eyes off the assemblage in the room. How did the four of us do this?

"I'm blown away by today. I need to thank all of your for being part of this from the sponsors to the volunteers and filmmakers and Eric Agren who closed the place for us. I know you got some drink tickets as part of the deal, but please buy a lot at his bar after dinner. There are three people I have to thank the most," I said turning toward Paul, Molly, and Sandy.

This wasn't about to be one of the go-through-the-motion appreciations I gave when getting magazine awards. I never could have expected it, but I started breaking down.

"I've been through a war with these people," I said, tears welling up in my eyes and voice cracking, just trying to hold it together so I didn't enter a full sob. "Sandy Marquis was the second or third person who heard about my crazy idea last summer and bought into it immediately. She always helped me keep things in perspective, except when I was able to overwhelm her. You have no idea how much work she put into this."

I paused while people gave her a round of applause and turned toward Molly, still gritting my teeth, trying not to cry.

"Molly is amazing. Those magazines some of you filmmakers got in your gift bags today . . . My name is at the top, but she's responsible for just as much as I am. She's not only a partner, she's a friend," I said, to another round of applause.

"Paul Roy . . ." I said and probably to my biggest surprise, my voice really started going.

"I've known Paul for 20 years, before he had gray hair. He was the only other person with me when we started the magazine. Most know him as our sales director, but I don't think people realize a third of his job is just handling me. These are the people at the heart of the festival."

I gathered myself while another polite round of applause rose and fell.

"I'm giving away the Producer's Award, as Molly said. We will give this award annually to someone we feel who has made a contribution to film that otherwise may not be acknowledged. This year, it took less than a minute to figure out who the first recipient should be. It's true this festival was my idea, but I had to get to a place in life where it was even possible to consider trying it. This festival grew out of *Lewiston Auburn Magazine. Lewiston Auburn Magazine* grew out of a newspaper in Windham called *The Independent*. It wasn't started by a big newspaper company or even anybody experienced in publishing. It was started by a man, a visionary, who owned the most popular sandwich shop in Windham. If you're looking for a person to thank for tonight, it's him. The recipient of this year's Lewiston Auburn Film Festival Producer's Award is Donato Corsetti."

The audience applauded as I turned toward Donato. He came to the podium and kept it short.

"This is quite an honor, thank you," he said and then returned to his seat.

I'd hoped for more, but we surprised a guy who doesn't like public speaking and prefers the background, not the spotlight.

The rest of the show went nicely and following dessert, many retired to the gallery for the viewing of a couple of the short award winners while others enjoyed the bar at Fuel. Chip Morrison came over and complimented us.

"'I don't know how you guys do it or where you find the time. I saw some movies I didn't understand today, but just phenomenal work," he said while Jane nodded. I don't know why, but it meant so much when Chip said he was proud of me. Maybe for just a moment, I didn't feel like a fraud.

I mingled for a few minutes, but was exhausted and knew that if I started to drink with any vigor, I wasn't going to stop until I passed out . . . and I was going to be a sloppy, sad drunk that night. With only about a quarter of the people still left, a few were trying to arrange an after-party at The Cage, a local spacious dive bar. I wanted ten more beers, but the drunken stupor part seemed like a bad idea.

"I'm going home," I told Sandy. "I'm tired."

"Why don't you knock off early on Monday and come to my house? We'll figure everything out with money."

"That sounds nice. I'm going to go home and sleep until then," I said.

"You deserve it. Nice work. Really nice work," she said.

I heard about the post-Fuel drunken escapades on Monday morning at the office. I was disappointed I hadn't been there, but knew it was for the best.

Monday was a lost day. We were all still beat, but happy, sharing our individual stories of the festival. Shortly after we went out for one of our long, gift-card lunches, we called Sandy, said we weren't getting anything done, and headed over.

Once drinks were in hand, we went through the task of counting stacks of cash and adding up credit card receipts.

Minus a few lingering expenses we came up just short of $4,000 for a profit. We put $2,000 back into the LAFF bank account and split the other $2,000. Considering we'd been meeting, watching movies, and planning for six months, it probably represented about 50 cents per hour for each of us, but it was a nice bonus since we just aimed for break-even. We agreed a second festival should happen, but we'd wait a few months to talk about it.

The other thing decided that afternoon was to spin the festival off into its own company, under the same structure as the magazine, an S-Corporation. It was for-profit and protected our butts as individuals. We decided to put off non-profit status until after the second festival. We wanted it but had no idea how to set it up properly. We decided to split ownership five ways with each of us getting twenty percent, including Donato. I called him the following day with the idea, and he told me he'd get Neil the Lawyer right on it.

* * *

It was obvious to most people I was a workaholic. I have no question in my mind that I am an alcoholic, but I think I hid it fairly well. Even after my arrest, I struggled with the idea I was a porn addict. It was easy for me to dismiss using porn as more of a seedy hobby than a legitimate addiction nobody knew about. For every minute of porn there was an hour of drinking and twelve hours of work. In my heart, I knew that my relationship with porn had never been healthy. From the moment I felt the chemical mixture of adrenaline, testosterone, and dopamine hit when my cousin Scott showed me a *Penthouse* at his family's summer rental in the mid-1980s, I knew I found something that would occupy a special place of prominence in my life.

Porn has always been my go-to sexual crutch. I thought it solved all my problems. When my first high school girlfriend—the one who took my virginity—broke it off with me a few months later, my stack of *Playboy* magazines were still there to comfort me. They didn't want to see other people. In my early 20s, when a long-term relationship with a woman I lived with in Portland was crumbling on multiple levels, including sexually, I never stopped and tried seriously to fix it. Pay-per-view was now bringing porn directly to our apartment via the cable box. I didn't need to have an awkward conversation because I didn't need to talk at all.

The collapse of intimacy between Melissa and I was one of the many casualties of my descent into illness. It didn't disappear entirely, but it had to be on my timetable, when I wanted it. With my growing emotional isolation from her, why would she want to still be doing that with me? There were many nights I was unsuccessful in waking her. At some point I just decided to stop trying. You don't have to wake up the Internet.

My mental connection of sex to some kind of dangerous, forbidden activity coupled with my inability to have an open and honest conversation about my personal sexuality with those I'm most intimate with is not a good combination if one is also looking to use porn in a healthy way. What turns me on is fairly basic, but even if I wanted to have an orgy with nothing but people over 6' 6" while being pelted with tater tots while loud Irish music played, I should be able to tell Melissa. My wife isn't going to leave me if I tell her something embarrassing or weird.

My brain historically told me that the upside with porn is none of these issues of real intimacy ever had to come into play, and it's that faulty thinking—choosing porn over a connection with a real person—that finally forced the logical side of me to admit I am a pornography addict. Logically, I know Melissa would chuckle and say, "I hate Irish music, don't want to do that with other people, and that's a waste of tater tots." That would be the end of it.

But my mind says that Melissa would say, "What the fuck is wrong with you, you fucking freak? Number one, you're married. Number two, where are you going to find a bunch of people that tall? Number three, that's a waste of perfectly good food and who the hell is doing the throwing? The other orgy members? Me? And you're just doing this because you want to be with other women, right??!! Well fuck you, go be with other women! I want a divorce! You're never going to see your kids again, and I'm taking the pets and the cars and the house—and you'll have to live with your parents. Then you can go hook up with your giant orgy friends whenever you want, but that will never happen. You will die alone in your parents' house!"

The obvious solution to my problems at the time was to just take thirty minutes and masturbate to pornography online. I didn't want to end up dying alone in my parents' house. My mind told me I was making the smart choice.

Chapter 9

As we entered our second summer in business, with ten issues printed, a successful film festival in our back pocket, and every award in the area captured, things evened out a bit which was OK. We were no longer seen as rookies to most people. I knew our job was not to continue raising the bar in quality of the magazine, but to stay relevant in people's minds.

The only way I knew how to raise the bar was by engineering some attention-grabbing stunt or doing something that made people stop to look at us. The response was always unanimously positive . . . or at least that's how I chose to interpret it. For someone who felt like a failure throughout life, it was surreal. From my point of view, I couldn't make a mistake, and if I did, people still loved whatever my error yielded. A feeling of invincibility washed over me. Most of the time, I was completely sold on the idea I was a charismatic local celebrity. It was only when I was alone, not doing magazine work, when things were quiet and I could get introspective that I said to myself, "The clock is ticking on this bomb. You're going to fuck things up eventually."

I can draw a direct comparison between how I needed to constantly raise the bar with the magazine and how I viewed pornography in the few years leading up to my arrest.

Most of my life, all I needed was a *Playboy* magazine or basic adult website, but I found that a photograph of an attractive woman wasn't enough anymore. I needed to start raising the bar to keep things exciting with porn.

It's textbook addict behavior. You build a tolerance, and the substance doesn't do for you what it once did. I couldn't sit and look at a website with photos of beautiful naked women and be satisfied. I needed to start looking at video clips.

At first, as with regular photos, I wasn't too discriminating and didn't favor the hardcore stuff. I could watch a handful of videos, and it would meet my cravings and my needs, but then they became mundane. Soon, I didn't need just a couple of clips, I needed a couple dozen. Then they started to become more explicit—although still completely legal at this point. Looking at them for twenty minutes soon became forty minutes, then an hour.

At the time a little later that I made the jump to live cam/chat rooms it was some kind of logical progression in my twisted, sick mind. Photographs were passive. Video clips were active. Cam/chat rooms were interactive.

Much like I wondered how to raise the bar with the magazine's visibility, I was starting to recognize the need to raise the bar in my pornography consumption to be satisfied. I'm sure I just dismissed it as a spike of stress, not the downward trajectory I had begun.

* * *

Noticing when things start going bad had always been a blind spot with me. I'd had enough failures that I should have learned to spot signs when things are starting to go awry, but I didn't have the capability at that point in time. Now, "Am I missing something here?" is a mantra that helps keep recovery on the right path.

Another blind spot I've had through life, that I only started examining after rehab, is my lack of ability to take social cues and understand how my words and actions would be perceived by others. I recognize my defense mechanism of joking to dispel tension usually falls flat, but my deeper understanding of how my words are being interpreted isn't as razor-sharp as I'd like to believe it is.

It took me quite a while after my arrest to appreciate the fact that there is a large amount of the population—probably a majority—who can never take me out of a box my crime has placed me in within their mind. I will not change their opinion, ever.

Much of the information in the media about my crime was vague, and some was actually incorrect. I've learned that if I try to correct it or give specifics and provide perspective, most jump to the conclusion that I'm diminishing, minimizing and rationalizing what I did. Upon being released on bail following my arrest, it was reported I was not allowed to be around my children. This was incorrect. I could not be left alone with my children, but if my wife or parents were around, I could be with the children as much as I wanted. The initial state police press release was incorrect, and the media simply reported what they were given.

Early on, I tried to correct wrong information and put things in perspective for people, but what I learned was that this was interpreted as an exercise to make myself look better. In most people's opinion, I should keep my mouth shut, even if they are judging me based on wrong or incomplete information.

People have an idea of what I did, and they don't want to hear me delineate the details. Whereas my mind once thought I could put things into perspective for others, explaining some of the gray areas, I now understand most view this in terms of black and white and certainly don't want me to be the messenger providing any fact-checking. The moment I open my mouth I'm seen as a bias spin doctor.

I've tried to explain why I think this is wrong to people but finally came around to their explanations that I'm at the center of this issue, not an impartial observer in this scenario. People not only distrust, but also dislike, when the source tries to be impartial.

The inability to recognize this big blind spot has been with me throughout life. I think it has a lot to do with having few close bonds with people. I've never understood when I should just keep my mouth shut and not make things worse. That was a constant, major blind spot.

Most in my family know better than to come to me for comfort at a funeral because I'm more apt to say something that puts death into perspective for myself, but not make the situation any better for them.

It's one thing to commit the crime of enticing a teenage girl to perform sexual acts on a computer screen, but it's worse to have done it and be seen as defending my own behavior. I've never defended what I did, but I've also learned that I can't say, "I didn't physically touch a child" or "Underage porn use was less than 1% of my overall porn consumption." Both of those things are true, but out of my mouth, they make the situation worse.

Maybe it was always being told to tell the truth as a child or all of those years as a journalist trying to be fair and impartial, but it took these horrible life changing events for me to realize how the truth is presented and who it is presented by is just as important as what the truth actually is.

Wanting others to know the hard facts is my way of hopefully softening what people think of me, but that's a miscalculation. Nothing from my mouth is going to change what people believe or don't believe happened—and it will never improve what people think of me.

These are the kinds of lessons I've learned about myself through the recovery process. Now, when someone asks about my crime, I make things as short and straightforward as possible.

* * *

Since the film festival took our attention away, we almost missed reserving a booth for the LAEGC B2B Trade Show at the Civic Center in 2011. It was going to be a big one as Calvin was trying to make a good first impression, and he had to remind us the clock was ticking when we returned from lunch one weekday.

"Everybody has boring displays," I said to Paul and Molly, telling them nothing they didn't know. "Ours was dull last year, but that was our first time. We need people to leave remembering us thinking that we're fun, adventurous, insane, and wondering what we're going to do next. They have to see us and wonder what we're thinking and see the magazine and wonder what's inside. Hey Calvin! Can you hear me?"

"A little bit," he said over the partition. He never commented on our conversations, but I knew he could hear them all.

"Is our booth space open from last year. Those two booths at the end on the left?" I asked.

"No. Energy Maine is having a race car in that spot," he said.

"Can you come over here and show us what's available?"

Calvin brought his schematic over. There were no double-sized booths on either edge of the map available, but in the middle of the floor, where booths were not only side-to-side but also back-to-back, a space of four open booths formed a square.

"We can't afford it, but can we work a deal for these four?" I asked.

"What are you planning?" he asked suspiciously.

"No idea, but I guess it's going to have to take up 400 square feet. It's not like we have to get the OK from you for our plans, right?" I said.

"You know, I own a pretty good size bounce house," he said.

We looked around at each other.

"Calvin? Why do you own a bounce house?" Molly immediately needed to know.

"When Mariah and I got married, we thought we'd rent one for the kids who came, but it was basically the same price to buy it so we did and figure we'd get our money's worth eventually," he explained.

"How much you want to rent it?" I asked.

"I'll just give it to you," he said.

"Sold," said Molly.

We brought the bounce house over to the civic center the day before the show to test it. Calvin delivered it to our booth space, and it fit perfectly, also allowing us enough room to still have a few tables to put magazines and LAFF press kits out for people.

During our test, people from other companies setting up their displays came over to marvel at our choice. It caused a reaction, but I could tell it was not always positive. The suit-and-tie types, the ones who longed for a business job that would net them the upper-middle-class life they could pretend was lower-upper-class didn't like it. Commerce was a serious thing, not to be taken lightly. In my eyes, the show wasn't about commerce. It was about saying, "Hey, come look at me!" I'd perfected that art form over thirty-five years.

The morning of the show, we arrived early, set up the tables, and re-inflated the bounce house. It was vacant most of the day, although those who brought kids were relieved there was something for them. There were the young cell phone booth workers who clearly hadn't committed to the corporate lifestyle who loved it, and I was all for letting twenty-year-old girls bounce around my booth as long as they desired. Molly and I also took turns jumping around to draw attention. Paul never stepped foot inside.

Sandy said she was going to split booth time with Marquis Signs and LAFF/*Lewiston Auburn Magazine*.

"You guys really know how to get attention," she said, shaking her head upon seeing the bounce house.

"I know you mean that as a compliment," I said.

"Most of the time, yes," she responded.

"I just want people to remember this. I want them to walk away and say, 'Now there are people who look like they have fun at work.' I don't know," I said to Sandy, searching for the right words. "It's like I always imagined a job where I could do anything and try anything I wanted."

"And you got it!" she said.

"Yeah . . ."

I dwelled on her statement a lot that day, especially when I was bouncing around in my socks, inside a giant children's toy. Then again, I was a giant child who felt like he was really pulling the wool over everyone's eyes. I couldn't tell if I was just lucky or had manipulated the community into a robust group of enablers. I knew it couldn't have anything to do with talent and ability. There I was for good chunks of the day, in my playpen for everyone to see, smiling, laughing, and waving.

My parents brought the kids over late in the day. Kaden and I immediately jumped in and started wrestling. I loved that moment because the world disappeared, and it was just my eight-year-old son and I playing WWE. I wish I had more time like that along the way.

* * *

Our morning routine usually had me as the last one to leave the house, returning to eat breakfast and take a shower after the kids were brought to school. Melissa worked in Portland, so she was gone much earlier in the morning.

I was looking at the *Sun Journal* website one day in the spring and saw an article about a joint meeting between Auburn's City Council and School Board. I lived in Ward 5 in Auburn. My City Council representative, Ray Berube, stormed out of a joint city/school budget meeting the night before, according to the newspaper. I knew Ray was one of the bullying majority who rendered Dick Gleason a figurehead as mayor. Something in me snapped that morning. I sent Ray an email asking to meet with him as soon as possible. He should have given me a day or two to cool off. Instead, he made the mistake of meeting me about two hours after I read the article at his small City Hall office.

"What can I do for you Mr. Shea?" he asked once we'd settled into our seats.

"You can call me Josh. Mr. Shea was my father. He was a teacher at Sherwood Heights School at the very beginning of his career. That's the elementary school in our ward. He taught there at the very end of his career, too, as did my mother, Mrs. Shea. My daughter is now at Auburn Middle School, but she spent five years at Sherwood Heights. My son will do all seven years of his elementary school there. I live a quarter mile from the school. What you did walking out of that meeting last night was disgusting and reprehensible. It doesn't represent me, and I'm guessing it doesn't represent well more than half of the people in our neighborhood," I told the gray-haired man who looked around seventy-five.

"Josh, you have to understand, their budget is ridiculous," he got out before I interrupted.

"No, you don't get it, Ray. The point is that even if they come to you with a $10 billion budget, you sit there and you listen. You be polite, you be courteous, and you sit there listening to every damn word they have to say. If you don't have the time, you shouldn't be a City Councilor."

"I thought about how I handled it on the way home. I should have stayed," he said.

"But you didn't," I said. "You got up and left with your two buddies to make a scene, to make a statement. Wrong statement. You looked like an angry little kid who was going to take his toys and go home."

And then, stone sober, I made one of those declarations you can't back off from unless you're at peace with looking like a major hypocrite.

"Ray, if you run again, I'm going to have to run against you. If you don't run, I'm going to run anyway. I will have everybody who liked my parents, I'll have everybody who reads my magazine, and I'll have everybody who just doesn't like you," I said, standing up.

"What magazine do you own?" he asked, standing up.

"*Lewiston Auburn Magazine*," I responded, knowing he was on the VIP mailing list, like all elected officials.

"I don't think I've seen it," he said.

"That's OK. Thank you for meeting with me. Some people may have hid. I disagree with you and I want you out, but you did face me like a man," I said. It's not my style to storm out of places angry.

"Thank you, it was good meeting you," he said.

As I walked to the parking garage, I had one thought: Now I have to run for Auburn City Council.

I didn't tell anybody at first about the meeting. I thought about it, convincing myself I could actually help point Auburn in a better direction, so why not run?

The first person I approached was Chip Morrison at the Chamber of Commerce. He said I'd make a "wonderful" councilor, but he also gave a key piece of advice: "If you run, you'll have to win." I never asked him to elaborate. What would happen if I didn't win? He made it sound frightening.

Next, I went to Dick Gleason, Auburn's mayor and owner of the only radio stations in Lewiston and Auburn. We didn't talk a lot, but I always listened closely. He likely never had any idea the weight his words meant to me. I wanted to know two things: Was he going to run again and did serving as an elected official affect his business? There were still a few months to decide to pursue another term, which he hadn't done yet, and he didn't think serving as mayor helped or hurt his radio stations in any measurable way. He said my running was a good idea, but the tone of his voice gave me doubts.

I heard through the grapevine another guy, Leroy Walker, was looking at a Ward 5 run. He was the closest thing to a boss/

icon/celebrity Ward 5 had. He worked for the City of Auburn a couple of decades and owned the most popular restaurant in the neighborhood, Andy's Baked Beans.

I arranged a meeting with Leroy and came to a good news/ bad news conclusion. The bad news was that I'd never defeat him. The good news was despite his gruffness, he cared deeply for the neighborhood, providing a level of business sense lacking on the council from Ward 5. We differed on education, but he was an upgrade from Ray.

Jonathan LaBonte was also from the neighborhood, living there since he was a child. Mostly loved, he was the only person who had a chance of beating Leroy, and I knew he had been quietly considering a run as he was already serving as a county commissioner. People said one-day LaBonte would be governor. If he threw his hat into a race with Leroy and I, I would finish a distant third.

Where did this leave me? I couldn't win Ward 5, and I couldn't run in Wards 1-4. The only other seats were two "At-Large" posts elected by the entire city. LaBonte pointed out to me I might do better in the more middle or upper-class parts of Auburn than I would in my own backyard. Since the magazine went citywide and my parents had taught at various schools in Auburn over the years, he made sense.

The problem was that the At-Large seats were locked-in. One by Belinda Gerry, a person whose "heart was in the right place" which was code people used to say that there was little consistency behind her decision making. Gerry had served many terms and lived in the largest subsidized housing complex in Auburn. She was actually quite smart, but because she masterfully played the poor, meek, and obese cards, nobody ever challenged her opinions. She was loved among the lower socioeconomic groups of voters.

Despite the fact she was part of the problem, I have long held the theory she always got a lot of votes because she was usually the only woman in the At-Large race in a field of six or seven male candidates. Voters were allowed to pick two candidates of the At-Large slate. If only 300 citizens cast their vote for her because they'd like a woman's "voice" on the council, it could sway the outcome. I have a suspicion if every person who voted for her thought deeper than "Look, there's a woman's name—I like diversity" she'd have lost years earlier. I would have loved to unseat her but didn't know if it was possible.

The other At-Large candidate was a member of the Androscoggin County Sheriff's Department, Eric Samson. He's served two terms and was one of the good guys. Replacing him would not make sense. He was plugged into the community and the council. But when I met with him, he told me he was not going to run again so he could focus on his career and family. He mentioned that he'd heard the three councilors I strongly disagreed with, including Ray, were not running again. I'm sure Ray heard Leroy, LaBonte, or I were running and realized it was fool's errand to challenge.

If everything Samson said was correct, it left the philosophical direction of the council wide open. Wards 2 and 4 already had decent councilors. If they could be held and two of the five other seats could be gained, Dick Gleason could be the mayor he always should have been had he not been stonewalled.

I told Molly and Paul I was running, explaining to them Dick said it had no effect on his business. Along with the bottom line, they worried about my objectivity changing. I figured as long as I didn't screw over advertisers as a City Councilor, I'd be fine. If it got dicey, I'd just abstain. Paul and Molly knew listening to their feedback was merely a courtesy I was extending. Should I win, I agreed to never mention I was a Councilor in the magazine.

I told my parents and Melissa that I was planning on running for City Council. My parents thought it was exciting but wondered if I had the time. Melissa just shrugged. She'd also started backing off attending as many events with me. Looking back, I don't blame her. I was just out there promoting myself for the sake of it most days.

She was pleased for me that things I worked hard for were coming to fruition, and I don't think she was mad that they necessarily took time away from the family. I think she was more disappointed that I either didn't notice or that it didn't matter to me. Sadly, she was right. I had tunnel vision.

I really loved those rare moments when I could be derailed long enough to do something fun with the family like go to the drive-in movie theater or have a date night with Melissa, but I was so focused it was hard to knock me off track.

I was always torn on Melissa not being outwardly, vocally impressed with much of what I did. It grounded me and showed me there was a "real life" outside of the public brand I was building, but a piece of me resented her for not thinking she was lucky for being with such a go-getter. Not everybody was married to a future City Councilor. Not everybody was named to so many lists of up-and-coming young entrepreneurs. If I took my success for granted, I felt she was doubly guilty and that was a slap in my face. I look back at this kind of narcissism, and it comes off almost like a cartoon villain, but it was very real and I believed every ounce of my own bullshit. I don't think I could have sold it as well if I didn't.

Her praise for the magazine came through her mother, who read it cover-to-cover when it arrived. Melissa would always report what her mother liked and that would sometimes prompt her to take a look and comment on what she saw. Melissa knew it was never wise to give me too much praise. I held onto it and spun it for much more than it was worth because, again, the narcissistic side of me was raging.

I'm sure it was difficult knowing exactly how to handle somebody who was obsessed with his job and was clearly getting so much more than just a paycheck and professional recognition. She could see that it was a feeding tube for my mental health and knew to tread carefully. The balancing act she pulled off was in many ways just as remarkable as mine.

* * *

I recognized I was beginning to spread myself thin and could even sense a little burnout on Molly and Paul's part. Our financial situation was still rosy, and I figured we'd be OK bringing on someone new at $10/hour. I needed a jack-of-all-trades: Someone who could sell a little, take care of the subscription database, take a photo or write a short story if needed, maintain the website, and handle a myriad of other tasks. I needed a mini-me, but I also wanted someone who had marketing experience or a degree in that area.

I thought there was an opportunity to create a tiny PR/marketing/advertising agency extension to what we were doing. I didn't want to be even 5% the size of a legit agency like Rinck, but I knew there were a lot of little design and consulting gigs floating around that we were either already doing for free or could tack on a small fee and let it grow organically from there. A new hire with some background in this area could help create and grow that division. While I knew $400 a week wasn't cheap, I saw it as an investment. This position would start by selling ads half the time, which might be able to get us closer to the $30,000 in ad sales every issue and cover for me if I ever wanted to take a vacation, which I was clearly needing.

I didn't post anything on Facebook, Craigslist, or tell many people beyond Paul and Molly I was debating a new hire. Social media, especially Facebook, was an integral part of the success of *Lewiston Auburn Magazine* as it was our most valuable tool for self-promotion and content idea generator.

One late August afternoon I was at home, working near my pool sipping on a Corona, taking a break to scan Facebook. I knew the moment I saw the post she was as good as hired.

Danielle Sicotte, the box office manager at Community Little Theatre and a part-time assistant at Encompass Marketing, posted she was getting desperate for full-time employment. I had seen her around enough that I could hold a quick conversation with her. I think Danielle was barely paid at the theater where she had been in productions since childhood, and she simply couldn't get the number of hours she needed at Encompass.

I noticed Danielle was online, so I began exchanging messages with her. She was getting married in a few months so the urge to begin "settling down" was weighing on her. She had a degree in marketing, was a fan of the magazine and film festival, and liked our work culture.

She came in for a formal interview the next day. I told her about the idea for the small marketing/PR/advertising arm of LA Publishing and how I'd want her to start with us selling advertising half of the time. I needed her to know there would be a chunk of rejection to come with the new job. I figured as an actress who had done auditions, she was familiar with the process.

I wanted Danielle to understand we were a "work hard, play hard" company. I think this interview was the first time I spoke the words, "I'm hiring you to live your life. This isn't a job. This is a lifestyle. You don't punch a clock."

I had Paul and Molly talk to her without me in the room. I wanted to hire her, but if either had strong objections, I wasn't going to do it. Paul was concerned about her lack of sales experience, but not enough to deny her the chance. Danielle took the job.

In the long run, despite a few false starts, we just didn't have time to diligently pursue the marketing/advertising arm of the company.

* * *

Just as autumn began, Kevin and Gabby, our new landlords, finished renovating the first floor of our new Lisbon Street office. The room was unique, about 20 feet wide by 100 feet long. The first 10 feet near the door was carpeted and served as a lobby. To the right, the next 20 feet was a tiled counter, sink, and refrigerator while on the left were our workspaces against an exposed brick wall. The last 70 feet was a wide-open space with white walls we decided to use as an art gallery to be curated by Kerry Landry and Captive Elements. In the rear to the right was a small office and to the left was a small stage. Bathrooms were tucked behind the wall that ran along the right side. Kevin and Gabby gave us the hippest looking office space in Lewiston or Auburn, which fit perfectly with the image of the magazine.

Properly outfitting the new location was going to be costly, but I felt like we needed to have an office people walked into and said, "I wish I worked here." The magazine wasn't brand new when we moved in, but the move helped keep the image of us as a progressive, growing company. We worked a deal for large bullpen cubicles for cash-and-trade and did a similar one for very expensive black leather furniture for the lobby area. We all shopped for other furniture, plants, a coffee machine, and everything else that makes an office come together. It wasn't cheap, but it was fun.

Molly and I purchased a strikingly beautiful—or hideous—set of chairs at a surplus store. We played good cop/bad cop and got them at half price. I never would have had the balls to try stuff like that a year earlier. Walking into a workplace that I created was like walking into a place where nothing could stop me. I just kept waiting for someone to come and say, "OK, I caught you."

Within a week, Kerry and company put art on the walls in the gallery portion. Instead of the clusterfuck of mediocre paintings I expected, he decided to highlight only a few artists at a time, including guests from around the country who were head and shoulders above the abilities of the Captive Elements stable. The first exhibit was beautiful and blended nicely with the eclectic mix of art we'd collected and put on the brick wall above our work area. Not only did I run a magazine, my desk was situated in the middle of an art gallery.

The office opened in time to participate in the last Art Walk of the year in late September. It was held the last Friday of every month May through September in downtown Lewiston. About a dozen restaurants and businesses turned into art galleries for the evening and let people stroll in and out. Now, we added a real art gallery to the list. Hundreds of people came through the new office, marveling at what Kevin and Gabby had done with the place.

A few weeks later, we held an official ribbon cutting ceremony drawing more people on a Friday morning than an average Business After Hours event. I think advertising that we'd have free mimosas resulted in a lot of early lunch breaks to attend the ceremony. Two television stations covered the event. I knew we were still in the front of everybody's mind, but I also knew we were preparing to release the November 2011 issue and were twenty months removed from our debut effort. Staying relevant was not going to get easier, and the election was looming.

Chapter 10

The day LaBonte and I we found out Dick Gleason wouldn't be running for Mayor again was a big one, calling for an immediate summit at Gritty's.

"You think any of the guys leaving the council are actually thinking about running for mayor?" I asked, knowing he was more plugged into the Republican side of things, which these guys all were.

"I don't think so. They all want out," said LaBonte.

"You should be the one to do it," I told him, pausing to let him soak it in while I took a long sip of my Scottish Ale.

I knew he didn't want to be the one to come out and say it, but the quicker one of us did, the quicker we could address the rest of the election.

"I don't know. I don't want to lose," he explained.

Nobody wanted to lose, but from a place of complete objectivity, he was the natural choice. The opportunity to be the mayor fell into his lap. False modesty aside, we both knew what he was going to do.

"I'll put it to you this way: If you don't take out nomination papers, I will and I'll win and you don't want me to be the Mayor of Auburn," I said.

I was only half-joking. I could moderate the meetings shown on television, cut the ribbons, and give the speeches. I knew the mayor also set the meeting agenda with the city manager but I had no idea what was actually happening in city government. I pretended to follow it but didn't. Like every previous endeavor in my life, I figured on-the-job training would suffice. LaBonte already had a handle on everything and was a much better choice. He knew it, too.

A few days later, we met at City Hall the morning nominating papers became available, and he took them out for both the mayoral race and at-large council contest. If somebody emerged as a tough competitor, he could simply not return those mayoral papers. As luck had it, he was the only person to take them out.

I took papers out for only at-large, not bothering to push my luck in Ward 5. Leroy Walker had that sewn up before the first ballot was cast.

I was no local political historian. That was more LaBonte's thing, but I knew that there hadn't been two younger guys to hit the scene together at the same time who had the energy and drive that we did in at least the last twenty years. I thought most City Councils were full of old men holding back progress or people who could do little else than tread water during their term. Not LaBonte and I. We were going to be remembered as the two guys who turned Auburn around. If we played our cards right, we could exert a lot of influence in Lewiston politics, too. We were going to make history. Then, when he became Governor of Maine, he'd feel an obligation to appoint me to some spokesperson or cabinet post.

Belinda Gerry was running yet again. I'd been told her strategy was to get all of the old and disabled people who lived in subsidized housing out to the polls in advance to vote absentee and collect enough other votes in Ward 5, where she also lived, to gain a victory. Many said that strategy—plus once again being the only female name of the at-large slate of candidates—guaranteed a victory. I couldn't say they were wrong until the votes were counted.

Instead of door-to-door canvassing, which scared the hell out of me, I tried to build a Facebook following. When Gerry called me out for forgetting to put a "Paid for and authorized by Joshua Shea, Candidate; Marc Roy, Treasurer" on a campaign flyer, I called her out in a vicious but totally accurate attack on Facebook. The only bad blood in the race was between Belinda and me.

I couldn't tell if it was intentional, but it seemed the *Sun Journal* wanted me to win. The candidates had four debates/presentations, all covered by the newspaper, and I was prominently featured in a photo or had the most quotes in every article. This could have been coincidence, or they could have subconsciously tipped things in my direction. The only disputable theory to that lay in the fact that I know how to give a proper quote. After years of quoting other people in stories, it's easy to predict what makes the paper and what never gets out of a reporter's notebook.

Along with Belinda, the at-large field of candidates was rounded out by Ron Potvin, a perpetual but rarely successful candidate; a liberal city planner named Jeremiah Bartlett; and an unknown guy. Most thought it was a three-way race between Belinda, Jeremiah, and myself since Potvin's "all taxes suck" platform wasn't going to play well that election cycle, but with the public's ability to vote for two candidates, a lot could happen.

I planned to spend Election Day pressing the flesh, starting at Sherwood Heights School near my home, but left quickly as Belinda and Leroy were there. Neighborhood people knew them more and Belinda was a shoe-in to win our ward in the at-large race, so I headed to Washburn School, the Ward 2 voting location. Jeremiah and I worked there together, later moving to Ward 4, his home ward at Fairview School.

After a quick dinner at home and some pictures with the kids, I went to City Hall, which doubled as the Ward 1 voting place for a couple final hours of saying my name as people arrived for ballot casting. Candidates are not allowed to say anything other than hello and their name. I compensated by wearing my *Lewiston Auburn Magazine* jacket.

Every few hours that day I'd check Facebook on my phone to see what people were saying about the election. Predictably, it was pro-Shea and pro-Bartlett. My favorite entry was a nice testimonial from Melissa asking people to vote for me. She largely stayed out of my affairs at this point. There wasn't animosity, but I was so busy and her priorities and mine were growing further apart. It was nice to see her rooting for me publicly on this one.

Once the polls closed, Auburn's city clerk said results would be posted on the wall of City Hall as soon as they were tabulated and phoned-in from the wards. I was touched when Melissa and my father came to watch the results get posted with me. The only other person there was Dan Hartill, a reporter for the *Sun Journal*

I knew in passing who liked to talk about the film festival. The four of us waited twenty minutes until the absentee and Ward 1 results were posted. I was first in absentee, beating Belinda by a handful of votes. The story was the same in Ward One. Jeremiah fell well short, finishing third in both. The other two guys were non-factors.

"I won. I'm going to be in the top two. I probably won the whole thing," I told Melissa.

"How do you know?" she asked.

"Belinda and I are so far ahead. It can't change that much anywhere else," I said. "I won."

Melissa and my father were both proud and excited while I sat surreally stunned. I called the kids and my mother to let them know. I wanted a little more confirmation, but I knew I'd done it.

Belinda won Wards 3 and 5 by a slight margin and I took Ward 2. Ward 4 didn't come in because of a voting machine problem, but it didn't matter once the others were counted. Jeremiah was almost always in third place by varying degrees.

By that point, friends kept texting me to join them at the Firehouse Grille, a bar not far from my house, for a celebration. Melissa went to pick up the kids and go home so I could meet my friends. I had no idea they'd all be there, but Dan, Sandy, Molly, Erik, Danielle, and her husband, Nate, were all there waiting. LaBonte was there celebrating his uncontested win as were a few others—both winners and losers—like Leroy and Ron Potvin. I have to give Potvin credit. I knew he didn't like me or my method of doing things, but he was a gentleman, seeking me out and shaking my hand, offering congratulations.

"You did it! You did it!" exclaimed Chip Morrison, who I didn't know was there, from off to my right. "I have never seen anyone come out of nowhere and achieve what you have done in such a short time!"

"It's been quite a run," I said.

Objectively, I knew what he meant. Subjectively, I was in the middle of the hurricane. It was calm, but I could see the storm swirling around me. What I'd won was a part-time job paying only around $150 per month I didn't actually have time for. After two beers and a tipsy Molly telling me she was proud of my win, I went home, fairly sure I could do anything I wanted.

And for the record, across the city, I defeated Belinda by a couple dozen votes. I finished in first place, just like I egotistically predicted to anyone who would listen.

* * *

That was the last time I saw Molly take a drink for at least nine months.

"I'm pregnant," she told me several weeks later while working on the next wedding edition.

I was genuinely happy for her and Erik but had a sinking feeling it wasn't my new City Council seat that was going to shake things up. Molly said nothing was going to change until the baby came the following summer. I hoped that was true.

We started meetings for the second Lewiston Auburn Film Festival around this time. There was something strange about it no longer being virgin territory. Nobody actually asked the question, "So you really want to do this again?" It was like a responsibility. We birthed the event, so now we had to raise it.

We decided a two-day festival made more sense and booked the Hilton's 220-seat ballroom for the awards dinner. I asked the group if I could produce it as an actual entertaining awards show like you'd see on TV and was given the nod. Or maybe I didn't ask. I was doing it either way.

Paul immediately redeemed himself from the previous year, landing Center Street Dental as the presenting sponsor for $5,000. While Molly and I were flipping around inside the bounce house months earlier, Paul was convincing husband and wife co-owners Carl and Rosemarie Sheline to put the kind of money upfront none of us expected possible. It gave us the kind of confidence to ask for large co-sponsorships from other companies.

Sandy invested some of our bank account to join WithoutABox (WAB), a web portal where independent filmmakers can submit their work to film festivals for consideration, posting their movies digitally. This meant fewer viewing parties and less taking DVDs home. While we had to cough up nearly $1,000 to use the service, filmmaker entry fees were divided between WAB and LAFF. If we had enough entries, we'd end up making money, although that was never a goal.

Watching movies at home on my laptop was so much more convenient. Going through WAB let far more legitimate filmmakers know about LAFF and increased the quality of what was submitted over the previous year tenfold.

* * *

The first time I worried about money at the magazine was at the end of 2011. We were still averaging $25,000 most months in ad sales, but with the new monthly costs of Danielle's salary, a rent increase, and paying off office and lobby furniture, our expenses jumped more than I mentally kept track of. We were also entering a time of year where it wasn't difficult to sell advertising, but it's wasn't simple to collect payment.

Thankfully, January is when major advertisers set their budgets for the year. I realized if we offered a few clients a decent discount for paying the contract up front, it's possible to limp through this time of year. An advertiser paying $8,000 in one check the first week of January can mean more than 10 checks of $1,000 spread through the year. I made the commitment to myself to calm the frivolous spending until the furniture was paid for.

It was still late 2011 and time for another Christmas party. We hired the same karaoke DJ as the previous year, but moved everything to our office and held it in the large art gallery.

We traded advertising with Davinci's Italian restaurant so they'd send over a mobile bar and bartender. Molly slipped the bartender grape juice early on, telling her anytime she ordered wine to give her the juice instead. I was still the only person Molly had let know she was pregnant. She wasn't ready to tell people, and I promised not to compromise her secret.

The year ended on an "eh" note. The party didn't offer anything special and fifteen issues into its life, trying to convince people we were still new was officially over. Hiring Danielle took the pressure off me in some areas, mainly sales, but it didn't bring the anticipated jolt to the bottom line. Nonetheless, our revenues trended upward all year . . . as did our expenses.

It was easy to pretend my porn usage wasn't becoming a problem because my drinking and overall workaholism appeared to be much more acute.

It's also easy to excuse the porn use as a vessel for the act of self-pleasuring. I want to dance, so I listen to music. I want to see competition, so I watch sports. If I want to relieve tension sexually, I look at pornography. It seemed that harmless.

At the end of 2011, I hadn't made the jump to chatrooms yet, but I was probably spending at least an hour every night with video clips of pornography that I discovered online. Most of the time, it was streaming, but every once in a while, I'd find a movie I'd have to download and then just delete off the desktop after.

I thought if people knew I had porn on my computer, they'd know why and that just seemed pathetic to me. What kind of winning city councilor, successful magazine publisher, lauded film festival curator, and totally amazing guy needed to porn to get off? The kind who wasn't actually winning, successful, lauded or totally amazing—and I didn't see myself as any of those things.

Chapter 11

The holidays were a good time to catch up on watching films for the next LAFF, and it was amazing how much more fun it was when they were good movies and how much more attention we were getting since we'd already had one successful year. It was a bit like the magazine. People needed to see it before they could believe. Since our first film festival was a success, people assumed the second one would be and were already excited instead of taking a wait-and-see attitude.

This was great, but it put additional pressure on me for production of the awards dinner. We weren't going to be cramped into a nice restaurant. We were going to be in a hotel ballroom, doing the stereotypical cheesy banquet that had to rise above. I could have said, "Hey, this is Lewiston and Auburn, Maine. Nobody is expecting anything great." But that's not my style. Unfortunately, the need to show everybody how awesome I was had hit, and I felt like I had to give everybody in that ballroom a Top 10 moment in their life.

I put the opening sequence on the back burner and thought about the end of the show. What if I spent $3,000 on a big deal surprise guest to leave people floored? I found a talent booking agency online and learned I was a moron in thinking $3,000 would get me anything. For $3,000, I could get the former lead singer of the 1980s band Flock of Seagulls, but it wouldn't get the backup band that I'd have to provide. The cheapest band anybody in the room would have recognized would have been Morris Day and the Time, the antagonists from *Purple Rain* and they were over $10,000 plus a few grand more in expenses. The "O-E-O-E-O" hook of their song *Jungle Love* would be recognized by ninety percent of the crowd, regardless of age, but even at my drunkest, I couldn't convince myself to approach the LAFF board with this idea.

Then it dawned on me if we put on a concert at the Franco Center with a notable act, charged $50 per seat and sold out, we'd break even with a $25,000 act. I contacted Kenny Loggins' booking agent and found out he was $40,000 and set my sights lower, asking the booking company for a list in the $15,000-$25,000 range. I realized if we booked an act at $20,000 and the place was only half-full, we'd take a hit, but it wouldn't be one we couldn't recover from.

As far as fame goes, the $20,000 names were not great. The remaining members of Bachman Turner Overdrive or The Mighty Mighty Bosstones would not draw 500 people at $50 each. Don McLean's name was mentioned. I knew immediately we had our winner because of his monster 1971 hit *American Pie*. The over 35-year-old audience, which made up the bulk of our ticket buying crowd would know the name. They were our VIP ticket buyers, too. If we guaranteed seating in the first three rows at his concert, VIP seating at the dinner, and a pass for movies on Saturday and Sunday, could a VIP ticket fetch $100? With the layout of the Franco Center, we could sell the first 300 seats at $60 and the back 200 at $50. We could actually make money if we sold 85% of the tickets.

This was one of those ideas that seemed like a good idea when hatched sometime between midnight and 3 a.m. some random morning between Christmas and New Year's 2011. Was I drinking? Likely, but not necessarily. I wasn't seeing a therapist at the time, but I think with the recent City Council win and growing belief I could do whatever I wanted and be successful, I had a low-level Messiah complex developing.

"What if we expanded the film festival to three days instead of one and do a concert at the Franco Center to kick things off on Friday night? We can get Don McLean for $20,000 plus some expenses," I told everyone at the early January 2012 LAFF planning meeting.

They looked at me like I was crazy.

"Hear me out, we want a celebrity. They are crazy expensive . . . tens of thousands of dollars. We can bring in a decent actor for $10,000, but we can't make our money back. We need someone who will draw money so that pretty much has to be a musician. Imagine VIP ticket holders getting a seat in the first three rows at the Franco Center for an opening night concert. Then they get seating up front at the awards dinner. Of course they get a pass to the movies. We charge $100 and sell a bunch upfront. It gives us some money to play with while the sponsorships come in. That's a real VIP ticket. We can do just an awards dinner and movie viewing ticket, too. We can also do just a Don McLean ticket," I said.

"What does Don McLean have to do with a film festival?" said Molly in a tone that registered her dislike of the initial idea.

"Oh, come on. *American Pie* has been in 100 movies," I said. I hoped she wouldn't call me on which ones since I could only think of Madonna's cover of the song from one of the *Austin Powers* sequels. "Instead of a musical opening act, we can show three short films. There will be a lot of people who have never been to a film festival before. Maybe they'll come back and see we're not experimental high art," making words up as they spilled out of my mouth.

"Finally, and I hope you'll give me credit for what I've done with the magazine and LAFF here, it's good marketing. It shows we're growing and it attracts more eyeballs. Don McLean will get us bigger headlines and better media coverage. He's probably going to be worth $3,000 to $5,000 in free media coverage. We could have a legit press conference to announce it," I pitched to them in full salesman mode. "It will impress Carl and Dr. Rose at Center Street Dental, and we could probably attach another sponsor who would help knock down the cost and put another business name on the festival. This is a community event. We're all about community. We'll be promoting the biggest name to ever appear at the Franco Center. Don't you want to say you promoted the biggest fucking concert ever at that place?"

If something in that impromptu speech didn't sell it, nothing would.

"What are you thinking for ticket prices?" Sandy asked.

"After the first 3 VIP rows, we do $60 for the lower section and $50 for the upper part," I said. "Take away your VIP seats and sponsorship and you've got just over $20,000 in seats. I did the math. And if we don't sell shit, we can pull the plug with two weeks' notice for a 10% cancellation fee."

"Do you think you could sell a sponsorship?" Sandy asked Paul.

"Probably. Maybe. It's a big deal," he said.

* * *

I was psyched to start my term on the Auburn City Council. The inauguration was held in the gym of a local elementary school because of the expected crowd. An ice storm kept it down, but over 150 people still showed up.

There was a receiving line for congratulations after the swearing-in ceremony. Dan and Sandy attended, which I thought was a nice gesture considering they were Lewiston residents. Dan brought his camera and I made sure he took several photos of me hugging and kissing my kids in the receiving line. I wanted them to have something to remember the night by, but I also knew if I threw them on my Facebook page, it would hit the "caring family man" button I wanted the public to see.

Once I started serving on the City Council, it was immediately clear I was going to be the swing vote in a lot of decisions. Balance and compromise was sorely lacking in this group.

The only impact the City Council could have on education was to approve the school board's budget and then send it onto voters for final approval at a special referendum that usually saw about ten percent voter turnout. My impact on education was clearly going to be nil. In economic development, nothing of note had happened in the last ten years, and it didn't seem I could change that situation either.

It took me only six months to recognize I'd make a mistake running, fooling myself into believing I'd done it for any other reason than to find out if I could win a popularity contest. I don't have the "work in a large committee" nor the "wait years to see the results of your labor" genes. Government is not the place for people like me. Deep down, I knew this but still wanted to find out if I could win an election.

While other councilors had to be reminded the limits of their power when it came to city business, the staff loved me because I left them alone and went with their recommendations ninety-nine percent of the time. I don't think most residents realize it's the people who work for the city who make the biggest contributions to residents' lives, not city councilors.

I hated serving on the Auburn City Council because I felt helpless. Government moves slower than a turtle walking uphill. It was not like my small business. The simplest change could take years.

When we had a decision to make, it was debated into the ground for no good reason. Spending sixty minutes of my life listening to out-of-touch councilors who had nothing better to do than debate raising non-profit snack bar license fees from $20 to $30 was fifty-eight minutes too long. The whole experience was just too frustrating and irritating.

I did enjoy the pre-meeting beers at Gritty's, just around the corner from City Hall. I made it a point to have between two and four beers before most meetings if possible. Workshops were held from 5:30 p.m. to 7 p.m. and the real meetings started at 7 p.m. I used the workshop time to sober up.

The magazine was going on two years. I was more wrapped up with LAFF than ever and spent every Monday night at city council meetings. Even when I was home, I wasn't really home. I could be found at the kitchen table working on something to do with the magazine or watching movies for the festival.

I had an hour with Kaden, who was now eight-years-old, in the morning. He'd either watch YouTube videos or Nickelodeon. When he opted for *SpongeBob Squarepants,* I'd join him some of the time. I'd get his clothes ready, make his lunch, and bring him to school. Katrielle was now in middle school, so aside from a quick goodbye, I barely saw her or Melissa in the morning. My nights home were rare, and nights that I paid attention to them were rarer.

The only family member who seemed interested in any of my exploits was Kat. I knew how proud of me she was and how she liked the rub of being my daughter when people brought up my name. Like everything else good in my life, I took it for granted.

Melissa said one thing to me over and over: "These are your employees. They can't be your best friends. You're in charge, and you're too close to them."

She was right. I denied it, but she was absolutely right. They weren't my staff. They were my daytime family who helped feed my ego more than my nighttime family. I could never imagine firing Paul, Molly, or Danielle for any transgression. I couldn't imagine a life Dan and Sandy weren't constantly a part of or where LaBonte wasn't almost always present. They got so much of my time and attention it still bugs me to think of the time I didn't spend with my family during this stretch of my life.

The April 2012 issue was released in early March. It was notable in that it was the third time we released one that had the word "April" on the cover. Along with longer durations of time spent looking at video clips of pornography, my drinking increased after Melissa and the kids went to bed. My taste in porn was not illegal, but that was not far from changing.

* * *

WithoutaBox.com coordination of the movies, Danielle handling ticket sales, and the fact we were attracting sponsors made the second film festival preparations run smoother than the first year. Once the Don McLean concert was in place, my over-the-top desires for the dinner entertainment were tempered. I was able to book the performance art duo AudioBody and the Maine Music Society's choir as the entertainment for the dinner.

A few weeks before the festival happened, I was introduced to a documentary Laura Davis of Rinck Advertising was in the early stages of co-producing with famous actor Patrick Dempsey which would be directed by local filmmaker Ramsey Tripp called *The Peloton Project.* The film would document a bicycle trek across Canada, ending at the annual Dempsey Challenge fundraiser held in Lewiston every October. The Challenge usually made over $1 million for the cancer resource and support center the actor, who grew up in the area, opened in honor of his mother.

Sandy and I met with Ramsey and Laura, and after some cajoling, I was able to convince Ramsey to debut *The Peloton Project* at our third film festival in 2013, still thirteen months away and let us announce that it would premiere during our awards dinner, months before the movie was even shot. He was nervous about having so few months to edit the project, but I think they saw the promotional value of attaching it to us a year in advance. I knew the Canadian cyclists, most of whom were very well-off financially, may return to see themselves in a movie if all went according to plan. It might also get a legitimate TV and movie star in Patrick Dempsey to attend our festival.

* * *

After twenty issues, it was hard to surprise or impress regular readers with the magazine stories, so I experimented with additional outside projects. I think that while the public may have enjoyed the end result, my co-workers didn't.

I don't think my team nor the Captive Elements artists appreciated my eccentricity when I decided to see how far I could push another insane late-night idea. I was watching television and saw a taxidermy giraffe. I don't like killing animals, but I think real-life stuffed animals look amazing up close. It's like being at a very safe zoo.

It made me wonder how much an interesting piece of taxidermy would cost for the office. I had no idea an ostrich was $5,000 and an African elk could go for upward of $12,000. The thought occurred to me that taxidermy was a form of art, and if I could find somebody who did the stuff locally—not deer heads and fish, but the cool stuff—I could let them put it on display and try to sell it.

I fired off what I hoped were sober-sounding e-mails to a few taxidermists in Northern New England who looked like they worked on big game. Despite the Red Bull and tequila-soaked communication, I was introduced to a high school teacher about two hours to the north who had the only taxidermy class in an American public school. Following a donation of dozens of large mounts in need of repair from the Smithsonian Institute years earlier, he had rooms full of exotic animals and was more than willing to lend them out for display. Since they were on permanent loan from the Smithsonian, he couldn't sell them but invited us to rent a U-Haul and come grab what we wanted.

Kerry and Captive Elements had no idea we were taking so much of the gallery floor space. On the stage was a killer Russian Black Bear mauling a giant deer. Between our bullpens was a Greater Kudu, a giant African elk close to the size of a pony. Five or six other animals were scattered throughout the room. We had a display from the fucking Smithsonian—including an endangered species. How could anyone not be impressed?

The animals were there the entire summer of 2012 and drew a lot of people for that summer's art walks. Paul, Molly, and Danielle never told me what they really thought about the taxidermy. They didn't need to. I knew, and I didn't care.

Chapter 12

Casalinova Development Group came on as the Don McLean concert sponsor which saved my ass because ticket sales were good but didn't sell out in advance as I had hoped. By the night of the show, the last two or three rows of the $50 seats were unsold. I figured we'd probably done $18,000 in ticket sales, but there were a few additional expenses. With the sponsor money, it would be close to break-even.

I was on the side of the stage, just behind the curtain when McLean launched into his final song, the classic *American Pie*. While recorded five years before I was born, it was one of those songs I grew up with and is second only to *Stairway to Heaven* as my favorite long classic rock song. It has always been one of those that makes me lament getting home early if it is still playing on the car radio, but on this night, it was being played live by the original artist twenty feet away from me.

Peeking out at the crowd I saw my parents in the second row, standing and singing along. Nearby were Chip and Jane Morrison doing the same thing. Looking over the first four or five rows, I recognized half the crowd who were all doing the same thing, especially the baby boomers. It was a moment of sheer joy for them, and once the song picked up tempo, people in the $50 seats literally started dancing in the aisles.

With the exception of the standing ovation I got at the first LAFF dinner, this was my favorite moment at any of the film festivals. It felt so organic and spontaneous. The biggest win of the night was not having to address what a Don McLean concert had to do with a film festival one more time. I still have no idea.

I don't think more than fifty walk-up tickets were sold for Saturday's movies, although we did manage to sell the 220-seat dinner out about an hour before it happened. It went very well, and with the thousands of dollars we spent hiring an A/V company that erected large screens and lighting, along with Colin's clip packages for nominees, it looked like a real awards show. I skipped going to Gritty's afterward, knowing that a drunken stupor would have followed—and we still had Sunday to go. Having a drink by myself, relieving the stress of the day with online porn, and going to sleep made the most sense.

"Best of LAFF" was scheduled for The Public Theatre in Lewiston on Sunday, but it failed on several levels. Mother Nature delivered the first 75-degree day of the year, so most people probably skipped it to be outside. I would have.

The five of us got together at Sandy's the next day to review notes and total things up. Once everything was accounted for, we suffered a small loss, around $2,000. Sandy wasn't the least pleased person as I would have expected. It was Molly. She blamed the McLean concert, but Sandy defended it, saying it broke even and likely even earned a little money. The loss came at selling so many dinner tickets to filmmakers at what we thought was cost, but turned out to be a loss when everything was calculated correctly.

I also pointed out we'd purchased a lot of things like backdrops, red carpets, banners, table centerpieces, and other items we'd not have to purchase again for years. It surprised me we made money the first year. Had we lost $10,000 the first year, and only $2,000 the second year, we would have seen it as a win.

* * *

Molly worked right up until her baby was born. I got a text from Erik saying she was in labor on a Thursday morning and that evening another text came saying she'd given birth. I wrote back congratulating them and telling them when they wanted company to let us know.

I had to invent a maternity leave policy. I decided to pay for six weeks and said the job was safe another ten weeks after, but it was unpaid. I have no idea if that was better or worse than the law demanded, but I didn't worry about it since nobody ever complained.

Before she went on leave, we talked about Molly's strategy for putting in hours once the baby was a part of her life. She felt she could maintain her solid work rate being home three days a week and working in the office on two. I never thought she couldn't keep up, but the Molly who returned wasn't the Molly who left us. This was Mother Molly, and as she should be, totally gung ho to take this little lump of flesh and turn it into an opponent of intolerance and ignorance as all good parents should do.

I'm a father, but by this point, my kids had been taking care of themselves for the basics for a long time. Mistakenly, I was also pushing them aside during this period. I never noticed my coworkers pushing their kids aside because they didn't have any. Once Molly had one, she was not going to do anything of the sort and deserves a lot of credit for that decision.

Molly's friend Josh let her set her new schedule. Molly's boss Josh should have been stricter. I should have developed a company-wide policy stating an employee must be seen in the office four days week. If you couldn't manage even a pop-in, you couldn't work there. Not having an employee handbook was starting to put me at a disadvantage, but I told myself Molly at 70% was still better than someone new at 100%.

Molly knew a lot about my life, as I did hers, but I felt far closer and more emotionally invested in Corey and Paul. I felt closer to Sandy than Molly most of the time. I could actually describe Erik's family tree with roughly the same accuracy as Molly's. She always maintained certain boundaries and looking back now, I respect her for it.

I think people mistook Molly and I being closer friends because Paul and I genuinely were, and the three of us were so much on the same page in those early years when it came to building the magazine and sharing a love for it. We also had the same self-effacing nature, and a complete comfort bordering on a need to be in front of groups of people. I don't think there were two co-workers in Central Maine at the time who appeared in public "celebrity" roles together as much as Molly and me. We were very good at having professional fun together, and it probably gave the impression we were closer than we were.

That said, it did give me a warm feeling when we were both drunk and she called me her "bestie." That warm feeling might have just been a martini, though.

* * *

I almost completely severed my relationship with *The Independent* around Labor Day. It was a joke to still call myself the editor of the weekly newspaper since Corey had been handling 95% of the job. I switched my salary to LA Publishing. Adding $2,500 worth of expenses monthly to the magazine's bottom line was rough. I knew it was possible but would be tight.

I hired Marc Roy, Paul's older brother and my best friend, as our accountant for the magazine and film festival. His message to me was direct.

"There are too many weeks you are having less money coming in than going out. This is a problem," he said.

"I know the expenses have grown, but we're still doing more than $25,000 in ad sales most months. We grossed over $300,000 in 2011, and we're on track to do $330,000 this year," I said.

"You're not taking in $25,000 every month," he explained. "If somebody writes you a check for $5,500 for a year of advertising, it's not $500 per issue. It's $5,500 once. You account for it as $500 per month as if it were still coming in. You account for it as if checks come in regularly."

"Spread across the year of issues, it's $500 per month," I reasoned.

"The moment you spend the $5,500, it's gone. If you saved it and only spent $500 per month, you could claim that," he explained.

"But, if I fall a little behind with the printer, sometimes I need to write them a $15,000 check," I said.

"That's fine. You just can't account for it the current way."

I saw his point there.

"I'm going to send you a budget spreadsheet. Plug in the real numbers and see what happens," he said.

I created a budget through the end of 2012. It showed a $3,000 loss on what I felt were very conservative numbers. The problem is my "very conservative" is still liberal. I mentioned the situation to a couple of people I trusted and almost uniformly they said it was normal. Most suggested I pursue a line of credit to get through lean times.

Banks said we were still too young and unproven with no real assets to be granted a line of credit. They said we should get a loan first, so we took one out through a non-profit called Community Concepts. The idea was if we took out a loan for $10,000, as they suggested, then paid it back over a couple of years, a bank would then give us a $100,000 line of credit.

In order to push this through, I had to sign 101 forms and get two years of tax returns for every owner, which was not easy to coordinate. Ironically, the day we signed the papers to get the $10,000, we had a banner day in the mail, as we did the following day. That week, our bank account swelled to $22,000 for the only time. I caught up on almost every bill and got us back to a point where I had a couple weeks of buffer.

* * *

Once we caught up on bills, I never looked at the budget spreadsheet Marc gave me for 2012 again. I ran things tighter but still knew there had to be a way for us to bring in $5,000 more per month. It's all we needed, and our problems would be taken care of, I'd convinced myself. We didn't need sweeping changes, just fine-tuning.

The return of autumn in 2012 meant time to think about the third annual Lewiston Auburn Film Festival. Rinck Advertising was in hype mode because they were crossing Canada and the US filming *The Peloton Project* for ten days, with the last shot coming the day before the Dempsey Challenge began in Lewiston. The riders arriving wasn't an official part of the festival but drew a small crowd of maybe 200 people, including Patrick Dempsey, who I'd met a handful of times by this point as we'd featured him in our magazine on a few occasions. Paul pointed out he was just hanging out in the back of the crowd.

"Let's go talk to him," I said.

"Why?" Paul asked.

"To invite him to the film festival, or at least plant the seed," I said. "We'll do the 'Take a picture' thing to get in there. He never says no to that."

Paul and I wormed our way over to where others were just noticing he had arrived.

"Excuse me, Mr. Dempsey, can I get a photo with you?"

"Sure. Sure," he said, turning toward Paul. I didn't care if there were batteries in the camera. I just needed the time.

"Are you getting the copies of *Lewiston Auburn Magazine* we're sending to your home?" I asked. We'd already done a long Q&A with him, so he was familiar with us.

"That's right. That's you," he said. "Yeah. I liked that food issue."

"So, since you're the producer of *The Peloton Project* and it's going to be the headliner at the Lewiston Auburn Film Festival next year, you're going to come to the premiere, right?" I asked.

"When is it?" he asked.

"Early April," I said.

Paul snapped the picture. Too soon, Paul.

"If I'm done filming *Grey's Anatomy* for the season, I'll try," he said.

"We'll keep Mary in the loop," I told him. Mary was his sister who ran the Dempsey Center.

Shortly after our exchange, forty cyclists and a bus of supporters came zooming into the parking lot with a police escort to loud cheers. There was Ramsey and his small crew filming every step of it. Laura Davis was running around making sure everything was just right.

These weren't professional cyclists. They were average people, young and old, all touched by cancer in one way or another. I was told participants had to raise a crazy amount of money to participate, and most came from the Calgary area and were from old oil family money.

Everybody on the film festival team liked Laura, but there were varying degrees of tolerance toward the way she did things and decisions she made. I was probably the most lenient. I think it was a combination of being cut from the same cloth of being big dreamers who had a vision, then figured out the logistics. I may have also gone easy on her because she was the cool sixth grade teacher back when I was still at Montello Elementary School. Her name was Mrs. Irish back then. I got stuck with a different teacher. Despite the fact she only knew me as the twelve-year-old who would hook up the Radio Shack TRS-80 computer in her room because none of her students could figure it out, I felt like we had a shared history.

I agreed to cover a booth hyping the *Peloton* movie during The Dempsey Challenge weekend so Laura could do other things at the festival. I knew that we would be the ones selling the tickets and making the money at the *Peloton* premiere, and this gave us control of the process. I also knew it was up to us, not her, to get those Canadian cyclists and their families to fly back in six months and buy VIP packages in advance. Laura only had to provide us with a film. I saw the booth at the Dempsey Challenge festival as a LAFF booth that hyped *The Peloton Project*, but not everybody on our team did.

It didn't help the weather was miserable on Saturday, but I tried to keep everyone with their eye on the prize. I didn't know what VIP tickets would go for, but paid in advance, it was going to be thousands of dollars if we talked up the cyclists, got them to like us, and made LAFF seem like a can't-miss event. By Sunday afternoon, when things were wrapping up, the riders were all telling us they were going to return. I wouldn't have wanted to leave the responsibility to get that kind of reaction in Laura's hands. LAFF was our festival, not hers. I appreciated she let us handle things.

Chapter 13

I felt a pain in my back the day before Thanksgiving. There had been a snowstorm the night before, which was a lucky break for me as I was scheduled for a ride-along with an Auburn Police Department officer for a story I was writing for the magazine. The shitty weather made things more interesting, and I knew the photos would be better, or at least whiter.

During the ride-along, I thought I pulled a muscle on the left side of my back, which was nothing new. In the last eight or nine years, I'd gone to the emergency room four times for back-related injuries. When Kaden was a baby, I took a hard fall on ice outside of the post office in Portland and had to be rushed to the hospital. Since then, bending just the wrong way would mean a trip to the ER, and I'd be laid up for a day or two.

It'd been a couple years since it flared up, but it wasn't surprising when I felt twinges standing next to the police cruiser. I assumed I twisted the wrong way. I bailed on the ride a little earlier than planned when my stomach also started hurting. A few hours of laying on the couch later and I was fine for Thanksgiving.

Jumping forward a few days, it happened again. I was sitting at the dining room table, working of course, when the pain hit, this time on both sides. Over the next thirty minutes, the pain expanded, creeping to the front of my rib cage, causing some nausea. I told Melissa it was unlike regular back pain, and I thought it made sense to go to the ER as it was getting worse.

By the time I arrived at St. Mary's Hospital, I was in agony. They hooked me up to morphine and called in the ultrasound technician despite the fact it was nearing midnight. If something was wrong, at least I'd find out if I was having a boy or a girl.

Shortly into Monday, the lady rubbed the cold wand over my lubed-up midsection and within seconds found a gallbladder more than half-filled with stones. Once the pain settled, they explained it wasn't a true emergency and said the surgery to remove the stones could be pushed until after Christmas. They wrote a prescription for Vicodin in the unlikely case of another painful flare-up and sent me on my way.

It only took a few days for the unlikely to become likely when the pain returned, again late at night, but this time faster and more severe than before. Vicodin couldn't touch the pain, and I knew I couldn't drive, so I called my father to bring me to the hospital.

They quickly pumped me with morphine upon arrival to stop the pain. I told the doctor what the issue was so they could get me right into surgery, but he brought up an interesting point.

"Plenty of people have had a gallbladder full of stones and died of something else," he informed me.

"Then test away . . ."

It was the gallbladder, but once the morphine hit, I didn't need immediate surgery, and I was scheduled for the next morning.

I started taking pictures with my phone and posting them to Facebook with foggy comments since I liked the attention. I had a small group of regular 4 a.m. Facebook followers since I rarely slept more than three hours a night anymore. Their responses were equal parts amazed I was providing updates when I should have been drooling (which proves alcoholism helps with a morphine tolerance) and those who passive aggressively saw it as a new low in attention craving. I even picked a fight with the DJ from our Christmas parties who said I should leave the hospital and seek holistic options.

My mother showed up around 8 a.m. when I was scheduled to go into surgery. Melissa stayed home to get the kids off to school. My mother told her to go to work, and she'd handle things at the hospital.

The morphine kept coming and while I was exhausted, it prevented me from sleeping more than thirty seconds at a time because the moment I'd doze off, I'd have a wicked nightmare.

"How are you, Mr. Shea?" a nurse said around the time it was to go for surgery.

"Tired. Weird dreams. No real pain," I said.

"We're going to have to put off your surgery a few hours because a couple of car accident victims were just transported here, but we'll keep you comfortable. It'll probably be just after lunch now," she said. "Are you the guy who does the magazine?"

"That's me."

"I love your magazine. You do such a good job with it," she said.

"Thanks," I said, as she left.

"Does that happen a lot?" my mother asked.

"Yes, for a couple of years now," I muttered. I didn't realize she'd never been around to see a stranger compliment me for the magazine. Her friends told her they liked the magazine, but she'd never seen a stranger recognize me.

It happened a few more times, and I answered a couple of questions about the magazine, including just as I was being given the final anesthesia to go into the operating room near 5 p.m. An emergency C-section pushed the operation back even further, causing me to have to spend the night.

* * *

I was released from the hospital at noon the next day, Friday, December 7, 2012. the day of the company Christmas party. Thankfully, I hadn't rehired the holistic-happy DJ. Despite being told by many people I shouldn't go, I wasn't going to let a few little incision marks stop me. I had a bottle full of Vicodin, and morphine was still pulsing through my veins. I agreed not to drink alcohol, nor jump around.

Molly, Paul and Danielle—who was now several months along in her first pregnancy—got the place in order, and I arrived a few minutes before real guests. I wished I could have helped more, but I think the fact I was there was a big enough deal since most people wouldn't have attempted it.

I remember some of the party, held at a local event center we did a barter deal with, but that may only be because of the pictures. I sang karaoke, danced a little, and delighted in showing the blood-soaked bandages on my chest. Melissa, Sandy, and Tammie said they were worried I was going to tear a stitch and need to go back to the hospital.

The next day, I was in pain. With the morphine and Vicodin wearing off, I settled onto the couch at home for a weekend-long marathon of *Survivorman* on The Discovery Channel, deciding to take a break from the film festival entries I should have been watching.

I momentarily forgot the pain when I got a surreal telephone call from Corey, who was going to attend the party the night before with Donato and Belinda, but no-showed. He explained why, and my jaw hit the floor.

As I was leaving the hospital that Friday afternoon, something was happening at the apartment building Donato owned next to his convenience store in Windham. A few hours later, he would be arrested on a Class A charge of arson.

Corey explained firefighters were called to the building when somebody reported seeing smoke. Donato was found on the first floor, coughing, loosely tied with a lamp cord, and with a nasty gash on his head. It looked too suspicious for the police, and when they dug into his financial records, including the fact that the building was foreclosed on days earlier, it looked bad.

Based on a few of his statements to the police that were printed in the *Portland Press Herald*, it wasn't hard to infer Donato had connections to some unsavory, potentially criminal, people in Rhode Island. I'd always wondered if he was involved with that kind of thing but obviously never asked. I told Corey to give me a call if he heard anything else and decided not to bother the Corsettis that weekend.

I managed a half-day of work in the office on Monday, still aching a bit from the operation. Sandy happened to be there, dropping off DVDs sent in for the film festival. I expressed the feelings about Donato I still hold to this day to everyone who was there.

"First, did he do it? Maybe? Probably? Of course not? The only person who knows is him. Individually, you can ask how it will affect any relationship you have with him, and I'm doing that, but the bigger question is how will it affect us as a whole? On a legal level, it won't. I always found it a little sketchy nothing was in his name, but it's good here. Belinda owns part of the film festival, not him. Belinda and the kids own most of the magazine, not him. Did Donato do it? It's none of our business and theoretically shouldn't affect us. The guy did a lot for us, and personally, I'm going to support him."

Even before everything happened with my legal situation, I believed people make mistakes, even big ones, and those mistakes should not define us. It's not even a matter of forgiveness. I think as a matter of survival we sometimes make bad choices we wouldn't otherwise and shouldn't have upon reflection. Maybe having bipolar disorder and knowing that the smart choice isn't always the natural choice makes me more tolerant of people having giant mental lapses. It doesn't make us bad people. It makes us flawed. Hopefully he didn't do it, but even if he made that kind of catastrophic mistake—the kind I was only months away from starting to make—I was not going to abandon him.

* * *

One Sunday while watching the NFL playoffs in early January 2013 I decided it was time to write a personal story for the magazine about the journey I took recognizing and accepting I had bipolar disorder and the struggles that exist maintaining a balance.

Following five or six years of immense highs and lows, in and out of cognitive behavioral therapy, often on medication, I was finally properly diagnosed when I was twenty-six-years-old. I've always known something was just "different" about the way my head operated back to being thirteen-years-old and knew that it had a dark side. When I was twenty, I started the process of figuring it out what it was.

The story was raw and sometimes emotional to write. I knew we had a health-themed issue coming out in mid-April, and if we could get quality content completed in advance, there would be no post-LAFF slump for the magazine there had been following the first two film festivals. When it takes a week or two to mentally and physically recuperate from the festival, that's a huge chunk of time lost in building a quality publication.

I cut the bipolar story down to about 3,400 words and let Molly read it. She said parts of it almost made her cry. I knew it might help stigma toward bipolar disorder in people's eyes, but I also thought it could help humanize me in people's eyes who may have been starting to grow wary of my attention-grabbing shtick. Showing myself not only to be human, but to have a giant hidden flaw I was overcoming would be good for the Joshua Shea brand. This was a fact that did not escape me.

As Danielle and I were working together in early January on the advertising/marketing agency idea, I mentioned a pictorial I'd seen in a European magazine a decade earlier that I wanted to try in our magazine but didn't know if we could pull it off. It featured beautiful, almost perfect models, completely naked in black and white. Near each model was a first-person passage they wrote about what they didn't like about their body. The message for the readers was when you see someone you think is physically perfect, they don't see perfection looking in the mirror—nobody does. The nudity was not sexual. It was almost artistically clinical.

We talked about replicating a version in our Health issue with appropriate modifications. Blatant nudity was out, and we knew we couldn't find perfect models because they would charge big bucks to pose. We thought it might be more interesting to find different shapes and ages and expand on the European idea. A fifty-year-old white male reader may actually have the same body issues of a twenty-eight-year-old black woman. A thin nineteen-year-old woman may have the same issues of an overweight forty-year-old guy. If we could put local people in the magazine, it would be even more powerful.

Danielle and I talked about handling the lighting and photography in-house, knowing we didn't have the budget to bring in photographers for a dozen shoots. We were both aware it was dangerous, could be handled very poorly, and blow up in our faces, but we were 80% sure we could pull it off and create a feature for the magazine people would respect. I knew the biggest challenge would be to sell Paul and Molly on the idea.

When it came to Molly, I told her and Paul immediately after she shared how much she liked the bipolar story. They both gave me the "We're preparing to accept bad news because we know you've made up your mind" face.

"I want to call the issue 'Healthy Mind, Healthy Body.' The bipolar story is the mind, but we need the body. I'd like to tweak something I saw in a magazine once. We get people of every shape, size, age, ethnicity, and sexual orientation, and we shoot them in very, very obscured nude photos—and they talk about what they do or don't like about their bodies," I said.

"And how do I tell advertisers we're now having naked people?" Paul asked, the first to object.

"We make this so fucking classy, so non-sexual, in such good taste with such a powerful message that nobody would dare say anything," I explained.

"It's still naked people," Molly said. "I don't like it."

I ran through the argument about people reading about their body image hang-ups in other people and think I was cracking through their icy stares a little.

"My bipolar story will be six pages. This will be around ten. If we get another three or four 1,000-word stories and place ads around them, we've got a thirty-page Health and Wellness section finished before we have to worry about the film festival." I knew not having to kill ourselves to get a magazine together immediately after LAFF would help my argument.

As expected, she said she didn't want to take part but was open to the idea after I explained it, assuring she'd have a fair amount of editorial input. I told her the worst thing that could happen was that we'd scrap the whole thing, and I'd be the first to say it wasn't working.

I wanted to see if this idea would work in Lewiston and Auburn. Yes, the promise of naked people would get curiosity seekers to open a magazine they hadn't looked at before— something that was actually a good business move on our part and is sometimes forgotten, but pulling off an amazing, non-sexualized photo essay and important accompanying text would show our readers we could do something edgy and handle it with class and poise. We hadn't tried that yet.

* * *

Despite having almost a year left on my city council term, I announced on my *Joshua Shea for City Council* Facebook page I wouldn't be running again. It was just a waste of my time in a place I was not flourishing. Less than thirty minutes after I posted the statement, the *Sun Journal* called, wanting more information.

Kerry Landry and the rest of the Captive Elements artists decided the gallery wasn't worth the cost or energy around this time. Kerry had recently become a father and his priorities were changing. He, along with his wife and newborn son, were actually models in our "Healthy Mind, Healthy Body" photo essay a few months later.

I saw us continuing the gallery as an opportunity. Instead of putting high-priced, bad local art on the walls, we could put a mix of decent local art at good prices and higher-end art we curated from further away. Tammie seemed to make that formula work at the gallery next to Fuel when it changed from Gallery 5 to Lyceum Gallery.

Whereas Molly was super-pregnant for the 2012 LAFF, it was Danielle's turn in 2013. She did a great job running meetings and our website looked better than ever, but her delivery date was so close to the festival, we knew that we couldn't count on her at crunch time.

It took a bit of convincing from outside sources, but I got the core group onboard with the idea of having Les Stroud of the TV show *Survivorman* as our celebrity guest. I simply fell in love with the fact he created an actual "reality show" when I was stuck on the couch watching a marathon on the mend from gallbladder surgery. Thankfully, Dan Marquis also loved the show and convinced Sandy, as did a pair of Molly's friends who flipped out at the idea of us bringing him in when she mentioned it. I could have said anything, but once outside people sang Stroud's praises, we were golden. Seeing the influence others had, which really sealed the deal, made me realize my influence was waning.

I worked a deal with Stroud, his band, and his photographer girlfriend to get a photo exhibit for our gallery, a book signing at the gallery, and a Q&A during the film festival. Stroud would accept an award at our dinner and his band would play a concert after the dinner. The entire price tag was $5,000. It seemed like a bargain compared to Don McLean.

* * *

A not-so-surprising call came from Donato. Out on bail, his family wanted to sell as much of the magazine as possible. They controlled 600 of the 1,000 shares. We negotiated a price of $35 per share, valuing the company at $35,000, which seemed very low at the time.

I brought it up to Paul, Molly, and Corey immediately since we were the existing owners. If Donato wanted to sell and a majority fell into the wrong hands, we were fucked. The *Sun Journal* could buy us just to shut it down. We all liked the opportunity to buy more and decided that we'd also present the opportunity to Danielle and Sandy and Dan.

It was a clusterfuck. In hindsight, I should have found somebody to front me a lot of money so I could have 51%. We ended up having eight owners, with Molly and I each owning the most—around 22%—down to Danielle owning 3%. While Belinda was out, Donato's kids retained small pieces, and Sandy was now a player, too. It was a mess, but I followed my inner mantra of doing what I needed to do to survive until the next day.

This upheaval caused me stress as did the fact we were falling below having a week's worth of buffer money for expenses in our checking account. By early 2013, local businesses had several years to determine if advertising with us helped. Most felt it did, but some were unsure and after a few years with us, were ready to try other things.

In early February, I deferred my pay for the first time but didn't tell my co-workers. I made sure they were paid, and our other bills were paid. I always made sure our loan with Community Concepts and health insurance, utilized by Danielle and Molly, were paid.

While the money was becoming tighter, Molly seemed a bit less engrossed in the work. I thought giving her more command of the product might bring her interest level up. Even if she was working from home a lot because of the baby, if she was named the editor, it might spark something in her that had started to fizzle. I hoped it would also give me a little less to do since I could hear my body telling me I needed to slow down. I relinquished the "Editor" title to her, hoping it would mean better things for us.

Chapter 14

The first time I felt like LA Publishing was no longer my company, no longer Donato's company—no longer the company that Paul, Corey, and I worked long hours to build—was when Sandy wanted to see a legitimate corporate structure she was comfortable with. We found a lawyer, Mike Malloy, who worked with a large law firm that made no realistic sense approaching. It just happened to be in Lewiston. They didn't advertise locally because they had well-known national commercial clients. He just liked the magazine and liked us. He was not loud or pushy. Despite keeping everything professional, it was clear he cared for us and the company on a personal level.

Paul, Molly, Sandy, Danielle, and I sat at a giant wooden conference room table at Mike's firm that I'm sure cost more than my car. Corey said he was too sick to attend, and the Corsetti kids were no-shows. Mike explained business structures, the minutiae of a legal board of directors structure with officers, and what our future should look like.

Paul, Danielle, and I stayed mostly silent. I knew we were digging ourselves into a financial hole doing business with Mike, no matter how nice he was. Sandy and Molly had 101 questions, 98 of them completely pointless in my opinion, just taking up our time and money. I should have said something, but I didn't. Sandy could get on a roll, losing sense of the big picture, and Molly probably didn't realize we were paying $5 for every minute we were there. The two people who complained about money the most couldn't see it melting away as they asked hypothetical questions about partners dying and their shares of stock transferring to next of kin. My answer would have been, "We'll deal with it when someone dies" but my answers didn't hold the weight they once did any more.

Mike organized new bylaws, issued stock certificates, and forwarded us a bill for money we didn't have. My attitude as the guy who ran the day-to-day operations was "I didn't approve the services on this bill. I'll get to it when I get to it." I was more concerned that Kevin and Gabby got their overdue rent.

* * *

I've always been very good at ignoring the negative and focusing on the positive, so with our hugely successfully press conference for the third Lewiston Auburn Film Festival held at our office gallery, which we'd renamed Prose Gallery, there was light in my professional life. Ramsey Tripp talked about the *Peloton* film, Jonathan LaBonte—in his role as mayor—talked about what a big deal it was for the two cities to have a festival like LAFF, and Les Stroud joined us via Skype. All three network news affiliates and two newspapers attended, along with many sponsors, or those who were considering. With our stage and professional looking backdrops, it came off like a real production.

As I was standing at the podium, announcing Stroud as that year's special guest, I had one of those moments where I looked around and genuinely wondered, "Is this just another great con, or am I genuinely pulling this off . . . and can I even tell the difference anymore?" I never shared that thought for obvious reasons.

Assuming nobody there was questioning the veracity of my song-and-dance, I wondered how many people in positions similar to mine had these exact feelings. I wasn't capable of the humility that a lot of people feign who actually buy into their own hype. I was long past that. It was a real inability to tell the difference between if I was sincere in presenting a film festival to better my community or if I was full of shit and playing the part of a guy who was putting on a film festival because it was an interesting role and more fun than being myself. Did I genuinely coordinate a legit press conference or did I fool a room of a people who should know better into thinking I did? Is there a difference? Does it matter?

Center Street Dental returned as the lead sponsor and several others jumped on board almost immediately. Canadian cyclists and their families bought several dozen VIP packages to spend the weekend at the film festival, and *The Peloton Project* premiere film at the Franco Center sold out in about two weeks.

* * *

Danielle and I would shoot photos of people for the "Healthy Mind, Healthy Body" photo spread in between all of our other commitments. The first couple of people were nerve wracking. I'd never worked around naked people before, but we coordinated three shoots on the first day and got any weirdness out of our system.

I didn't worry about handling myself in a classy way, because I can always do that when called upon. I was more worried I'd get an erection. Once we started, it was not like porn. Porn was a means of self-soothing privately. This was actual work.

I bought a bunch of small lamps and a variety of lightbulbs. It was fascinating how people's skin reacted to different types of light and the challenge of how much light and what kind made them look best against white or black backdrops became the fun part of the shoot. The fact they were naked was quickly forgotten by Danielle and I most of the time.

By the 12th or 13th person, the whole process was kind of boring, and we were glad to be done with it. What I thought would be a "dangerous" and "creative" challenge quickly became mundane. Helping the models write their blurbs was also like pulling teeth. I would pick my four favorite photos of a shoot and make sure the models were OK with the four, knowing one would get into the magazines. There were a few vetoes and two bailed out of the pictorial after their shoots completely, but I gave them that right.

The larger battle, as usual, was over the cover. My first choice was the side of one of the models who had a fascinating fish hook and ocean tattoo. Inside, she explained it was a tribute to her grandfather, so it tied the story and the photo together. Molly,

Paul, and Danielle thought it was a little too sleazy for the cover. The colors were beautiful and the line of the models arching back from top to bottom of the cover, not seeing her head or butt, was artistically striking, but they were right and I admitted it, which was becoming a rare phenomenon. I didn't want people to think they were getting *Tattoo Digest*.

The cover photo had to be as classy, but even tamer than the super-tame photos on the inside. I found a photo I thought was powerful in color but didn't translate in black and white. It had a thin model sitting cross-legged, her back to the camera. The black background was overpowering, with the only light being a warm incandescent just outside of the frame illuminating a little bit of the side of her leg, following up a sliver of her back and arm reaching her slightly-turned head. You could just make out her face in the glow, giving an intensity, but vulnerability, too. We didn't put any teasers or any other words on this start cover other than "Healthy Mind, Healthy Body".

When the issue came out, we didn't lose a single advertiser and positive-to-negative comment ratio was 20-to-1. I think it was one of the cover model's greatest moments when she saw the issue for the first time.

LaBonte liked the risk we took, telling me: "They'd never try this in Portland. This says something about Lewiston-Auburn."

* * *

I had to design most of the well-received "Healthy Mind, Healthy Body" issue, which meant I was working until 1 or 2 a.m. almost every night of the week. A few months earlier, what Corey thought was a back injury led doctors to find a host of other issues including a highly distressed liver from a level of drinking I was completely unaware of. He asked me not to tell anybody at the magazine about it. I had absolutely no idea Corey was a problem drinker.

Once he let me know and I started covering for him and picking up his magazine slack, it didn't take too many issues for Molly to recognize I was always designing the cover or for Paul to realize I was designing more of the ads than Corey to show potential advertisers. I eventually told them most of what I knew, which still wasn't a lot.

Being at an event until 11 p.m. or working at home until 2 a.m. wasn't uncommon, and I didn't resent doing it. I still loved *Lewiston Auburn Magazine* even if it wasn't the new kid on the block. I've always needed at least an hour or two to unwind after working, usually watching TV by myself before going to bed. With Melissa and the kids traditionally in bed by 10 or 10:30, I was in bed by midnight before the magazine began, usually not needing porn to help unwind. Now that I had to take on Corey's design work in addition to juggling other magazine and LAFF duties, I started making a horrible series of professional and personal decisions that began the bad, bad run that would eventually take me down.

When people would come up to me and say something like, "You're a magazine publisher, you run a film festival, and you're a city councilor. How do you find the time to do it all?" I had a standard response that was meant to make people laugh but was on the verge of becoming true.

"What's ironic," I'd tell people, "is that aside from doing all those things, half of my energy is spent just making sure I don't completely lose my shit and go crazy."

I stopped having that half of my energy.

Even if I didn't have a meeting, I'd find a way to finish my day at a place with a bar like Gritty's or Davinci's. If I couldn't wait that long, I'd end up having a lunchtime 12-2 Happy Hour. Soon I added a 5-8 Happy Hour. Once everyone went to bed at home, I drank as I designed pages. Then I'd use porn for somewhere between 30-90 minutes and go to bed.

I wasn't sleeping the proper amount, but instead of drinking less, skipping the porn, and getting more hours of sleep, I decided I could roll the dice and hope that if I stopped taking my bipolar medication (ironically, just as the story about being bipolar was released) I might be able to tap into my manic side and get through this hectic time right before the film festival.

People with bipolar disorder don't want to take their medication. It's just one of those things. You think you're normal, you feel normal most of the time. Not taking the meds is like a test because you remember those manic times without the meds that felt great. It's easy to forget the depression. It's easy to forget the carnage manic episodes cause. Through the lens of nostalgia, mania is recalled as nothing but positive. I never remembered how bailing on my meds always ended messy. So, with a horrible memory and an earnest belief it could help the situation, I pulled myself off of my Wellbutrin and Lamictal.

The drinking was mostly about quelling anxiety, and it escalated to compensate for the loss of bipolar medication. Anxiety has always been an issue, but it was at an all-time high. The largest version of LAFF was coming up, revenues were stagnant at the magazine yet costs were rising. I had almost no connection to my family, and it felt like there was more magazine work than ever. I had no enthusiasm toward any of it.

To offset the alcohol, my caffeine intake was equally unhealthy. I probably drank eight to ten cups of coffee per day, and my nightcap was a tumbler or two of Red Bull and tequila. As the weather warmed over the next few months, I would stop at McDonald's on the way into work and buy a tray of iced coffees to last me through the day. I was ingesting either liquid depressant or liquid stimulant around the clock.

Panic attacks suck, but they became a regular part of my life that I tried to hide. During an attack it's hard for me to breathe, my chest and stomach tighten. I become hypersensitive to everything happening to my body and five or six scary real-life thoughts rotate, offering intense terror. Any one of those thoughts, like Les Stroud cancelling and not appearing at the film festival, become unbearable. I could envision a scenario of events which led straight to bankruptcy, jail, abandonment, and death. When these attacks happen, I know to just lay there and let them run their course. It can take five minutes or two hours, but I always come out on the other side just fine.

Manic episodes are different, and I don't realize they are often happening until well after they're done and I'm analyzing a time period as a whole. There were plenty of manic episodes working in tandem with panic attacks in mid-2013. I'm not talking about moments where I think I can fly or that I'm God. That's different than mania. My manic episodes could last for days at a time. I could sleep six hours in three days and show no signs of fatigue. I'd get grand ideas and act on them without thought. Physically and mentally, manic episodes feel good in the moment. I could never feel nor see my body deteriorating. I'd lose the capacity to naturally understand the differences between right and wrong or good ideas and bad ones. When you don't know you're sick . . . you don't know you're sick.

* * *

When I needed physical intimacy, I'd find it online with myself with a legal porno site and call it a night, but this was when I made the transition to live camera sites. They featured people sitting in their homes, broadcasting to the world. They were people who ranged in age from eighteen to way-too-old mostly just being naked and talking to people who would type comments to them in an on-screen chat. I found the concept of just sitting there conversing with naked people about normal things fascinating. There were other rooms on the extreme end of the spectrum, with people performing sex acts with their real-life partner. I didn't visit those kind often, but always wondered, "How does one person bring up the idea of doing this to the other?"

Some of the films we received for the festival were in formats I couldn't watch, so I'd need to find software to view them. On an early March 2013 night, I used a torrent site looking for a specific application to download. Among the search results was a folder with something that sounded like the video player I needed. Inside, there were eight or nine video files. Most had labels which should have sent me running because they clearly advertised young children naked, but one intrigued me. It said "16 and 17-year-old girls at the beach."

I knew it was a folder of child pornography based on the other file names, but this seemed close enough to legal and non-sexual in nature. I never should have pushed the button. I wasn't craving anything like it at the moment. I don't know why for 99% of my life I would have gone running, but instead, began the download of the folder. I knew from using torrents that if I wanted that one file I had to start the download of the entire folder. Once the files began their way onto the computer, I canceled the downloads of the other seven files before even 3% of any of them were downloaded and threw them into the trash can on my desktop.

When the desired file finished downloading about ten minutes later, it was exactly as advertised. Two young, post-pubescent teens were playing paddle ball on a nude beach and weren't having sex. I told myself as long as they looked like women, it was OK. I could trust the file name or I could actually be watching "19 and 21-year-old girls at the beach" I rationalized. What I needed to realize was that I had entered a critical phase of a pornography addiction I didn't recognize I had.

That was the day my mind—already beginning its descent into very unhealthy territory—first blurred the line between young women and older girls. I watched the short clip, deleted the file, and didn't touch underage pornography again for several months.

* * *

A very pregnant Danielle couldn't participate in LAFF the first few days of April 2013, but she did a hell of a job coordinating tickets. She delivered a daughter a few days after the festival.

LAFF was shaping up to be a financially positive experience, helping to take my mind off the magazine, which never returned to a two-week buffer of money in the checking account. Diverting some of my paycheck for a few days happened more often. One week shortly before the festival, we all took $100 on a Friday instead of our paycheck to get through the weekend to allow client payments to come in the mail. By Tuesday, everyone was paid in full. It was just how we got by.

It was embarrassing another week when I had to call Sandy and suggest we increase the LAFF advertising budget to the magazine by $1,500. I told her we fell short on payroll. We both knew that the magazine, at least according to the rate card, had given LAFF tens of thousands of dollars of free advertising, so it was not hard to rationalize payment, but it had never been part of the film festival budget.

"If we have to do it, we have to do it," she said. I could hear her question the investment in the magazine in her voice.

This was the first of a couple of periods of time where Molly and I started drifting apart. I think it had to do mostly with the fact we had much less face time than before. We only talked magazine (or film festival) and almost only via e-mail since she worked from home more than half the week. All of our friendly downtime was gone.

Money was a bigger issue with her than any of the owners. She had a broad idea what was going on financially but couldn't appreciate some weeks were harder than others to pay every bill. She expected her full salary and benefits, every utility, rent, and all of the freelancers to be paid every week. Most weeks we could. It's not a crazy thing to expect, but I felt so much pressure on the weeks it was close. At that point in the early spring of 2013, it just wasn't happening.

"If you'd like, I won't pay you this week and pay the freelancers," I'd say. That would send her away frustrated. I knew she resented me for the money issues and was scared to death the loan wouldn't be paid but I assured her it was No. 1 on my priority list.

Along with the deterioration of a friendship, I began resenting Molly because it was obvious to me she didn't love her job or contribute at the quality level she had in the past. I didn't resent her baby. I resented Molly making the same money but giving me less quality work. When I feel like I'm taken advantage of, I instinctively start to give people the cold shoulder. I know it started before the film festival in 2013, and by mid-July that year, we'd almost completely stopped talking in person when we found ourselves in the same room. Communication was by email, all business. I think this breakdown happened because we didn't say the negative things on our minds to each other like we would have in the past. Bottling it up was toxic.

Marc Roy met with me shortly before LAFF, and his message was clear.

"You've got to stop bouncing checks!" he said.

He was right. It was happening more often. Each time we did, it was a $30 overdraft fee.

"You've got $300 in fees so far this year!" he exclaimed. "You've got to do something!"

"What?" What do you want me to do?" I got mad at him. "Danielle is gone, and when she's here, she's not selling very much. Your brother seems like he'd rather be anywhere else lately because he hates when we work on the film festival. Molly and I are barely talking. Corey is sick with God knows what. Donato's probably going to jail. I'm up 18 hours a day trying to keep this fucking thing together. What do you want me to do?"

"You need to take care of yourself. It's just a magazine. It's going to kill you. You look like shit. You're all so stressed out there. You have to find out how to spend a lot less, or you have to find out how to make a lot more. It's the math."

"I know. I know," I said.

Chapter 15

The 2013 Lewiston Auburn Film Festival was the last great thing that Paul, Molly, and I did together. Les "Survivorman" Stroud and his photographer-girlfriend Laura Bombier came in for their Thursday night book signing/gallery show blowing away our best expectations. When the door opened at Prose Gallery for what was technically the first artistic installation we attempted featuring Bombier's nature photography, the line extended from the stage at one end of the building, 100 feet to the door, outside and down a city block, wrapping around. I thought we might get 100 people to come, but it was probably closer to 600, with plenty of others telling me in the weeks to come they saw the line stretching down the street and kept on driving by. It was a positive shock and provided a morale boost that allowed any interpersonal resentments to be put on hold a few days.

The next morning, word came Patrick Dempsey had flown in. Laura Davis told me, as expected, he wanted no interaction with the public and didn't want to say anything to the media. Since the event was sold out, it's not like shunning the media was going to hurt ticket sales. As long as we didn't have to pay to get him there and he'd take a picture in front of our backdrop on the red carpet, I didn't care who he talked to one bit.

I briefly went to the pre-show cocktail party at Lyceum Gallery, but it was too packed for me and my manic energy was not allowing me the focus to schmooze with anyone. Sandy and Laura had that well in hand. I was proud of Sandy, who notoriously hated speaking in public, doing an interview for TV news. Back at the Franco Center, Paul was taking care of the box office, and Molly made sure volunteers knew their jobs. I kept lookout for Dempsey, so we could sequester him downstairs before the movie began.

I knew he was supposed to arrive at the side door at 6:40, but I made sure to be there at 6:30. My former colleague from the *Sun Journal*, Mark Laflamme, who was covering the event, saw me and came over.

"Rumor has it Patrick Dempsey will be here tonight," he said.

"That's the plan, but I won't believe it until he's sitting in the front row," I said. "And before you ask, I can't allow media to approach him. Of course, whoever you have taking photos could always get a picture from the side of the stage."

"Do you want to give me some quotes? You know the kind of stuff I need," Laflamme said.

"Yeah sure. We're thrilled Patrick Dempsey is able to be a part of LAFF this year, Hopefully we'll have him back in a larger role in the next few years. *The Peloton Project* has been a labor of love for many people, especially Ramsey Tripp. Tonight is the night all of his hard work and his crew's hard work pays off. You can try to call me after the show, but unless you hear there's a fire or something, let's say it was a great success. We sold out, and I don't think there was a dry eye in the house. Having the actual stars of the movie, the cyclists come out at the end was a powerful moment that I don't think anybody is ever going to forget. Based on advanced tickets sales for the festival, we've already surpassed last year, but there are still plenty of Saturday and Sunday film passes available. Good enough?"

"It's so much easier to interview someone who is a journalist," said Laflamme.

Les Stroud and Laura Bombier arrived. I showed them to the downstairs area. As I got back to my spot, Patrick Dempsey arrived at 6:45 with several family members.

"Thanks for coming," I said, holding out my hand.

"It's Josh, right?" he said.

Holy shit! Patrick Dempsey either knows my name or remembered it for the five seconds it took from someone telling him in the car to shaking my hand at the door. It didn't matter. I was counting it!

"It's Patrick, right?" I asked, jokingly.

I lead the Dempseys downstairs where the after-party was going to be and where they could meet Les Stroud and Laura Bombier prior to finding their seats. After a few pictures in front of our banners with the celebrities, we went upstairs to start the show.

As the opening video Colin put together played, the Dempsey family settled into their front row seats. Before the lights came up, I introduced Molly, and the night was off and everything I forecasted for Laflamme came true.

Saturday was easy, but like the year before, didn't result in a ton of walk-up sales, which disappointed me. I promised myself not to expect it the following year. I'd learned my lesson. The biggest ticket disappointment was the lack of a walk-up for the "Q&A with *Survivorman*" at the Public Theatre. We offered it as a standalone ticket, as a bundle with a ticket to his concert that night, and as part of the day pass with all of the other films, so I figured at least 150 people would attend. It was closer to 75. Just as it was set to begin, I got a message there was an issue at the Ramada ballroom where the awards dinner and concert was being held later that night, so Les actually offered to host the Q&A himself since it was a small group.

When I got to the hotel, the technical issue had been ironed out. It allowed me to go to the room we were using for changing our clothes. I put on a pair of shorts and a T-shirt and fell backward onto the bed, turning on the TV, watching a few minutes of the Red Sox game. I wondered what would happened if I just took my clothes, left and went home for the night. How hard would anybody really try to get me to return?

I presented the Producers' Award to Les that night at the awards show. I also gave the "Humanitarian through Film Award" to Ramsey Tripp. It was intended for Patrick Dempsey if he stayed, but I was so much happier to give it to Ramsey, who actually deserved it. I read off a list of his good deeds that makes the rest of us look like heathens. In my world that was shades of gray drifting toward black, he was bright white good. Need to solve the world's problems? We all just have to act like Ramsey.

Les' concert was fantastic afterward. We cleared several rows of tables away and set up four rows of chairs and let in the extra ticket holders, really packing the ballroom for the show. I spent a lot of the concert in the rear of the room where people who wanted to talk could hear each other. It was there I got the best compliment of that festival, from one of the Peloton riders who said they'd been to the big national awards shows, and while everything always looks better on TV, we put on a hell of a show considering our budget.

The last time I can honestly say I ever felt terrific for the next several years was immediately after Les' show. He had a meet-and-greet with fans which kept us there late, but it also meant more money rolling in as we got a cut of his merchandise sales. There were also so many filmmakers, Peloton riders, and concertgoers in such good moods they just wanted to hang out. I fear that I will never be at the epicenter of creating such positive energy again. Molly and I were getting along. Paul and I were joking like nothing was tense at the office. I knew Sandy saw nothing but dollar signs with a day left of the festival. Even Dan Marquis seemed giddy.

There was a short get-together for the core group of us in the hotel room we used, but like every other year, I took off early, shortly after Les left. It wasn't lost on me that less than four months earlier I was nursing a gallbladder operation on my couch watching this guy's TV show, now I'm hanging out in a hotel room with him drinking beers after a hugely successful day at the film festival.

It was hard to sleep when I got home, especially after looking at my Facebook page, which had blown up with compliments, photos, and recollections of the day. It blew my mind and not just in an ego-massaging way. It was a super-concentrated wave of appreciation and love. I think it's the only time I ever felt what I was always searching for. I was up until 4 in the morning reading posts. Before I went to catch a couple hours of sleep I posted: "I hope everyone can experience the joy I have right now at least once in their life." I still mean that. Even in my worst moments, of which there were so many just around the corner, I was able to think about this night. I know that I helped create a lot of once-in-a-lifetime moments for people, but this was one for me.

Sunday was slow, but we expected it. It was more of a victory lap and cool-down for people who had been in it for the long haul since Les' book signing on Thursday night. It still amazes me people came in from a dozen states and handful of countries for this festival that was growing exponentially. Despite the magazine's foundation showing cracks I didn't know if I could fix, LAFF looked healthy.

The Monday after LAFF, Paul took the day off. Molly, Sandy, and I gathered at Sandy's house for cocktails and money counting. Expenses were lower than our second year, but the gross was even, which meant a tidy profit was turned.

We then did something arguably defensible, but kind of shitty in retrospect. Since the festival was a for-profit business, we could pay ourselves as we wished. Letting a tipsy trio—who felt other team members didn't pull their weight—make payoff decisions put all the power in our hands. We gave Paul and Danielle half of what we each took. We then paid both Marquis Signs and *Lewiston Auburn Magazine* a chunk of the in-kind services they had donated. The magazine used that money to give bonuses to Molly and I for the next several pay periods. While this may have all been shady, it wasn't illegal since the three of us comprised more than 50 percent of the voting stock in both companies.

* * *

In mid-May, Paul told me he was going to be leaving *Lewiston Auburn Magazine* in the next couple of months. His wife, Kate, was either going back to school for a doctorate to help her career and would need to leave the state for school, or she going to find better opportunities outside of Maine. Paul had mentioned this off-and-on over the years, but he always said it in a tone which never worried me.

A few quiet days later, he and I met at a coffee shop. I was hoping a change of scenery might allow us to tap into the piece of our non-professional relationship and communicate better than we had been.

"Are you staying with us until Kate finds something or do you want to set a date for leaving?" I asked.

"I'm going to go either way. I'm just burnt out," he said.

"What's your plan?" I asked, trying to make my tone sound more like a friend than a boss.

"I'll sell cars again until Kate finds something. I'll figure something out from there," he said.

"Sure you want to go?"

"It's been a lot of fun, but the driving is killing me and doing the same thing over and over is burning me out," said Paul.

I asked Paul to give me a date he was leaving so I could begin the search process. He said August 1. More than two months' notice was appreciated, and I could tell in his voice that it would have taken a ridiculous amount of money to keep him there. I didn't make an offer.

I'm of the belief that commission drives some salespeople and pride drives others. Paul was a pride guy, and I went that route with him from day one. Paul and Danielle always knew they could count on their salary every week. I've worked places where salespeople have had three or four weeks of bad commission checks—which are not always their fault. That's a recipe for depression, deflection, and low self-esteem. It's also hard to keep a consistent payroll that way.

With Paul planning to leave and the simple fact my productivity was dropping on all fronts, I was no longer convinced pride was a better route than security. I started to wonder if security was just what they didn't need.

* * *

My porn use at night would see peaks and valleys over the next few months. There were two very different types of porn sought out for two very different reasons. The first was how I think most people traditionally view porn. They find something that arouses them, get off to it, then move on with their lives. I still mostly preferred sites that had video clips. Whatever I wanted to see that night as far as a genre of porn, I could just type into the search field, and I'd get a ton of clips to go along with it.

I wasn't somebody who spent hours surfing porn sites. I had too much to do. I've met guys who have told stories of sitting in front of a computer for six, eight and ten hours at a time or who masturbated three or four times a day. I don't know how they did it. If I was watching video clips longer than ninety minutes, I usually quit. Watching porn was a nice diversion from work and an escape from the real world where people now seemed to enjoy being mean and disappointing. The ladies on the computer screen weren't turning on me the way people were in real life.

I noticed some of the better video clips came from a site called Omegle I'd never visited. When I went to look at the site, I realized it wasn't a traditional cam site where people watch a performer. Instead, like the more popular ChatRoulette, it was a site where people connected one-on-one. If the two people who connected via their web cams wanted to chat (out loud or typing) great, if not, one could hit the "NEXT" button and a new connection was made.

I'm sure some people just chatted, but this site was clearly utilized by a vast majority looking for naked people. I never used this site as traditional porn. This was something else. This was about manipulation and exerting what little power I felt I had left in my life. When I discovered Omegle, I was probably fooling around with it for thirty minutes a night on most nights, maybe four or five nights a week. I was undoubtedly drinking, and I told myself it was just another distraction from my work, like regular non-interactive porn.

I wasn't about to show my face on camera, so nobody stopped that first night or two. When I finally got the guts to turn my camera on, still nobody stopped. The ratio of men-to-women was 20-to-1 and seeing some of the buff guys on the site, I couldn't hold a candle to them in the looks department. As I was about to give up on the site, I realized many of the men repeated again and again. Considering the site often claimed to have over 40,000 people viewing at a time, it seemed the odds that the same man would repeatedly appear were small, even if the site was lying about its numbers tenfold.

Eventually, I got one of these good-looking guys to stop and explain that he wasn't the guy I saw on screen. He told me about a website I could find videos of attractive people who looked like they were sitting at computers typing and explained the software I'd need to bypass my laptop's camera. I played around for a few days and eventually found a video of an attractive guy, probably 20 or 21 years old in a white T-shirt and basketball shorts. In the 25-minute video, the guy waved, made a peace symbol, smiled a few times, stood up, showed his abs, showed his penis for a few seconds, and looked like he was typing the rest of the time. I was able to time things out where if a woman said, "I think you're fake, wave at me" I could have this guy wave that second, or if she said, "you never smile" I could click to the right part of the video, and he'd smile immediately.

I could get probably every 10th female to stop and talk to this guy. This was not about porn from almost the first conversation. Since I used Omegle between midnight and 3 a.m. almost exclusively, it was usually women in their early-to-mid 20s I found who were looking for the type of guy I was pretending to be. Within the first few women, I had a backstory for this guy that stayed mostly the same until the day I was arrested. He was a wannabe model from the northeast who was in Miami trying to make it as a model. He spent his days auditioning and had a real job as a personal trainer. The twist was that he was the valedictorian of his high school and turned down Ivy League scholarships to the dismay of his family to follow his dream. I usually called him Antony.

There were nights when I was feeling depressed that I would simply sit there and talk to a woman for an hour and the topic of sex never came up. Some nights I might even steer the conversation away from it. Other nights, I might see how quickly I could get her to disrobe and see how far I could push her before she'd object. It really had to do with my mood. I just looked at the woman on the other end of the computer as there for my needs, whatever they might be that night. Even when I was able to push them in a sexual direction, it wasn't mainly for my carnal gratification. It was about my ego and my ability to control and manipulate. I felt like I had so little control in my life that I wanted a puppet on the other end of the computer.

Asking them to wave, or hold up a pillow, or make a silly face . . . they wouldn't object to that. If I was going to prove to myself I had any real power or any real control, it had to be in areas that they didn't want to go. Obviously, I couldn't force a woman to take off her shirt, so I had to convince her. That was the challenge. That was how I could prove to myself despite things going to hell in real life, I still was somehow special and could accomplish what most would never be able to do.

* * *

After the film festival, most of the team was physically exhausted. They would get so amped up that in the aftermath, they let their guard down and crashed. It almost stands to reason that for me, the crash was mental.

It was in the middle of May on a Saturday that I opted to do my work at the office. I could have stayed home but knew I could drink beer and isolate at the office. I didn't avoid Melissa and the kids, but it was clear they didn't really need me around . . . and didn't expect to see me anywhere but the kitchen table. I contributed to the household budget most weeks (I paid myself on time 75% by this point I'd guess), but I was not very active in their lives otherwise.

Sitting in the darkened office with only a bit of natural light coming in from the front window, I took a long look at our giant 100-foot-long office space. We had dozens of pieces of art on the walls, furniture worth thousands, copies of 30-35 issues we'd produced, a bunch of awards on a shelf. I knew we'd begun the journey to the end. How did I mismanage it so poorly? How had I made myself so miserable with all of it?

I knew my personal friendship with Paul would be dead the moment he left. The only director of sales I'd ever had was leaving. What was I going to do? The professional relationship I had with Molly was eroding like a beach during a winter storm. Danielle's mediocre output wasn't going to suddenly improve with a new baby.

I broke down. I broke down hard. The intensity of the tears, wailing, and body convulsions were as loud and violent as my worst anxiety attacks were silent and crippling. I needed someone who could understand. I called Sandy.

She was very good at calming me, sharing a little about anxiety she'd experienced in her life. I told her how I felt everything was falling apart around me. She appeared understanding, told me to take a few days off, and do what I needed to pull myself together so I could come back and devise a plan for rebounding.

I called Melissa next. She wasn't too concerned, but she shouldn't have been since I gave her no context about my life for months. I told her I just needed to jumpstart my mind and didn't know how to get that done. She suggested a long drive.

After debating visiting the Baseball Hall of Fame in Cooperstown, New York, I decided to go to Foxwoods Resort and Casino in Connecticut because I could sit at a poker table and be forced to make decision after decision in the heat of the moment. I told Sandy I felt like I was paralyzed to make decisions in the month following LAFF and hoped the poker table might jolt me. I was letting bills add up, not sure which to pay. After dropping Kaden off at school, I'd sometimes go back home to sleep, not hitting the office until lunch, for fear I'd be confronted with something I'd done wrong. Before this slowdown in my mental capacity, I could pay $1,200 in bills with $1,000 and wiggle my way out of any situation. I just didn't have it anymore.

For the first time ever, I started soothing myself with pornography in the morning. I didn't use chatrooms and the length of an online session of browsing porn was much shorter than the evening, but I still made that jump to looking at porn more than once a day.

Over that Friday and Saturday at Foxwoods, I bought myself only one good meal, spending almost all of my time at the poker table. I lost $150, but that was far from the point. I was forced to make decision after decision in the moment based on my cards. By Sunday morning, thirty minutes into playing, I was done. My mind was back on track. I had a vice-free couple of days: No alcohol, no porn, no work. It was what my brain needed.

On the way home, I crafted a plan for the magazine. It wasn't going to fix everything, but it would be a start.

- Once Paul left, we'd ride out the rest of the year without a sales manager. I'd run some numbers recently and knew Danielle wasn't pulling her weight as a sales person, even if that was only supposed to be half of her job. Neither had a contract so when I returned I was going to present them with a base salary plus 10% commission. Paul would get roughly the same money, she'd make less (forcing a need to improve) and I wouldn't take commission on my sales.

- It was time to cut the extras. No cases of coffee. No cases of beer and once the gift card contracts ran out, we'd renegotiate to 50% gift card and 50% cash or we didn't take the contract.
- I decided to take a $50 cut in pay per week, starting immediately. It was only $3,500 in savings per year but would show the others I meant business when it came to cutting costs.
- Kevin and Gabby knew we were having trouble because I never got them a rent check on time. If we couldn't get them down $200 to $400 per month, we didn't need that space. We were no longer on a lease and could use it as leverage.
- Prose Gallery needed to become a source of revenue. Instead of expensive, beautiful works, like Lyceum Gallery, we needed to put pieces on the wall that could sell during ArtWalk season. I also knew with the stage and open space, we could promote small entertainment shows and events people would pay a few dollars to come see. If we could do $1,000 per month, rent would take care of itself.
- Finally, I knew the magazine had to get better. I could hypothesize why the decline, but with the exception of the "Healthy Mind, Healthy Body" issue that I handled most of the content for, I felt the Molly-edited magazine was bland.

I had a martini meeting at Sandy's house a day or two after I got home. I told her how much better I felt and told her it was time to fix the magazine.

"There are people talking, and they're saying the magazine has been getting boring," said Sandy. "And I have to agree with them. Is it Molly? Is it you?"

"Both of us. But I'm going to try and write a feature every month. I've been thinking about maybe getting a little newsier. It needs to be a magazine people are excited to get again," I said.

"I'm so glad to hear you say this," she said. "After your meltdown, I was getting worried about you."

I commented that I was worried what Molly may say when I confronted her about the content lacking something lately.

"If Molly isn't pulling her weight, you may have to make a tough decision," Sandy said, clearly trying to mentally prepare me for firing Molly. "But, she needs to be told things are bad and be given time to fix it."

She agreed with moving to a commission structure, tweaking the gallery, and not funding the extras. At least it was a plan.

* * *

Danielle came in for a meeting during her maternity leave so I could unveil the commission structure. I told her and Paul that we'd be moving to that set-up on July 1, explaining that if we didn't, we'd probably would have trouble making payroll over the traditionally challenging late summer if advertiser checks weren't coming in. They both understood, and she left to return home to her new baby, leaving just Paul and I in the office.

"Can you just pay me the same way in July since I'll be gone on August 1?" he asked.

"Yeah, sure," I said, giving it no thought, knowing the numbers were the same. "This is more about putting a system into place that makes Danielle more accountable and whoever comes in after you to start with it from Day One. We've evolved and need something new. Something here is broken right now."

"It is. And a big part of it is you. And you and Molly need to figure out what your issue is. The magazine sucks with you two not talking to each other," said Paul.

Two weeks later, a couple of days before Danielle was set to return from maternity leave, she came into the office and told us she had taken a job elsewhere and was leaving without notice. After she walked through the door, we looked at each other out of shock that somebody left us with no notice, collecting a salary and benefits while on maternity leave.

"It is what it is," I said to Paul, quietly impressed how she gamed the system. "I guess instead of just advertising your position, we are advertising for two. Even if she'd come to us two weeks earlier, objectively, she was due the maternity leave money. At least we save some money immediately moving forward."

* * *

A once-in-a-lifetime opportunity, the kind of thing a narcissist like me dreams about but knows is too egotistical to even wish for out loud, came true when I was asked to give the commencement address for the Lewiston High School Class of 2013. It was in that list of honors in my head (along with a Key to the City, a street named after me, and an Honorary Doctorate) that I don't share with people because there's nothing I can really do to achieve them and sounded insane to have hope happened.

A few days later, Katrielle said she was going to be in the Auburn Middle School talent show the same night. I explained to her that daddy had the biggest speech of his life to give. She said it was OK. I think neither her nor Melissa were surprised I'd skip the talent show at that point. I didn't see how I could say no to speaking in front of 3,500 people.

The commencement address took place a few days after coming home from Foxwoods after my colossal meltdown, to illustrate the duality of my inner and outer worlds at the time. I had a couple of beers at the office before I left to give the speech at the civic center, but was sober several hours later when the time came to deliver it. The theme was about knowing who you really are and that expressing love and gratitude were the keys to having a quality life. Following the ceremony, there were the typical "Always wanted to meet you" handshakes that still happened. Lately, most had been around my bipolar disorder story. I was very popular that summer in mental health circles, even being roped in by Laura Davis to shoot a public service announcement for the NAMI mental health group in Maine.

After the commencement ceremony, I returned to the office for the tail end of the first ArtWalk of the season. I texted Melissa to find out what happened with the talent show. Kat won first place. I told Sandy, and she gave me the look of somebody who made the wrong choice of which event to attend. Kat won. I lost.

Chapter 16

About a week before Paul left, he blew up at me to such a vehement and random degree I had the feeling it was something he'd saved up a long time. I don't remember how it started, he just started blurting.

"You need to start listening to other people if this is going to survive after I'm gone. You don't do that anymore," he said late in the morning, unprompted.

"OK, I'm listening now," I said.

"We're stuck in Lewiston and Auburn. There's Brunswick. There's Augusta. There's a lot we don't go after," he said. "There are good stories outside of here."

He'd made mention about Brunswick in the past. It really never made sense. Molly and I had casually discussed it in the past, when she'd bought a house closer to Brunswick, but we didn't want to dilute the product.

"It doesn't make sense to have those places in *Lewiston Auburn Magazine*," I said.

"That's what you always say!" he responded angrily, knowing this would be his last chance to make this argument. He knew he would end up on the losing end of it. Maybe it helped the transition out of the office feel easier.

Augusta is Maine's state capital, so during the day, there are probably 75,000-100,000 people in the small city. At night, though, there are about 18,000 and once the museum closes, there's nothing really of note there. Brunswick has about 20,000 people but is crawling with tourists a good chunk of the year. If you're looking for one of those stereotypical coastal Maine towns with the quaint Main Street and smell of the ocean in the air, it's Brunswick, located halfway between Lewiston and Portland, but socioeconomic demographics—probably because it's a coastal city—are much higher than Lewiston. The people there don't come to Lewiston for anything, they go to Portland.

"How many times have you spent the day in Brunswick trying to sell ads?" I asked.

"It's not worth it if we're not running stories," was his chicken-or-egg response.

"Wrong. Everyone travels south to shop. There are tens of thousands of people who go there. Look at *Portland Magazine*. They've got advertisers from Bar Harbor to Boston. You're wrong," I said.

"You tell people they're wrong all the time now," he said.

"Yes, but I tell them why. We're never going to write stories about Brunswick. Brunswick people won't read us and people in Lewiston and Auburn don't read us for stories about Brunswick. They know where to go to get stories about Brunswick. Brunswick businesses have ways to reach Brunswick residents. If they're interested in getting a higher-end Lewiston and Auburn crowd, they should be advertising with us. We haven't even approached Portland restaurants in our entire time being around, have we?" I asked.

"What about the ad placement?" he asked.

This also had been something he brought up in the past. It was like a death row inmate going through his greatest hits grievance list.

"Jesus. This again?"

"You've got all of these rules that don't make sense. There's no reason an eighth-page ad can't be on a page by itself. There's no reason a one-third page vertical ad can't be on the same page with a regular quarter-page ad," he complained.

"Yes. In both cases, that would look stupid. Feel free to ask the others," I said, although Molly was pretending not to be in the room. "I'm sorry if you don't agree, but it's the style guide that we've used and it's not changing."

"It's your style guide. I don't remember ever voting on it," he said.

"Well, I assure you that Molly and Corey would agree with me," I said.

"OK, well whoever sells next, don't tell them when you've got three quarter-page ads sold on a page and you need to fill a hole to go sell a quarter-page ad for whatever they can get for it. It makes us look cheap and desperate," he said.

"I could have Corey just make a filler ad, but I figure $50 is $50. That pays for the Keurig for a month," I said. "If it makes us look cheap and desperate, we're presenting it to an advertiser wrong. It should be like a reward for being loyal."

"Or we could just put stories there!" said Paul.

"That would look stupid. You don't fill a quarter page hole with content," I said. "Paul, I've explained why we don't do things that way, and it's going to stay that way after you're gone. I'm sorry that you don't agree."

There was no reason for me to get heated, and I think my calmness might have made the situation worse. I was going to win this argument not just because I was the publisher, but because I was right.

"I'm going to go have a cigarette," he said and left through the front door.

Molly swiveled her chair in my direction.

"That was out of nowhere," I said with a surprised look on my face.

"He's been complaining about everything for a few weeks," she said. "Especially about you."

"Why?"

"I don't know. Maybe he doesn't want to leave. Maybe he doesn't feel appreciated," she guessed.

"Was I wrong about anything I said?" I asked her.

"No, although maybe you could have said something nicer than his ideas were stupid," said Molly.

"OK, I could have been nicer, but Jesus Christ. Is he trying to make me fire him?"

"I don't know but fix it so his last week isn't full of tension," she commanded.

When he returned, I offered a simple, "I'm sorry."

"It's fine. I'm just sick of this fucking commute," he said. We worked in silence and went our separate ways for lunch. I don't think we ate together again before he left.

* * *

I hired a guy named Jim O'Rourke to take Paul's place. He was either in his late 40s or early 50s. His background was TV production, sales, and was a bit of an entrepreneur. He was tentative in the interview but made a good impression. Paul spent his last few days teaching Jim the ropes. Paul and I didn't say much to each other after that last big argument, and his goodbye party was me saying, "Goodbye."

Corey was back in the hospital, which meant more design work for me. Aside from trying to handle publisher duties and now morphing into a sales manager, I was keeping an eye on Molly's content, hoping to produce more of my own and now taking on a bunch of design. I hired an intern named Jen McLean who was a seventeen-year-old go-getter still in high school to help a bit. She had a lot of energy but was green. She reminded me more of myself when I started at the *Sun Journal* 20 years earlier than any person I'd worked with to that point. She could design, take photos, update the website, and wanted to learn anything we'd teach her.

Corey had his mother bring his computer to the hospital, where he contributed a bit but couldn't be counted on. Regardless of his output, I still tried to pay him his full salary.

It didn't take much time to see Jim wasn't a great fit. He could maintain contracts but felt no connection to the product. I didn't have much other choice than to give him time to find that stride because I still needed a new salesperson to take Danielle's spot before I could even think about a better one to replace him.

The physical act of doing the work was such a slog for me at this point. Because of summer vacation, the kids slept in, so I did, too. I truly missed having Paul around, and while we did save money on salaries, the art walks and gallery entertainment weren't generating the kind of money I hoped they would. Ticketed events, like biweekly comedy nights, would do anywhere from $40 to $150. Sometimes we rented it out for a flat fee of $200, but with only four or five events a month, it didn't equal the time spent promoting and running it.

One evening that August, Sandy, Tammie, and I were sitting at one of the tables outside of Fuel, enjoying a cocktail in the warm air. Both mentioned it was smart that I was letting my final months as a city councilor come to an end, and I admitted I barely paid attention at meetings on Monday evenings.

"Josh, the magazine, isn't very interesting lately," Tammie said during a conversational lull.

"Sandy and I had a conversation about this several weeks ago," I said. "I'm trying to fix it."

"Did you talk to Molly yet?" Sandy asked me.

"No," I admitted.

"You need to," she said.

"I hate having 'Come to Jesus' meetings," I said.

"But Josh, don't you already think you're God?" Tammie asked, only half-jokingly.

I thought about that for a second. I once did. Now I was just a tired guy.

"My God complex has disappeared," I said.

"I don't think so," said Sandy.

"You know," I said, "If I never won another award or had my name in the newspaper again, I'd be fine."

"No you wouldn't," said Sandy.

"I believe him," said Tammie, examining me, almost giving me a visual polygraph. "I know what he means."

"If you just picked me up and dropped me in another city and asked me to start a new life, I don't think I'd miss any of this," I said without realizing it.

"I don't think you would," said Tammie.

I probably shouldn't have said that in front of Sandy, looking back. I'm sure it was just another red flag that my heart and mind were drifting from her investment.

That night, between Red Bull and tequilas while I tried to work at home, I asked Molly via email for a meeting to clear the air. She offered her home the next day since it was one of the days she didn't come to the office. We both admitted that our relationship had got away from us and that communication needed to return.

We said how important we were to each other and promised things would change. Saying it felt even better than hearing it.

Nothing changed. I think we were simply too far gone and too many resentments had built, especially on my side.

* * *

I wish I could say I never downloaded another folder of pornography with teenagers after that first "girls on a beach" file months earlier, but it wasn't the case. I don't remember how I ended up back on the torrent search engine, probably looking for some kind of pirated graphic design software, but there I was and remembered it.

I never wanted anything of young children. I'm not attracted to males, nor pre-pubescent females. Like the average heterosexual male, I'm hardwired to be attracted to sexually mature females. My lack of judgment at the time blurred the line between an "older girl" and a "younger woman". That's an important line. Physiologically, I'm not a pedophile, but legally, I am a sex offender.

I don't understand the mindset of people who are pedophiliac or violent sex offenders because I'm not wired like them, but I don't judge them as harshly anymore now that I have spent time with so many of them and can tell you not a single one decided on their own to be that way. They have an illness and that's not a cop-out. What every sex offender did, no matter the specifics of the crime, is heinous. It's horrible to think of the pain of the victims, but it's not excusing the behavior to say there is usually mental illness and addiction behind it. I'll also tell you for every one that has been caught, I shudder to think just what the ratio is of those who are not. I bet 50-to-1 is lowballing it.

My mind was in a place where it was OK to sift through file names that I knew contained pornography that I didn't want just to get to the kind I did. Unfortunately, there were several times a mislabeled file led to me seeing something I didn't want. I found it disconcerting, and those are the images that haunt my mind daily. Thankfully, I didn't see a lot, having only downloaded a handful of folders over several months, and only actually completing the downloads of a few files in those folders.

It was reported shortly after my arrest that I had hundreds of images on my computer of children under twelve years old. This was one of those facts that I wish had been further clarified in the media. If I found a folder with one film clip I wanted to see, I still had to start the download of the entire folder, even if there were 99 other files I didn't want.

Once the download began, I would stop the downloads of the 99 files I didn't want and go into my computer's download manager and delete those 99 incomplete files. In most cases, less than 3% of any individual file was downloaded. They were unviewable at that point. However, it still counted to law enforcement as a file that was downloaded.

I shouldn't have had any of it, but I have a sense the overall volume of what I was downloading in most people's minds based on the first media reports, far outpaced the reality of the situation. Nonetheless, one is too many. One is 100% too many.

In my deteriorating condition, if I wanted to see younger women, a 16- or 17-year-old was just as good to me as a 19- or 20-year-old. It all blended together. I don't make the laws, though, and that's a good thing. There is a line of demarcation when it comes to viewing pornography. It's 18 years old, and I strayed below it. There's no rationalization that makes that OK. I broke the law and can't massage the facts to change that.

When it came to the specifics of a female's age, I don't think I cared as long as they looked like a woman. When a female popped up and looked like a 15-year-old, I'd hit "NEXT" quickly. I never got so sick that I was physically attracted to pre-pubescent children. I didn't have the good sense to appreciate there are children who look like young adults.

I started taking screen captures of the women who would undress or masturbate at my request, at least the ones I worked hard to convince. I never used these for sexual gratification later. I rarely ever looked at them except when I needed an ego boost. The real rush in my broken mind was grooming them and then watching them do what I wanted.

The folder I kept the screen captures in acted as a box of trophies, like some illegal big game hunter. They showed that I could manipulate someone into giving me what I wanted. There were nights I didn't need to see anything sexual, or if a woman was steadfast against that, I would try to get her to try on outfits for me, or move the furniture around . . . anything to somehow gain control.

If I couldn't get a woman to stop and talk to me, or I didn't get them to follow my commands, I considered that night a failure, like most of my days were. If I was able to get them to stop and they did what I wanted, I was successful. Since things were faltering in every other aspect of my life, it was nice to have one place where I could still get things right on a somewhat regular basis.

There are rituals around addiction, and they contribute to the rush that comes when one knows they are about to indulge. Simply beginning the process of indulging in an addiction brings some level of relief.

When it came to drinking at home, I always needed a giant plastic cup for my Red Bull and tequila. I'd pour in a splash of tequila, add the ice, then the can of Red Bull. Whatever space was left at the top was home to more tequila. I'd pop in a colorful straw, take a mighty sip, and then refill the empty space with more tequila. This all took place in the kitchen, always in that order.

Porn rituals changed for me over the years depending on what was going on in my life, but they were always important to the process, indicating it has always been an addiction. Porn and masturbation were completely entwined. I never looked at porn without self-gratifying, and 99.5% of the time I masturbated in my life, porn was utilized. I couldn't see a reason to watch porn unless using it as an aid for gratification, and while I have an imagination, there was no need to use it when visual aids were so readily available.

In the months leading to my arrest, I looked at legal porn most nights after everybody had gone to bed, and my buzz had kicked in. I visited the same few sites, in the same order, almost every time.

When it came to talking to females through the Omegle site, I had to first set up the video that hid my true identity. I'd almost always move from the kitchen table, where I did magazine work, to the living room. It was odd to go looking for people anywhere but the couch. Settling in, with the alcohol at its peak, these simple routines prepped me for the truly addictive behavior—but were just as much a part of the overall experience.

Whenever the question of if I was cheating on Melissa entered my head, I managed to escape elsewhere, as I did with any other question that had an answer I didn't want to face. The answer was a resounding yes and I knew it, but I rationalized if I was ever caught that I would deny it ever dawned on me such a thing was infidelity.

I'm not a jealous type and neither is Melissa. I'm also a little oblivious to when a woman is hitting on me, as happened once in front of Melissa at the gallery. I recognized it once Melissa pointed it out, but since it's a phenomenon that's happened so few times in my life, it's a blind spot.

I could say it's fortunate she never caught me, but I wish she had. I would have rather dealt with that fallout. I think I would have broken down and confessed to her how completely out of control everything was after trying to put up a front. Most men are happy they got away with cheating. I'm not one of them.

* * *

A late September meeting with Kevin and Gabby over rent did not go well. I acted as hostile toward them as I had started to with everyone else. My mind was telling me that people were out to get me, but in the throes of paranoia, everything seems crystal clear. They threw a bunch of proposals at me, but I didn't want to sign a lease. Even if they had said $250 per month, but it required a lease, I would have said no. The office vibe was different now. I'd hired another salesperson, Abbie Luttrell, who was good but still not one of the originals. I needed a new space to reinvent things.

Jim and I never clicked. I think I tend to like people when I see they are trying hard to contribute, but new clients were few and far between and he had no outward passion. He did a decent job maintaining the smaller old accounts of Paul and Danielle, but I never felt comfortable handing him the large accounts I now managed like the hospitals. I didn't want him to bungle them, and I couldn't afford to pay him the commission.

Molly and I fell back into a tense relationship after a few weeks of getting along. She regularly told me I treated Jim poorly and needed to work at building a relationship with him, but something in me didn't want to create a bond with someone who wasn't doing a good job in my eyes. I resented his performance.

He once told me that he was afraid to speak too much in the office because of the obvious tension between Molly and me. She offered him encouragement, but it came off as hollow praise, I think. All of this said, she was correct. It was up to me to get off on the right foot with Jim, and I didn't. My resentful silent treatment was never going to help things.

* * *

Despite the fact there were too many owners of the magazine, I was the only one who was working in the office full time and of all the others, Sandy seemed to the be the only one who asked about the financial state of the company. Once I got her to sign-off on the idea of leaving our large Lisbon Street gallery/office behind, we told ourselves things were looking up because despite everything else we were poised to have our best revenue generating issue ever with a "Women in Business" themed effort, but the phrase "too little, too late" exists for a reason.

In leaving that amazing Lisbon Street office, I played it off as a business decision based on the financial reality of Prose Gallery not generating enough revenue. I made the announcement on Facebook, writing about what love I had for our gallery, recounting the goofy taxidermy, and Les Stroud's book signing, the comedy nights, and the thousands of people who had streamed through over time. I mentioned we lost money, even in the summer with ArtWalks and events. I think people appreciated the honesty, with it ironically getting more likes and comments than anything else ever posted to the Prose Gallery Facebook page. The magazine relocating was an afterthought, treating it more as a casualty of the gallery than a business move of its own.

I sent Kevin Fletcher, Millett Realty's big commercial real estate guy an email telling him what I was looking for, saying I still wanted a cool space in a well-traveled location, but didn't want to spend more than $500 per month and would trade ads if needed. He showed me a few spots, but the one I loved was in the same building as Gritty's, right next door to the Androscoggin

Land Trust. Yup, I was just upstairs from a bar that I had endless gift cards for and next door to my buddy, Jonathan LaBonte. City Hall was just around the corner, our bank was across the street, and it was a nice section of downtown Auburn.

The office was roughly the size of the space we used for our work area, minus the gallery, in Lewiston but felt small because the ceiling was eight feet high, not 15, like on Lisbon Street. There was a small separate office to the side and a few little nooks and crannies. I never liked having my own office, so I stayed out in the main area and figured Molly could take the larger private office. Sales would be on one side of the room, and Corey, who was rebounding and wanted to be in the office more days of the week, would be on the other.

I brought Molly and Sandy to see the space after I chose it. I told them it was the best I'd seen for the deal we could get.

"This should be the place. For price and location, it's got what we need," I explained.

"We really should look at others," Sandy said.

Inside, I wanted to scream, "I'm the only one who does anything around here anymore! I write! I design! I sell! This is turning into a one-man show! Do you realize how shitty I feel? Do you realize I sleep two or three hours per night maximum? I take the time to find a new office, and you want to look at other fucking places? Is Josh not fucking doing enough already? Fuck my life!"

Apparently, my face went through a series of expressions as the monologues raged in my diseased head. I knew I was on the edge of a panic/anxiety/crying attack.

"What's wrong?" Sandy asked.

I took a breath and in a tone that couldn't hide the equal parts anger and frustration, I said "I've looked around. Kevin Fletcher showed me other spots. This is the one. We don't need anywhere else. I'm the one who is going to be here all the time. Not you two."

"OK, you're right," Sandy said, able to read my body language.

I could also read Sandy's body language. It said: "I'm giving in because you're about to lose your shit. Fighting with you just isn't worth it."

Molly acquiesced as well. I let Kevin Fletcher know we'd take the space as of November 1. I let Molly and Abbie pick the paint and carpet as a peace offering.

I agreed to let Sandy talk to Gabby about us transitioning out of the old office and how much of our deposit we'd be getting. I'd really left a bad impression when I said we wouldn't sign a new lease and with the overall way I'd treated our landlords for months.

I spent that weekend, alone, tearing apart all of our workspaces at the old office, transporting them to Auburn and rebuilding them. The only break I took was to run over to The Dempsey Challenge and take a quick private picture of Patrick Dempsey, his sister, Mary, and their mother, Amanda. I wanted a photo of the three of them for a Dempsey Center cover since we hadn't run a story about the cancer center or the fundraiser in a few years, and I didn't know the next time I could get the three of them together. They agreed to take a minute to pose for me between events.

"How's the film festival coming this year, Josh?" Patrick Dempsey asked me.

"Slower than usual, but fine," I said.

"If I can help in any way, let me know," he said, just being nice, as he was whisked off to the next thing. I didn't tell him just how slow.

Molly, Sandy, and I had met months earlier in July or August to talk about making the festival a non-profit finally, but put that discussion on the back burner. Sandy had made a few subtle hints she might want to take a year off after three solid years.

We stopped talking about LAFF entirely that October after a strange argument over funk guitarist Bootsy Collins.

I knew with Paul and Danielle out of the LAFF picture there would be a lot of 2-1 votes between Molly, Sandy, and I. That meant I'd be the tiebreaker most of the time.

In early autumn, I happened upon the opportunity to have Bootsy Collins, who was James Brown's guitarist and was in the 90s' psychedelic group Deee-Lite, perform a concert at a fair price of $10,000 with his band. I knew we could put him at the Franco Center and make half the money back, if not more, in tickets and get a sponsor to kick in a few thousand. The director of the center,

Louis Morin, was psyched. A guitarist himself, Collins was his idol. He committed to sponsoring the show for $1,000 and was going to put as much promotion behind the show as possible. I didn't think we could lose.

Despite our frostiness, I told Molly about the idea, and she loved it. She knew a lot of musicians, and they were excited about the idea of someone of Collins' stature coming to play.

I called Sandy, and the brakes went screeching. She vaguely knew the name, and Dan, despite being a drummer in bands in the 1970s and 80s, didn't. She didn't like the $10,000, so I asked her to talk to her musician friends and see if they'd drop $20-$40 on a ticket.

Molly and I talked to friends and came to the same conclusion that $30 would bring people in. After seeing the response to Don McLean at $50/$60 two years earlier, we thought it was a safe gamble.

If we drew a house of 200 at $30 each, plus the Franco's $1,000, and got a $2,500 sponsor, we were looking at a $500 loss . . . it was a gain when you figured how much publicity and new blood it would bring to LAFF. If the sponsor was $3,000 and the show sold 300 tickets, it was a nice profit.

I sent those numbers to both Sandy and Molly, but Sandy responded saying most of her musician friends never heard of Bootsy Collins and those who had would never pay $30 to see his band. She said we may get no sponsor and sell 75 tickets. She also, wisely, reminded us of things like hotel rooms and plane tickets. I agreed it was a risk but nothing like Don McLean's total that was north of $22,000.

Sandy responded negatively. She said that if we wanted to go that route, she wouldn't participate in LAFF in 2014. Sandy's email tone suggested there would be no changing her mind.

The next day at the office, Molly and I agreed to let Sandy have her way on this one, but we should watch for these kinds of ultimatums moving forward.

All talk of the festival kind of ceased at that point. When Patrick Dempsey mentioned it to me that afternoon, a month or so after the Bootsy Collins discussion, I knew we had WithoutABox set up, so films could be submitted, but despite it being October

2013, real planning had to start for the fourth festival coming up in April 2014 sooner than later—or we'd be screwed.

* * *

I had another full-on breakdown in mid-October but tried to hide it from everybody. Despite our "Women in Business" November 2013 issue finally cracking the $30,000 level in ad sales, there was no denying that *Lewiston Auburn Magazine* was as much a sinking ship as I was. I knew both the magazine and I couldn't stay on their current paths very long.

A couple of major advertisers who were putting together their budgets for 2014 had already told us they would be scaling back and that included Millett Realty, our largest advertiser. Sharon Millett said she might go back to her full purchase but cut it in half for the first few issues of the new year. She said the market was softening a bit, but I think she was just always ahead of the curve and could sense that we weren't going to be around much longer. She is a smart lady.

The idea of continuing on this hamster wheel of producing a magazine that was a fraction in quality of what it once was only a few years earlier was depressing. I rebuilt the office furniture in a new configuration and felt deflated nobody offered to help. So, that Sunday night—just hours after talking to Patrick Dempsey for what turned out to be the last time—instead of looking at porn or talking to women on Omegle, legal or illegal, I planned a trip. I told Melissa, Sandy, and Molly early in the week I was taking a long weekend starting the following Friday and that I just needed time to drive. I sensed they knew I had another breakdown.

I made sure the magazine wouldn't be affected by my short absence, and we were 90% moved out of the old office. Molly and Sandy said they would take care of the cleaning the last of the old place on Lisbon Street while I was away. I just wanted to drive for two solid days, stop for a day someplace I'd never been, and drive for two more days. I realized my options were pretty much Milwaukee or New Orleans. New Orleans sounded like the most decadently fun, so I chose that.

An interesting thing happened five or six hours into the drive, before New York becomes New Jersey. I didn't drink the night before I left, so maybe it was just twenty-four hours of detoxing, but I started feeling great on all fronts: physically, mentally, and emotionally. Listening to a massive iTunes playlist louder than usual and heading back into warmer temperatures far from home perked me up. As the first day grew longer, the scenery grew less familiar. I called it a day at the Tennessee/Virginia border, amazed at how far someone can go in the same amount of time that slipped by me unnoticed every day.

On, Saturday I didn't want to stop driving. My mind was just being cleansed with every passing minute. By early afternoon I hit a state I'd never stepped foot in before: Welcome to Alabama! Within a couple of hours, I'd broken the border of a new one, Mississippi. It was around 3 p.m. when I realized I had already passed the general area where I expected to stay the night. My original plan was to pull into New Orleans around noon on Sunday, but I was now less than four hours away. I figured I'd just go all the way until I found out my $109 room on Sunday was $349 on a Saturday night. I couldn't get within an hour of NOLA for under $200, so I settled on a room in Hattiesburg, Mississippi, just after 6 p.m.

I called home and told Melissa where I was, and I'd made it amazingly fast, almost too fast. She was in a good mood. Having me out of the house will do that. The Red Sox were in the playoffs, so I said goodbye and went to watch at a sports bar near the hotel. It was heaven. Had I been in Lewiston or Auburn, somebody would have wanted to talk about a City Council issue or pitch an asinine story idea for the magazine while I ate. This was the "being picked up and dropped in a random town" fantasy I mentioned to Tammie two months earlier. I had a steak sandwich, two beers, and the Red Sox captured the American League pennant.

The next morning, I pulled into NOLA round 10 a.m. I was staying in one of those typical French Quarter touristy hotels. I got settled and hit Bourbon Street without a plan.

With its mess of bars and strip clubs, you'd think I'd have been all set, and fifteen years earlier, I wouldn't have needed more than a block, but I walked the street's length, bumped into the "real" New Orleans and surveyed my options. I could turn around and spend 10-14 hours drinking myself into oblivion and putting dollar bills into G-strings or I could check out a city I drove like a crazy man for two days to see. Like a grown-up, I opted for the latter, taking a double-decker bus tour of the city.

The air felt great whooshing through my hair, which I'd washed the night before for the first time in a week. The lack of work, alcohol, stress, porn, and responsibility reminded me that there was still this dormant Josh alive deep in a place the current anxiety and addiction couldn't touch. The tour stopped in the Garden District and at a cool looking cemetery. I toured a warehouse where Mardi Gras floats were stored and walked along the waterfront. I walked into a Harrah's casino, played slots for three minutes, and won $64. I stopped, cashed out, and bought a nice catfish strip lunch while watching the New England Patriots at a nearby bar.

Instead of catching the tour bus back to the French Quarter, I kept walking along the riverfront, thinking about the magazine, finding myself surprisingly positive. I knew that it was still early, but the financial changes made over the last few months were showing small signs of working, not to mention we did just have a $30,000 issue. I realized it was time to find out what Molly really wanted, and if it didn't jive, to part ways. I knew if we increased the ad-to-content percentage ratio, it would save a lot of money on printing monthly. I was excited about our new office and Corey working by my side for the first time since the newspaper in Windham. I also wanted to figure a way for he and I to be paid regularly, every week, since it wasn't happening.

I knew if we could do $30,000 on a "Women in Business" issue that a springtime "Healthy Mind, Healthy Body II" issue could do the same. If we got working on the film festival soon, that could make another good profit. Revenue was there for the taking. I just had to shed this fucking malaise and get others to shed theirs.

I also realized that everybody who owned or worked for the magazine should be at a meeting together. That was like 14 or 15 people, and we all had a stake in things. The people who were silent owners had an interest, as did the people who did the work and got a paycheck. I wanted Abbie and Jim and Jen there as much as I thought Paul, Danielle, and someone from the Corsetti family should attend. I knew it could be awkward at first, but if we could get as many people as possible with an interest in seeing the magazine succeed together, we could come up with solutions by committee.

Once I got back to my room, excited about the meeting idea, I texted Molly about it. She responded with something like "We will have a meeting of the owners when you return. It's not the business of the others."

I asked if everything was OK. She said she and Sandy were cleaning the last of the old office. It sounded ominous. I knew with the Corsettis and Corey on my side they couldn't do too much other than force a meeting.

I didn't let that black cloud bring me down. I took a nap and went back out. I walked up and down Bourbon Street, but returned to the riverfront for dinner. I walked around after, in and out of a few bars, but wasn't drinking like I expected. I just wasn't a recreational drinker. I was more anxiety-free than I had been in months. I didn't drink for pleasure. I drank to numb the fear, and it wasn't necessary that night.

I stood on a terrace overlooking Bourbon Street from which beads are tossed during Mardi Gras on that quiet Sunday night in October and realized it was not the place a 37-year-old husband and father of two should be. We should have been on vacation together. I felt very guilty for being alone. I walked back to my hotel and was in bed by 9:30 p.m. I called Melissa to say goodnight and fell asleep watching an edited version of *Goodfellas* on TV.

The next morning, I took off, taking a more southerly route along the Gulf Coast, then turning toward Atlanta, finding I-95 in the evening. I found that driving Zen zone again, not coming up for air until I'd reached Doswell, Virginia's finest La Quinta Inn, across the street from King's Dominion Amusement Park, about 1,050 miles away from where I started my day. It's the only time I can say I've ever driven 1,000 miles in a day by myself. The suite I stayed in would have run $400 on Fourth of July weekend but was $69 on a random off-season Monday night. The suite was nice, but I was so numb, I barely noticed.

I pulled into Portland, Maine, around 7 p.m., the next night, stopping at the Apple store to pick up an iMac cord. Ninety minutes later I was home. I hadn't been happier to see my wife and kids in a long, long time.

Chapter 17

Those few days after I arrived back to the office from New Orleans had a weird vibe. It didn't kill my renewed spirit, but I could tell something was afoot. Mike Malloy, our lawyer, contacted me and suggested we get together for lunch to talk about a meeting he wanted to facilitate between the owners. I told him I didn't think it was smart to rack up his hourly fees. He said lunch would be free, and he'd charge less than usual to facilitate.

I met Mike for lunch on Saturday. He said he'd let all of the owners know a meeting was planned but hadn't heard anything from the Corsettis, still embroiled in Donato's arson case, or Corey. He said he'd spent time communicating with Sandy and Molly in the last week and let Paul and Danielle know he was available to answer their questions prior to gathering as a group. I couldn't imagine the bill.

He said they had been expressing concern about the company's financial situation. They'd looked at the books, as was their right, and didn't like what they saw.

"They wouldn't have liked what they saw over the last 18 months. I never hid anything from them, but they never asked to see anything. Molly just wanted to make sure the loan was paid," I told Mike.

"Well, they have concerns now they'd like to address," he said.

"Would it help if I created a budget for the rest of 2013 and for 2014?" I asked.

"Yes, it would go a long way. Make it conservative," he requested.

"We just had the best issue of the year. Nothing screwy is going on. I'd actually like them to see how Molly gets paid weekly, yet Corey and I defer our pay all the time," I said.

"That's something they should see. There is clearly a level of animosity, even mistrust among the owners," he said. "That can tear a company apart, but it can be fixed. You're not so far gone."

"Mike, it's been like this a long time. It was starting to get like this when we first sat down with you. Hiring you was not a wise use of our money and I can only imagine what Sandy and Molly think I'm wasting money on. I've blown up my friendship with Paul that goes back twenty years. Danielle only owns like 3%. I'm close to Sandy, or at least I feel like I was. I was once close to Molly, but I don't think that can be fixed."

"Why?" asked Mike.

"I'm mad at her because the magazine has been so dull the last year. When I've tried to address it, nothing has really changed," I said.

"Maybe it needs to be addressed as a group," he suggested. "How do you really feel about the magazine where it is now, with the staff you have?"

"I'm always going to want to be optimistic. The 'Women in Business' issue was actually a good read. Molly and I both did a good job, and it made more money than any other one we've done. I've got a 'History of Local Hockey' cover story coming up for our Holiday Issue that's going to be a big deal. And we're going to do another 'Healthy Mind, Healthy Body' issue, and I think that will get us a bunch of new advertisers. The classy nude photos made a splash last year," I said.

"That's good. That's real good. Does everybody know these things?"

"I don't think so. But nobody has ever needed to know," I said.

"Maybe that lack of communication needs to change," Mike said.

"They can all go into our Google Docs and see the stories planned or the ad schedules," I said.

"They can't read your mind," said Mike.

"OK, point taken," I admitted.

"Let me ask you one other thing. I know this is your magazine. You created this. How do you feel as the guy who built this whole thing?" he asked in a way nobody before had, like he wanted to know how I was personally feeling.

I paused, unsure if I should speak openly. I didn't know if it was a trap, but by the time the words started, tears were already welling up in my eyes.

"I love this magazine. I love it. It's my biggest dream come true. This magazine has been my life to the detriment of the relationship with my family. I've been a shitty husband and a shitty father because of this magazine . . . but I love this magazine," I said speaking slowly, voice quivering. "They can all bail on me. I'll figure out a way. Everybody knows; the other owners, the community, everybody knows this is MY magazine. This is MY fucking magazine. I will fight anybody for it. They need me more than I need them. That's a fact, and they know it. This is MY fucking magazine. If they all go away, that's fine. I'm not losing this. I love it too much."

It was the most emotional I ever got explaining my feelings about the magazine. I'm not sure I even knew it meant that much to me.

"This is your baby. I understand. You're right. It probably does mean more to you than anyone, but you are all better as a team than individuals," Mike said.

I didn't tell Melissa the specifics of the meeting with Mike, but after having barked at her a few days earlier that my medication intake was none of her business and I was taking them at the office so I wouldn't forget, we had a few icy days between us.

All I felt was shame. I couldn't admit my plan to tap into my manic side failed. She would have looked at me like my foolproof plan to pull myself off my medication months earlier was insane. She threatened to start counting my pills, suspecting that I was not taking them, so I came up with the excuse that I took them the first thing in the morning at the office.

She was always on my side, always hoping I'd make things work, but it became harder and harder for her to keeping rooting for me as I not only pushed her away but outwardly resented her for simply looking out for me. At the time, I thought her concern was an opportunity to prove me wrong. It seemed to be what everybody in the world was doing.

This was the time of my most frequent pornography use. I looked at it a couple of mornings and always at night. I rarely was looking at video clips as the high of the manipulation in the Omegle chatrooms felt like the only fuel I had.

Based on the evidence I received later, this was around the time that I spoke to the 14-year-old girl who eventually became the center of my legal case. I wish I didn't sound like just another sexual harasser who says he doesn't remember the person, but I genuinely don't.

If they looked like a sexually mature female and were able to be manipulated, I spent time with them online, but they blurred together since I was doing it so frequently.

That lack of memory extended well beyond my porn use. I look at the last half-dozen magazines we created, and I don't remember writing several of the stories with my name on them. One of the last stories I wrote was about what it's like to be a snowplow driver for the city during storms. Aside from a photo I took of myself in the side view mirror that proves I was there, I don't remember any of it.

Later on, in rehab, I was able to point to the autumn of 2013 as my rock bottom when it came to pornography addiction. When I was able to manipulate a woman into doing what I wanted, it reminded me of the power I had at the beginning of the magazine. On the nights where they would not acquiesce to my demands, it was an exclamation point on the basket case I had become.

* * *

I prepared for war, or at least as if I was being put on trial. The budget for the last quarter of 2013 I devised showed a total loss for the year of just under $4,000. My budget for 2014 showed an overall decline in revenue of $30,000, but an overall decline in costs of $65,000, forecasting a profit of $35,000.

I'd always kept track of our revenue over the years, specifically ad sales and subscriptions. I could show that we were doing about even on ad sales, but our subscriptions, especially renewals, were taking a hit. For me, when people say, "We don't want this anymore" it means that it's not a good product. I thought those figures would help prove the argument the magazine was dull in readers' eyes.

At the meeting, Mike said he was there simply to facilitate but wanted us to try to run things and he'd jump in as needed. Sandy brought out a stack of bank statements. She'd clearly spent a lot of time looking for something to nail me on. It made me smile because while I was a lot of horrible things, an embezzler or skimmer wasn't on the list.

I thought their grievances were trite. She mentioned they were concerned about a recent purchase of a backpack for $100 at Eastern Mountain Sports. It was for a blogger on our website who was traveling the Appalachian Trail. He was going to send us dispatches and instead of just paying $20 for five, by purchasing his equipment, we were now a sponsor and mentioned whenever he promoted his trip. I thought it might get us some out-of-state hits on the website.

This "We gotcha! Oh, you have an explanation?" went on a few minutes, and then they got to the one they thought they could really nail me on.

"What about this one? $400 to CN Brown Oil last winter?" Sandy asked.

"I used the company card and was going to pay it back in two $200 chunks. Do you know why I had to use the company card? Because I didn't pay myself that week, and I only took half my pay the next week. Everybody else got paid, including their benefits, but I didn't. I apologize for shitty bookkeeping on that one. But if you want to talk about people getting money from the company for fuel, we can talk about that."

I glared over at Paul, hoping he remembered all of the times I pulled a $20 bill from petty cash for gas so he could get home or make it to work the next day. I don't think he put it together.

"I forgot to pay it back, but I can pay it back now. Do you know how? Corey and I have been alternating taking hits on our pay. The company owes both of us right now. I'll just take it off the top. You can call Corey if you'd like to confirm this," I said.

"You can figure that out later," said Mike, recognizing nobody wasn't going to nail me on any financial misdeeds. I may have been sloppy at recording things, but I wasn't a crook. "Josh, do you want to hand out future financials?"

I gave them the history report, the end-of-the-year budget, and next year's budget.

"As you can see, there was basically no major sales hit when Paul and Danielle left. We just did the first $30K issue. I'm not worried. History shows us improving month-to-month from the previous year 80% of the time. I don't need to explain the up-and-down seasonal cycles, we all know how they go," I said switching to the budget.

"There are a few differences in revenue centers. There's no gallery revenue this year. I used the same revenue numbers on ad sales just in case we're flat, and I actually went down on our subscriptions," I explained.

"Why lower?" said Sandy.

"People aren't renewing like they used to and I'll get to that," I said. "In the expenses category, things drop a lot because of rent and salaries. I kept most things the same. No frills. It's printing, benefits, and salaries. That's all we buy around here."

"I think this works," Sandy admitted.

"What can we do moving forward to keep things transparent?" Mike asked. "Maybe if somebody else kept the books?"

"I would love that," I said. "But who? Marc is our accountant. He's not a bookkeeper. You want to hire one. Great. With what money? Do you want to do the books like you do for LAFF?"

I looked over at Sandy, who knew she didn't have the time.

"No, no, I don't."

"So who does that leave? That leaves me," I said.

"OK, let's stop here with this. I can see Josh feels like he's being attacked. Why don't you try to find some way to keep the stockholders more in the loop but not get down to the 'I just bought thumbtacks' detail?" Mike suggested.

He switched topics to the magazine itself. He talked about how much it meant to the area and what an impressive thing we created from nothing. He asked if anybody had anything to say.

"You're giving Jen too much autonomy. Her designs are terrible," said Molly. "She's in high school. She shouldn't be making any decisions that you just rubber stamp."

"You have a high school girl working here?" Paul asked.

"She started after you left. She's a good designer. She's getting better, and she's got more passion for this magazine than anybody in this room," I said. "Corey has been working with her on her designs, and she's picking up a ton of slack in other areas."

"Dan and I don't really like her designs," Sandy chimed in.

"That's fine. I don't expect everybody to love everything. I think having three designers is good because it mixes things up and like being a writer or photographer, there needs to be a level of creativity allowed," I said. "I haven't loved all of her layouts, but I haven't loved all of Dan's photos. I haven't loved everything in any issue."

"I should have a say in what the design looks like," said Molly.

"Why? The design isn't the problem with the magazine lately," I said.

"What do think the problem is, Josh?" Mike asked.

I froze. "Never mind."

"This is a time for all of us to talk," insisted Mike.

"The magazine is boring. It's been boring for months. Why do you think people aren't renewing?" I said angrily toward Molly.

"You never say anything. You won't talk to me. You won't talk to Jim. You talk to Corey. You talk to Abbie. You talk to Jen," was Molly's response.

"Is she right, Josh?" Mike asked.

"Yeah, she is. This magazine is dull. It's boring. I've had people directly say those words to me, and I know I'm not the only one," I said.

I looked at Sandy for back-up. I made it obvious. I hoped Molly's eyes followed me to Sandy. Sandy was willing to chime in about backpacks and page design by high school kids, but she just looked ahead blankly.

"Whatever. The subscriptions are dropping. The renewals are dropping. Less people want to get this in the mail. That's a thumbs-down vote, isn't it?" I asked the room.

"How am I supposed to know this?" Molly asked.

"How long have you known this, Josh?" Mike asked.

"I've watched the trend since Danielle left, and I took over the mailing list," I said.

"But you didn't tell anyone?" Mike said.

"I told a few people, but not Molly," I said.

"The communication issues are between these two," said Paul pointing at Molly and I.

"I guess Molly and I need to sit down again and try to hash this out," I said.

"I agree," she said.

"I want everyone to know I'll try to communicate better, but I'm doing my best. I'm the only one here in this office more than twenty hours per week. You all know how much I work. This is my magazine I'll be goddamned if anybody is going to take it away from me or micromanage it. I'm not going to let anybody fuck it up," I said, realizing just how bad the declaration probably came across.

"Nobody is saying you didn't start the magazine, Josh, and yes, you feel closer than anyone else ever will, but you need these people and they need you," Mike said.

"I know. I'm just exhausted, and I feel attacked," I said.

"Well, before anything else happens, I think we need to break here. It may not feel it, but you did get through some things. I'd suggest a meeting like this every month. I can come or not, but I think you've all got things to think about," he said.

Mike left with Paul and Danielle right behind him. Molly asked me to meet with her the next day at the office and I agreed, leaving just Sandy and I in the office.

"What do you think?" she asked.

"I wish you would have backed me on the boring thing," I said, annoyed.

"I don't work here, so I didn't think it was my place," she said.

Sandy never held her tongue. It's one of the things I liked best about her. I knew at that point I'd lost Sandy as an ally. Had I not mentally checked out so long before that meeting, I would have been able to read between the lines and see these people were doing the best thing for themselves trying to create distance with me. I would have done the same.

Chapter 18

Now that it took roughly ten seconds to get to Gritty's and I held an almost endless supply of their gift cards in trade for their large contract with us, I ate lunch alone downstairs almost every day, even if Jim or Abbie was at the office. I didn't want them to see me drink two pints of beer. I shouldn't minimize the two pints. They were "tall" twenty-ounce pints. In the afternoon, business meetings, either with other people or by myself, started around 3:30 and ran two hours. I'd try to find business reasons to drink, as it made it seem more official. If the beer hit particularly hard, I'd head to the office and drink water until the buzz subsided a bit, but I can't lie about never driving home drunk. I rationalized my home and Gritty's were a straight line, only about two minutes apart, reducing the chances for both police intervention or an accident. That's stupid. When I was in my first rehab, I did an exercise where I estimated the amount of times I drove drunk in my life. It was disturbingly in the mid-hundreds. I'm lucky I didn't kill anyone.

I don't remember the last half-dozen City Council meetings of my failed term. On my last night, LaBonte gave me an outgoing appreciation plaque for the Council work and the Key to the City of Auburn. It was yet another notch on the egotistical bucket list of treasure marked off. He gave it to me for my civic service including the magazine, film festival, volunteerism, and altruism. It should have meant so much more, but I don't remember getting it. I've seen a video online, and I look like an exhausted, unkempt mess.

In my last speech as a member of the Council, immediately after getting these honors, I talked about how the councilors, myself included, didn't listen to the public and voted the way we wanted. I told people our minds were almost always made up before we sat down and what they saw on public access TV was exactly that, a TV show. If they wanted to have a say, they should run for office and win. It was mostly accurate, but in watching the video, it's very clear I'm drunk. If I were sober, I would have pretended to be gracious if for no other reason I was glad to have that monkey off my back on Monday nights.

* * *

Once again, Molly and I put in some effort, but our relationship could not bounce back. I think on the days she was in the new office, she felt out of place. Corey was in the office more often, and he, Abbie, Jen, and I were developing a good rapport that made being at work tolerable.

It reached a point where I think it just wasn't worth it for Molly anymore.

"I think it's best if I took a break from here," she said one late morning when it was just her and I left at the office. "It will help the finances and maybe we can talk about things in a few months. I'm hoping you'll lay me off so I can collect unemployment," she said.

It was only 25% surprising, like when your 88-year-old grandmother dies unexpectedly. How unexpected was it, really? I wasn't going to fight hard to keep her because this was an opportunity to steady the ship.

"Are you positive?" I asked.

"Yeah, I don't like the way things are around here," she said.

"It's changing for sure," I said. "Of course I will lay you off. Will you stay until deadline next week on the Holiday Issue so we can get that out the door?"

"I can do that," she said.

"I appreciate that. I'm sorry you're not happy, but as I think you know, I'm not either. Everything around here and so, so many other things are taking a toll on me. I've got to start spending more time with Melissa and the kids. I'm not taking care of my mental health," I said in a moment of candor that we rarely shared anymore.

"You really need to start taking care of yourself," she said. "Family is important."

"What about the film festival? Are we doing one this year?" I asked.

"I don't think so. It's something we need to talk about with Sandy," Molly said.

"Well, I think that sucks. Maybe, like you said, we can figure out a way to make this work again in the future," I said.

"It will be for the best," she said.

"You're right. It will financially help a lot. I think you're entitled to benefits for another thirty days, but you can call the number on your card and check," I said.

I told Sandy about Molly's decision a few hours later. She said that it was going to be time for another monthly meeting soon. I sent her a late-night email saying I was excited things were going to turn around. I was hoping that even though it took months longer than it should have, she saw the departure of Molly as a chance of renewal.

Instead, I got an email cashing in. She said that with Molly leaving, she and Dan were going as well and that he would not take pictures for the magazine any more. She also said they wanted to sell their shares of LAFF and wanted to have a meeting as soon as possible.

I told her that I'd hoped we'd be able to be friends because I did value her friendship. She really did understand how I looked at the world in ways that few people I've met did. But I also knew with her leaving the company, our friendship was likely over. I told her I'd send an email to each owner about a meeting.

Corey and the Corsettis couldn't make it, but Corey said he trusted me to make the right choices.

I contacted Marc Roy. I reminded him he was the accountant of LA Publishing and the Lewiston Auburn Film Festival, but I knew as Paul's brother, there could be a conflict, so if he had trouble giving me straight answers, he should tell me. He said he could answer factual questions without issue and met with me on the morning of the meeting with the owners and explained either company could buy back stock and hold it as general stock. I realized this would be the best idea.

There was leverage for LA Publishing as an entity since nobody owned a majority of the stock and there was no money floating around. It would take a unique voting block to shut it down, and there was no upside to that for anybody who owned stock.

I told Sandy through email the company would buy back her stock at pennies on the dollar. She asked if we could work an advertising trade deal, which we did and agreed to sign papers at the meeting later that night. I knew the film festival would be different. Paul, Molly, and Sandy owned sixty percent, and we had plenty of money in the bank. The fate of it was in their hands.

I didn't drink that afternoon. I knew I needed to be clear-headed that night. I told Melissa I knew I was walking into a bad situation and had no idea what I was going to be walking out of, but knew it was going to be better.

Once Sandy, Molly, Paul, and Danielle were there, I started.

"Let's cut to the chase on this. Sandy is trading her LA Publishing stock for ads. The company will retain the stock as general stock. If anybody wants to buy it later, it will first be offered to anybody who is a current owner at the time, per our bylaws. If any of you are interested in also selling, the price is going to really suck, but we can work something out, especially with you Danielle, since you have so few shares," I said. "The Corsettis, Corey, and I are not going to sell our shares."

"OK, I just want to get out of this," Danielle said.

"OK, we can work out a deal over email. Are you good with a little bit of cash and gift cards?" I said.

"Yeah," she said.

"OK, I'll send you an offer later," I said, turning to Molly. "What are your plans?"

"I'm holding on for now," said Molly.

"Me too," said Paul.

"OK. Anything else?" I asked.

"We need to talk about the film festival," Sandy said.

"I'll leave for that," Danielle said, almost as if choreographed.

"We've all decided we'd like out of the film festival," said Sandy once Danielle was gone.

"So are you looking to kill the whole thing?" I asked.

"That's up to you," she said. "We currently have about $11,000 in the bank, but we also have a little debt to pay off."

"So we pay off the debt, blow it up, each get $1,500, and it's dead?" I asked.

"That's one way," she said. "If you want to keep the festival and run it yourself, you or the festival company could buy the shares. Either you or the festival would cut us each a check here tonight."

"What do you want for your shares?" I asked.

Molly and Sandy turned to Paul, who was clearly responsible for telling me the figure they agreed upon.

"We were thinking . . ." he said, drawing out all of his words as if he didn't want to say it. "That $3,500 each was fair."

"You really want to take it all," I said, smiling, expecting as much. I knew they'd want to empty the account, but I also knew I wanted to keep LAFF going. Weeks earlier it had been called one of the "25 Coolest Film Festivals in America" by *MovieMaker Magazine*. I also knew that I could tell them to fuck off and just run the same-named festival, but all of the banners, signs, e-mail lists, financial books, and everything else that would be needed to continue the illusion of seamless continuity were stored at Sandy's house. I would never get my hands on it if I didn't purchase the festival the proper way.

"I want it, but I don't want to empty the bank account. If LAFF buys back the stock and it's held as general stock by the company, I want to make sure I get everything. Every last banner, DVD player, sandwich board, everything," I said.

"Yes, it's all in my basement. You can come get it and do whatever you want with it," said Sandy.

We already had a logo, name recognition, and calling the festival "Fourth Annual" meant cutting down on a lot of rebuilding. What was the name, reputation, website, Facebook page, and WithoutaBox account worth? What were the relationships with sponsors worth? Who would be lost with a name change? An argument was easy to make LAFF was worth well beyond the $10,500 they were asking.

"$3,000 each," I countered. "I need to leave some money in there."

They looked around at each other, I think trying to figure out who would be the first one to flinch. I don't remember who it was, but we had a deal.

"As the acting treasurer, you have to write the checks," I said to Sandy. "I'll fill out the bills of sale."

They were out the door three minutes later, and the entire meeting took 20 minutes.

I went back home and had the first nice conversation with Melissa I'd had in a long time.

"I'm in charge of the film festival now. Sandy and Danielle are out of the magazine," I told her.

"Good, I'm glad," she said.

"Now I just have to create a film festival. I'm only a few months behind schedule," I said.

"I know you can do it," she said.

It was so wonderful and important to hear her say something like that at that moment. It made me believe I could pull it off.

Molly stayed like she said she would another week. We got along fairly well, I think because we both saw the finish line. At the very end, there was an awkward hug and a "See you soon." We both knew that was never going to happen.

* * *

I knew for the sake of energy in the office, we were better off having Molly gone and came into work the next morning early with a minimal hangover, ready to tackle whatever came at me. I opened the door and flicked the lights on. I saw the wall to the left of my desk, bedazzled with the awards that either the magazine or I had won over the last four years. It was a wall that proved just how special I was.

A sick feeling came over me. Those trophies—be it the Young Entrepreneur of the Year or the Key to the City—technically meant nothing, yet I finally recognized they had been what I was striving for over the last twenty years. Something in me had thought if I could have a wall of validation, I'd feel complete. Now I had one, but it didn't.

A mini-panic attack ensued. I found my way to the couch and tried not to break down crying. Abbie wasn't far behind me.

She was usually the first in the office after dropping her daughter off at school.

"Struggling today?" she asked.

"Yup," I said, unable to even come up with a lie. "One of those mornings."

Objectively, the wall of plaques was impressive. It was a testament to the hard work over the last several years. It showed I could set a goal I didn't know how to achieve, but somehow nail it. There were a dozen pieces of proof I was special on the wall.

When it dawned on me the last twenty years had really been about trophy acquisition and that they didn't make me happy or complete, everything suddenly seemed meaningless. I'd wasted two decades and didn't find what I was looking for. The idea of starting a new path to happiness seemed laughable, exhausting, and impossible.

The porn and drinking weren't tools to try to make me happy. They were just there to cope with the unhappiness. I couldn't imagine spending another twenty years on something new to maybe find happiness. What if I did go down a new path and failed again? That thought was soul crushing. When I looked at porn, especially when I was drunk, the addiction took over the brain so there was no space to contemplate how bad things were. When I was deep into searching for explicit video clips for self-soothing or getting an equally depressed woman to take off her bra online, it's not that it made me feel great. It's that it subtracted the negative feelings of real life. I was never going to feel good. The best I could feel was numb.

My professional career had always been about advancing to the next level, but I knew that I was now at the proverbial glass ceiling. There were no more brass rings to grab. My family would never leave if I were to find a job outside of Maine, and the prospect of that happening without a college degree at my level was miniscule. For a long time, I felt like the magazine put me on top of Mt. Kilimanjaro and I had been beating my chest, screaming, "Hey, world, I reached the top! You're looking up at me now!" Walking through the door at work that day, it was like the universe turned around and said, "Yo, Josh! Hey, dipshit! I've got a hill in Nepal I want to tell you about! You've done nothing!"

* * *

The staff seemed relieved Molly—and the tension she and I brought to a room—was gone. I'd act as editor until the spring and figure out what to do after the film festival. I was contemplating the idea of a part-time editor, but there was no point for a while. Saving the money on Molly's salary and benefits was an early Christmas present to the company.

I started working feverishly on LAFF. I told the staff if they wanted to help that was great, and if not, I wasn't going to force anyone. Jen, unsurprisingly, wanted to do as much as possible, and Corey said he'd pitch in where his health allowed.

I put a solid team of volunteers together, some from previous years—other people I knew were interested in lending a hand that I trusted. I raised the price of submissions to hopefully keep the crap away, and our slowly-building national reputation brought in films that were better than ever.

I felt a renewed vigor, especially with the film festival. I still used legal porn some evenings to satisfy myself, but instead of trying to find females to talk with five or six nights a week on Omegle, I was doing it one or two times. Unfortunately, my drinking stayed roughly the same, as did my sleep patterns. This was not a true renewal. It was more of a plateau.

I restructured the festival with fewer films and multiple viewings. Instead of a gala awards dinner, we were going to have a party that more people could attend at a lower price and introduce acting and writing awards. When I started working in earnest, sponsors were easy to come by.

I ended up with around $10,000 budgeted for airline tickets, hotel rooms, and small stipends for certain filmmakers to attend. Many filmmakers paid their own way, but for certain films, I wanted the creative people there, and with that year's crop of high-quality film submissions, it meant we could have a handful of writers, directors, and actors who were also working on television and in movies that were mainstream. I thought instead of putting $10,000 behind one big name, if we spread it to fifteen smaller names, a few might become big over the years and remember us. If nothing else, we'd have pictures of a few stars at our festival before they were famous.

Corey wanted to help more, but he was tired. He made it into the office two or three days a week once Molly was gone. Before that, he tried to avoid her as much as possible.

He had lost so much weight since his first trip to the hospital a year earlier. Back when I first met him in 2005, when I worked with him daily, his 275-to-300 pounds hid the fact he was over six feet tall. He never gave me a number, but I'm guessing he dropped 100-125 pounds with his illness. At his heaviest, he looked ten years older than me. Now, he just looked unhealthy.

The biggest reason the weight came off was because he'd stopped drinking, but it also had to do with his organ damage. I didn't know how bad it was until he told me he was on the donor list for a new liver. I didn't ask a lot of questions because I didn't want to know, as a friend, just how bad it was. It didn't seem real.

I remember when Corey uttered the words to me, "This happened because I'm an alcoholic." That label hit hard. None of my friends or contemporaries were old enough to be alcoholics, I thought. If he could be an alcoholic, what about me? I peppered him with questions about his drinking, and while he was into exclusively hard liquor, I drank hard liquor and beer. The sad truth was ounce-to-ounce, I drank just as much if not more.

For the fifth year in a row, I attended the Business After Hours holiday party at Lost Valley. Jim came with me to man the small gift subscription table we'd set up a few years in a row. I did grow to like him more and our communication did improve with Molly's departure, but we just never clicked. I couldn't tell you how many subscriptions we sold, but I remember sitting there, taking stock of five years and thinking to myself, "I never want to come to this fucking thing ever again."

Abbie was the only salesperson who brought in new accounts, but that came to an end when she took a job with a car dealership she'd ironically been trying to get as an advertiser. I guess they liked her tenacity. It was a $10,000 raise with better benefits. I didn't try to counter-offer. Since the holiday issue was the double issue and a new one didn't come out until February, the timing was perfect. I had no problem with short notice, though I hated to see her go.

When people think about *Lewiston Auburn Magazine*, I know they don't associate Abbie Luttrell with it, but she almost singlehandedly kept that place financially afloat in the second half of 2013. If we could have hired her back when Danielle first came on board, I think things would have ended differently.

Chapter 19

L ate Christmas night of 2013, into the early morning of the 26th, I watched the *Doctor Who* Christmas episode as I did every year. For whatever reason, during the closing credits, I broke down crying, a quivering mass of sadness and despair. The only thing that felt right at the moment was to stop it all. I'd never had that feeling before, but it was crystal clear.

While I'm sure everyone would deny it, most people have probably pondered how they'd kill themselves. I always thought carbon monoxide poisoning was the logical choice. You painlessly fall asleep and don't wake up. I don't know if I planned on killing myself, but the idea of going into the garage, starting the car, and sitting in it seemed like the right thing to do. It didn't feel like I was getting ready to go kill myself. It felt like I was getting ready to see if I could perform a dress rehearsal of killing myself.

I went toward the garage but realized we took separate cars to Melissa's parents' house earlier in the day. Both cars were in the driveway. Even in my darkest hour, I'm a lazy piece of shit. Putting on my shoes, going outside in the cold, opening the garage door, getting a car in the garage, shutting the garage door, and starting the process was too much work . . . and I knew Melissa might hear me. I looked through the window of our mud room into the garage at a beam but realized you can't rehearse a hanging. I didn't know how to tie a noose or if we had any rope. The idea of hanging did not sound peaceful either.

Then the thought hit me, "It would not be cool for the kids to find their father dead in the garage the day after Christmas."

The fog, almost a buzz of sorts, lifted, and I went back inside. I sat on the couch, in mild shock over the last few minutes. How serious had I just been? Had I let the thought of suicide become an actual possibility? It wasn't a bad idea for a few minutes. I was legitimately suicidal for a few minutes and didn't recognize it as it was happening.

Despite the drama of the next several years to come, be it in a courtroom, rehab center, or jail, I never once returned to this dark place. I've told myself if it happens in the future, to think of my kids, but I was so detached from rational thinking, I don't know if that will happen. When I look back, those few minutes are the scariest of my life.

* * *

I knew I was addicted to alcohol and work, but I also know when it came to relieving stress and seeking relief and momentary calmness, I had few outlets other than pornography. Despite the fact my usage lessened between late fall 2013 and early 2014, it never completely stopped. I couldn't envision a scenario where it wasn't a crutch in my life.

In December and January, I didn't download illegal pornography, opting to view LAFF movies that needed to be judged before the deadline. My use of Omegle dwindled to almost nothing. Maybe I felt control over what was happening at the film festival or I just grew tired of talking to women online, I'm not sure. Whereas I had reached a point in August or September of 2013 where I had been in these chatrooms two-to-three hours almost nightly, I was only using it perhaps once a week come January because I was so engrossed with putting together the fourth film festival, the first totally under my supervision.

I wish all of the pornography of every ilk disappeared completely from my life, but without the unexpected intervention that was to come in the near future courtesy of the Maine State Police, I'm not sure if it ever would have on its own. I think that the Omegle stuff probably would have come to an end naturally since my use was steadily diminishing. When I felt like things were spinning out of control, it was a place to go and remind myself that I could engineer certain outcomes in my life—however twisted that logic was at the time.

But, in organizing LAFF on my own and not having to manage the resentment toward Molly or my other co-owners on a daily basis anymore, I felt something of an empowerment I hadn't in a long time. I wasn't adding to the folder of screen capture "trophies." I believe given more time, I would have had a much-needed moment of clarity and deleted it.

It's hard to say what would have happened to my pornography habits if things turned out differently. I've had habits and obsessions in my life that have faded on their own, but they are usually replaced by something else. Maybe I would have dropped the illegal porn entirely. Maybe I would gone into one of the dormant phases of this long addiction. Or maybe it would have got much, much worse.

I tell myself everything turned out for the best. Most of the time I believe it.

* * *

Knowing that major changes needed to happen in both my professional and private lives sooner than later or there would be real repercussions, I had a brainstorm sitting at work one afternoon in January when I read the just-released lineup for Coachella, a massive music festival near Palm Springs, California. I went to the festival in 2002 with my brother. The 2014 lineup was terrific with diverse acts I'd never seen like Outkast, Motorhead, and Pet Shop Boys along with current artists Katrielle, who was now fourteen, listened to like Lorde and Lana Del Rey. Melissa and I were chatting on email about the lineup, and I floated the idea of going as a family.

She said neither she or Kaden would want to go and thought a three-day grind at the festival at $400 per ticket, was a waste for them, but it might be something Kat and I would enjoy.

I looked at the calendar and saw Coachella started twelve days after LAFF ended. We were doing much better than I expected with both sponsors and ticket sales. My super-conservative profit guess was $5,000. My liberal one was $20,000—and that was after taking a $2,000 salary and providing a couple volunteers with stipends for their hard work. Either way, a bonus could bankroll a road-trip across the country I hoped Kat would want to take and give me the two-week vacation I'd needed for years.

I bought the tickets and printed the receipt, then texted Kat to see if she was home from school yet. I told Melissa to play dumb if Kat texted her on anything I said. Kat responded she was home. I wrote to her: "Don't go anywhere. I'll be home in a few minutes. I just got an email you're going to have to explain to me, young lady."

As expected, she texted Melissa, who played along. I entered the house and told her, "Go sit on the couch!" in an angry tone. I then handed her the receipt with the Coachella logo. She looked at it, then looked at me, then looked at it.

"Is this Coachella tickets?" she asked.

"Yeah, you and I are going to go this year," I said.

She was excited, giving me a big hug, and posted a photo on Facebook. I felt like the father I should have been more often.

"Do you want to fly or drive?" I asked.

"Drive!" she responded.

"OK, well, you'll miss a week of school, plus there's April vacation. I think it'll only be two weeks. Figure out if there's anywhere in the country you'd like to visit along the way. No Florida and no Seattle. Stay out of those two corners. Anywhere in between," I said.

That night, Kat told me she wanted to see a cemetery in New York she'd read a legend about and also mentioned Las Vegas. Only my daughter would pick a tombstone and Sin City. She said she trusted me to make it a fun trip. I was in heaven that night planning the road trip, carefully picking a few places along the way, but making sure we'd get to Coachella in time. The ride back would be a little more leisurely. I had us visiting my brother Patrick in Los Angeles, seeing the Grand Canyon, the arch in St. Louis, Carlsbad Caverns in New Mexico, and New Orleans. I wanted to see Austin, Texas, and of course, we made sure Las Vegas and the New York graveyard were on the map.

It would coincide with the "Healthy Mind, Healthy Body" issue, so a lot of the content would be done in advance and I trusted Corey to hold things down. Ad sales were starting to slump, so I knew we were looking at 64 or 80 pages, not 96, even a few months in advance. I wasn't worried about my absence. Knowing I was going to take a cross-country road-trip with my daughter was all the fuel I needed to get through the next couple of months until after LAFF ended.

* * *

I had a financial meeting with Marc in early February at his office which was only a ninety-second walk from mine. It was in the same office building as Rinck Advertising. LA Publishing showed a net loss of $6,000 in 2013. He figured it out a second way, including existing debt and it came closer to $30,000. He told me if my conservative budget for 2014 was correct that I shared with the other owners, we might end up break-even by year's end. It was hard to imagine a magazine Paul and I sat down to begin work on in late 2009 only being a break-even enterprise heading into 2015. Marc caught me gazing out the window of his office.

"Are you OK?" he asked.

"Break even. Sounds good," I said.

"No I mean, how are you doing?" he asked.

"Fine," I said.

"You look really tired," he said.

"Film festival stuff," I said. "It's not that far away now."

"OK, but you need to take it easy soon," he said.

"I'm taking a few weeks off after LAFF from everything," I said. "Taking a road trip with Katrielle."

"I guess just try to hang on until then."

I asked Peter Rinck, who worked with plenty of companies, if the landscape of advertising was changing locally or if the magazine sucked. There was a reason we were suddenly having trouble selling ads, and I needed to figure out what it was.

He said people were tightening their purse strings for whatever reason more than he'd seen since the announcement of the housing crisis back in late 2008. As for the magazine, he said it took four years, but we did finally reach the point we were dependable, which was good in some ways, but meant that we couldn't claim to be a new, hip cultural shake-up any longer. Businesses knew what we could offer them, and some were learning that a $300 full-page black and white ad in the freebee shopper you picked up leaving the grocery store did more for them than a $400 half-page color ad in our magazine.

Peter and I exchanged emails a few times for a couple of weeks. He had so much insight into the way business owners were thinking it helped me not feel like a total failure. He made me see advertising in *Lewiston Auburn Magazine* was no longer a speculative venture since years of data now existed for advertisers. The warm feelings of "help these scrappy dreamers and their new magazine" couldn't be generated during sales calls anymore. Like it or not, we were just another advertising option. We still had the best looking product, but we also had one of the more expensive and lowest circulated options. I still saw us as underdogs and rookies, but our clients didn't.

I also know with the way Molly, Sandy, and even Danielle left the company, I was developing a poor reputation in the business community. Like any largely insular group, the business owners of Lewiston and Auburn talked, and they weren't saying as many nice things about me as they once did. I can't say it wasn't deserved.

* * *

As January became February, ad sales continued to stall. Corey was worried about my vacation plan, but I told him that if the magazine got out the door a few days late, whatever, nobody would notice. That's not the kind of thing that would have been OK to me a year earlier.

The issue that came out in early February was the lowest grossing issue in years. I hadn't replaced Abbie, and there were major advertisers who neither Jim nor I convinced to renew their contracts. We weren't bringing in new blood, either. Those who stayed negotiated more for less.

It probably was a blessing I was exhausted because I would have been having complete breakdowns looking at our projected ad sales over the next several issues, which were hovering around $20,000. How we could lose $10,000 in billing in only a few months was beyond me, but I didn't have the energy to figure it out. With Abbie gone, I knew we were in trouble and needed the universe to drop a salesperson into my lap.

Bills started piling up except for the loan payment, which I always took care of, but one of the biggest kick in the pants was when the printer said they wouldn't process our next issue if we didn't pay down our debt, which had ballooned up to around $20,000. Corey and I deferred our pay for two weeks, but it was just a drop in the bucket.

I did the only thing I could and had the film festival loan some of the money to the magazine. I also got lucky, and the universe delivered Adriane Kramer, who most knew as the local celebrity Zumba instructor, who needed a job. She jumped in as a salesperson and started crushing it almost immediately.

She knew everybody in town and got people on board we'd never had before. She was also excited about the film festival and had volunteered with LAFF in the past. I had a great feeling about her and asked if she could get checks from new clients in advance. Every day, she walked in with hundreds of dollars. Somehow, about ten days after the printer told me we had to take care of our debt, he agreed to let us keep printing when I transferred $12,000 to their account.

Problems like this felt almost otherworldly. I had no point of reference for this kind of dilemma. Find the $20,000 or at least enough to shut the printing plant up, or we'd be sunk. I knew in my heart we were probably months away from being sunk anyway, but my survival instincts kicked in. Since I was a little kid at that babysitter's house, I've just had this instinct that says, "Survive until tomorrow."

It's not a great philosophy for long-term success, but as a short-term method of making it, not worrying about tomorrow's problems is a good way to get yourself to tomorrow. When I was younger, there was a manager for the Boston Red Sox who was being peppered with 101 questions about bullpen pitching. He finally stopped everyone and told them that a lot of what they were asking was going to sort itself out on its own. If he took care of the few problems of the here and now, those problems that needed to be worried about tomorrow would take care of themselves, and when they became today's problems, if they still existed, he'd deal with them then. Without ever really articulating it, he made me realize that's how I lived.

The most scared I've ever been in my life was at that babysitter's house and in the closing months of *Lewiston Auburn Magazine*. At the babysitter's, I never knew what crazy thing she was going to say or do. Her mental issues forced me to always be on guard. I didn't know what to say or do to avoid being left in a pitch black room or ignored outdoors for three or four hours at a time—or if I even could avoid it. I didn't know what to do when she'd cry for an hour, then yell for the next, or call me by the wrong name all day. At the magazine, I didn't know how to hide the fact that I couldn't make sure every employee and bill was paid with the money that came through the door. I didn't know how to hide the fact I wasn't sure there would be a next issue. I didn't know what to do at the babysitter's or at the magazine office, so I made it up as I went along. I survived. I dealt with today's problems and hoped tomorrow's took care of themselves.

Chapter 20

I was visiting Dick Gleason's radio station in late February to see if I could barter LAFF tickets for commercials when he mentioned starting a morning drive radio show and asked what I thought about his choice for a host, my old friend, Matt Boutwell. We met ten years earlier as woefully underemployed call center employees, and I'd used him as a freelance sportswriter through the years.

I explained to Dick how Matt and I had great chemistry and a playful banter—which he also knew. Before I realized it, I was pitching myself for the job of Matt's co-host.

I told Dick I thought Matt was technically sound and certainly knew sports, but I didn't know if his interviewing skills were up to par or if he had the charisma to carry a show by himself. In retrospect, it's easy to see Dick was just reeling me in. I started telling him about how I had a radio talk show at Bates College twenty years earlier when I was in high school and what a success that had been. I told him he could look up a story about it in the *Sun Journal* archives. I didn't mention that their student board of directors that ran the radio station fired me after finding out I was drinking in the studio and smoking weed in the yard behind the station. Now I can see it was an early red flag.

"I have a name around here, and you know what a promoter I am. If I'm involved, there will be plenty of ads in the magazine and between myself and the magazine, I have thousands of local Facebook followers," I reasoned.

"Are you saying you want a job?" Dick asked.

"I don't want the job if you're hiring one person. I'm saying Matt and I would be good together."

"It would only be part-time, four hours in the morning," he said. "Very little money at first."

"So don't pay me the first month and see if it works out," I said. I felt my creative juices flowing in a way they hadn't in a long time.

"I'd have to pay you something. Minimum wage at least, but would you be interested in selling advertising for the station? Maybe we could put some kind of bundles together for the magazine and the radio," Dick suggested.

"That's an interesting idea. When are you looking to start this?" I asked.

"Late April," he said.

"I'll be on the road with my daughter, traveling cross country to a giant music festival after LAFF," I said.

"That sounds great. You could call in from wherever you are in America and do reports," he suggested. He seemed excited about his new project. We agreed to talk about the prospect of me doing something with the station closer to April. Neither of us were going to commit then and there.

As I drove back to the office, feeling really pumped about this new prospect, the universe told me the new path I should follow:

- Once back from the Coachella trip, I'd give the owners of the magazine my notice that I wanted to transition out of the editor/publisher job into something else. It was no longer hyperbole to say the job might be killing me. The magazine was a viable product. I hoped that I could still contribute as a freelance writer and would help with a transition. If it meant Molly coming back as editor, I was fine with it. I just needed to take a giant step back. It was someone else's turn, and I was doing more harm than good.
- If Dick did hire me, I would work the radio show and see what radio ads sales was like and if it could be combined with whatever the magazine would be doing moving forward. Cross synergy between the companies might mean new advertisers and tens of thousands of dollars to each of our bottom lines.

- Make LAFF a true non-profit and make Film Festival Director a year-round job. For most nationally-recognized film festivals, there was at least one full-time, year-round position. I could work ten hours per week or a hundred, depending on what time of year it was. I was on my way to nearly $40,000 in committed sponsorships for 2014, including a couple of national brands, and that was with only a few months of part-time work. If I could work at it year-round and take a 20% commission on sponsorships and 10% commission on tickets sold, I could draw a salary that way.

- After LAFF, I would begin to eat healthy, exercise regularly, and resume my prescribed mental health medication. Once back from Coachella, I'd also start seeing a therapist weekly. I would not allow myself to work more than ten hours in a day, and I would make more time for my family than I had in the last five years. The kids were getting older and my marriage needed work.

Assuming the magazine kept going, I figured I'd be able to conservatively make $5,000 writing stories, make another $5,000 at the radio station, and make $20,000 as LAFF director. I'd probably make more money with each, but I knew I wouldn't do worse—and I'd be physically and mentally healthy for it.

* * *

Corey and I didn't take a paycheck the last week of February, and the magazine charged LAFF $1,000 for advertising to cover printing and payroll. Adriane was doing well, Jim was Jim—which I learned wasn't a terrible thing—and I was just too busy to do much to help turn things around. The April issue we were sending to the printer that was going to be arriving in people's mailboxes in mid-March was delayed about a week to let more money come in the mail. On paper, it was another $20,000 issue, but in reality, it was probably closer to $15,000. It was Issue No. 40, but we hadn't seen a revenue number that bad since Issue No. 2. Despite the fact Issue No. 41 was "Healthy Mind, Healthy Body" it was only currently scheduled at $23,000. I didn't have a lot of hope we were going to get it much past $25,000. The magazine was not going to survive on those numbers very long.

The first week of March, LAFF loaned the magazine a couple thousand dollars. Corey was paid that week, but I wasn't. The following week, there was another loan. Corey missed his check, and I got about half of mine. With each passing day and every trip to the mailbox resulting in a big strikeout, the anxiety of the magazine potentially closing in a few months weighed heavy. I didn't know how to close a magazine. What about the subscribers who bought a year of issues but were only half-done if we closed? What about the advertisers who pre-paid for four ads but we only ran two if we closed? We didn't have the money to give these people refunds.

I'd try to focus on LAFF, which was going to be a success by all counts, but my anxiety over the magazine imploding within the next few months was devouring me. It seemed surreal how it got exponentially worse from day-to-day and week-to-week. At night, I went home and promoted the film festival on Facebook between breaks to drink, watch legal porn (which made a bit of a return after the movies were done being judged), and play online games. There didn't seem any reason to try and save *Lewiston Auburn Magazine* anymore by working eighteen-hour days. Mathematically, I couldn't see us putting out more than three or four more issues unless things took a turn for the better.

I was out of ideas to generate money. The magazine held Sandy and Danielle's former stock as general stock, but I didn't think I'd be able to find anybody stupid enough to buy it to raise funds quickly. The idea of a Kickstarter campaign came to me, but I knew that would be the final nail in the coffin, publicly announcing we were in trouble. I'd rather have died with dignity.

The printer said they'd deliver the April issue on March 20 as long as we had a check of $6,500 for the driver. With a little maneuvering and another loan from LAFF to LA Publishing, I had the money and let the printer know on March 19 that we were all set for delivery the next day. I needed that issue to go out because it was a giant commercial for the film festival. If the issue could get another hundred people to attend LAFF, it would be worth it, though it was pretty blatant how cross-promotional it was.

I picked up Kaden from my parents' house the night of March 19. He liked going there after school to hang out. Did I drive drunk with my son in the car? That night? I don't remember. Probably not. But I had before, and I can't take that back, which really gnaws at me.

That night was one of many when my mother expressed concern for the way I looked.

"You really need to slow down," she said.

"I will after the film festival," I said.

"You look like you're going to die. I'm not kidding. You don't look well at all," she said. "Promise me you'll get some sleep tonight."

"I'll be fine," I said.

Melissa got home after me that night as she still worked in the Portland area. She brought home some groceries, including a Red Bull, which I asked her for almost every night. On the nights she forgot, I became almost irrationally angry and would go to the corner store to buy my own. I had perked up for a few weeks in January and early February because of Coachella and the potential radio job, but now facing the end of the magazine, unsure if there was even going to be a "Healthy Mind, Healthy Body" issue since I knew we'd need $12,000 to $13,000 to cover payroll and printing in the next month, I was in the darkest of days. I should have been taking my medication. That would have made such a difference.

As Melissa cooked dinner, I did a little bit of research on bankruptcy. I needed to know if we could restructure logically since I had a feeling my partners would just want to pull the plug. I didn't get any clear answers and knew I'd need to have a meeting with somebody who could give them to me, but it shouldn't be Marc Roy or Mike Malloy since they might tell the partners what I was wondering about.

That night, when everybody went to bed, I drank an average amount of Red Bull and tequila. I didn't engage in any porn and didn't go on Omegle to try and find women to manipulate. I was just too exhausted. I went to bed around 2 a.m., early by my standards.

Chapter 21

I woke up on Thursday, March 20, 2014, as Melissa and Kat were leaving. School had been delayed a couple of hours for weather, and everybody was getting late starts, so I let Kaden sleep in a bit.

My four and a half hours of sleep was like twelve. I didn't feel as down or freaked as I had the night before and was more open to the idea of bankruptcy. I also knew that if they were going to shut down the magazine, I wasn't going to get in any legal trouble. We'd made sure we were covered in how the corporation was structured. Stepping down might actually make the most sense in convincing everyone to keep the magazine running.

I woke Kaden up, made him toast, and set him up in front of the television while I tackled email at the kitchen table. I was still getting nearly 100 a day and letting it pile up was perpetually a bad habit.

I looked out the window and saw two cars and a van pull up in front of my house. While they were "unmarked," it did not take a genius to recognize they were the police.

People have always asked, "Did you know what they were there for?" No. I knew they were cops, and I had a sense I'd done something wrong, but if you'd given me three guesses, I wouldn't have been correct.

"Joshua Shea, I'm Detective Jason Bosco with the Maine State Police. I have a warrant to search your property."

I looked down at the paper and saw the words "unlawful," "underage," and "pornography" leap out from different parts of the page. I was able to piece together what the rest of the document said on those three keywords. As I let the men into the house, my first two thoughts were: "Oh my God, my life is about to change forever, and Thank God, my life is about to change forever."

I brought them to the rear of the kitchen where Kaden couldn't hear us, and Bosco explained why they were there. I asked if I'd be allowed to bring Kaden to school in ten minutes but was told I wouldn't. I asked if they could escort me. I wasn't going to run, pass a note, or do anything stupid. I just wanted to send my son to school without him being a ball of anxiety. They said they would bring him, and I then just asked them to not divulge details and back me up on what I told him.

"Kaden, these men are with the Maine State Police. I have to help them with an investigation, so I'm not going to have a chance to bring you to school. There's an officer here who is going to be happy to take you, so run upstairs and get ready," I said.

"OK," he said, peeling up the stairs. I asked Bosco to hold off discussing things until Kaden was gone and he had no problem with it. One of the guys brought Kaden to school, and I don't think he thought too much was out of the ordinary.

Bosco asked me to collect all of the computers and devices which could connect to the Internet. I used two iMacs for work, which were the only ones that had been used for any illegal purposes. But, I also had an iPhone, and we had three other laptops in the house which were seized.

"That's it," I said.

"No flash drives?" he asked.

"There's one in the XBox or PlayStation, but I only used the iMacs. There aren't any illegal photos on either right now, anyway," I said, actually forgetting about my folder of screen captures. Nothing I had downloaded months earlier from a torrent site folder was still on a computer.

"I believe you, but we need to do a sweep of the house," he said.

"I understand. Please don't trash it. I promise this is all there is," I said.

One of the officers did a quick sweep of the house while another took the computers and iPhone to the van.

"It's going to help a lot if you tell the truth," Bosco said, telling me that they had been watching my computers since November, five months earlier.

This is the point where you ask for a lawyer. I should have known this, but nobody said it was a formal interview. I'd not been read any Miranda Rights because I wasn't yet under arrest. I thought if I told the truth, it would help. I knew the guy in the van would see that there were folders that started to be downloaded, but that with 98% of the files in those folders, they never were downloaded beyond three or four percent.

Bosco never asked about Omegle, chat rooms, or posing as somebody else, so I didn't volunteer any of that information. I answered their questions for about an hour about my pornography habits before the guy in the van came back. He confirmed almost everything he could recover was partial and unviewable, but said he was able to pull up enough from fragments of what I had completely downloaded and deleted to arrest me.

One of the officers asked me to change into normal clothes as I was still wearing pajamas. Bosco led me outside, where I was arrested. I asked if he could arrest me indoors, but he said no. I still don't know why. He put me in the front seat of his car and told me that since I had no prior convictions and there was no evidence of anything hands-on, my bail would likely be set by the commissioner at $500. He asked if I wanted to use my phone to call anybody to come bail me out.

I called Melissa and said I looked at porn of girls who were under 18, but weren't little kids—and the police found out. I asked her to leave work and get $500 and bring it to the county jail. I knew she'd have to drive from Portland, so it would be a while. On the five-minute ride to the jail, Bosco told me to keep my head up and said in a few years, I'd probably be glad this all happened. I told him in a way I already was, because change was needed. It was just not knowing what the next part was that scared me.

I was brought to the county jail and given an orange jumpsuit. A Sheriff's deputy fingerprinted me and took my mugshot. I have never seen a photo where I look more unhealthy. I had probably not showered for at least a week leading up to it. My skin was blotchy and it looked like sleep hadn't been part of my routine for months despite a hefty four and a half hours the night before.

Until Melissa arrived, I was put into a private holding cell. That was the first time I was able to collect my thoughts in a couple of hours. Immediately, I thought about how disappointed Kat would be about missing our road trip to Coachella and that I'd have to tell her we couldn't make the journey together. I thought about facing Melissa and the kids. Then I thought about my parents and my family's lives moving forward, related to the guy who got caught for having the kiddie porn on his computer. I wondered what school would be like for the kids.

Then I wondered about the film festival. Could it still happen? Forget my labor or my profit. There were all these filmmakers and volunteers. Was there any way for me to step aside? And how big was this all going to be as a news story? I wasn't on the city council anymore. I was a local celebrity, but in the last year, it seemed to have faded, hadn't it? Obviously it would make the newspaper. Was it front page worthy?

The bail commissioner arrived around the same time as Melissa. He had my conditions listed. At first I was to have no contact with anybody under 18, but he amended it so I could be allowed to be around my kids with adult supervision. I was allowed to have a non-Internet friendly cell phone. I was told Melissa paid the money and was waiting out front. I walked out the door of the building, and she was in our Jeep, already running.

"If you want to divorce me, I totally get it," I said.

"I'm not going to do that. Was it little kids?" she asked.

"Of course not. It was older teenage girls," I said.

"That's what I figured. Were you downloading? You know that keeps a record, don't you?" she asked.

To this day, I don't have an answer. Yeah, I know everything that's done on the computer is kept somewhere. You can't do anything on the Internet or on a computer and expect it to not be recorded, no matter how well you think it is deleted or how unimportant you are. I knew that then. I know that now. I didn't know what to say then, and the only answer that makes sense looking back is that I wasn't thinking about the consequences of any actions because I'd let who I was on a mental, intellectual, spiritual, and emotional level rot to a dangerous level.

The jail was just up the street from the magazine office, less than a minute driving. I suggested we stop there briefly so I could tell them I'd be in the news for some charges and not to answer questions if anybody asked. When I got there, only Corey was at his computer.

"Hi," I said, heading to my desk to gather a few things.

"What the fuck did you do?" he asked.

"OK. It was that fast. What do you know?" I asked.

"The *Bangor News* posted a press release forty-five minutes ago, and a reporter from the *Sun Journal* was here about thirty minutes ago. It's all over Facebook," he said.

"So much for controlling the story," I said. "OK, well, don't talk to the media. We'll figure something out later. Call me before you leave."

I got back to the Jeep and looked at Melissa.

"This is going to be big, and this is going to be bad. It's already all over the Internet. The State Police must have sent out a press release the second I was arrested, even before I got to the jail," I said.

"No way. Let's go home," she said.

We made it to the top of our street, but there was a news van in front of my house, so we kept driving. I called my parents and my mother was understandably shaken. I told her we'd be over soon. My grandmother had already called her because the noon news reported on the press release with a live shot from the front of my home.

I don't remember most of what I said to Melissa that day and barely remember the visit to my parents' house. I remember telling the kids, "I looked at some pictures I shouldn't have."

The only other thing I really remember saying to Kat in those first few hours was that our trip to Coachella had to be cancelled. She said she knew and understood, far more sad for me than herself. She has a big heart.

I talked to one person from the media that day, and it was Dan Hartill, one of the reporters from the *Sun Journal,* who came to my door. He and Mark Laflamme would be the only two reporters I'd ever have answered for. Dan covered the film festival for the paper and grew to become as good a friend as you'll make at another publication. I wish we were still in touch.

"Are you OK?" he asked, notebook in hand.

"Everything is off the record," I said.

"Of course, I figured," he said, putting the notebook away. "A lot of people are worried about you back at the office. You must be totally freaked out."

"Yeah, I'm in shock. I know what I was arrested for, but I really can't comprehend it. I don't really know what happens next. It's surreal," I said.

"Do you know what's happening to the film festival?" he asked.

"To be honest, I've barely thought about it. I hope it can happen some way, but I'm not sure how. Because you're my friend and you cover this stuff, you're the one I'll call when I figure things out," I said.

"OK, Good luck, man" he said, offering his hand.

I shook it and said goodbye. He's one of the very few people I ever had closure with.

Corey called, and I invited him over. Melissa and the kids left for a little while.

I tried to tell Corey that I wasn't sure exactly what was going on but knew it had to do with stuff that came onto my computer when I was trying to download software for the film festival. I wasn't ready to tell my story, and he didn't seem to really care whether I was innocent or guilty, which I imagine was how he felt when Donato was first brought up on the arson charges.

"I don't think you should talk to me about this stuff," he said. "I don't really want to know."

I told him I thought that if I just disappeared for a couple of weeks, I could probably quietly come back and help out at the magazine once the initial burst of media exposure died off. It was one of my most naïve thoughts that day.

He was understandably uncomfortable and didn't know what to say. Had I known it was the last time I'd see him alive, I would have told him that he'd been one of my best friends over the previous decade.

That night, my family had to make a mad dash to our bedroom twice when news vans appeared. They'd ring the bell, the dog would stand on the couch and start barking, letting us know when they left by quieting down. Seeing the house, with our dog barking in the window on the 11 p.m. news was unbelievable. The whole day was.

Between dodging media and just trying to stay upright, a phone call came to Melissa's phone from Molly I agreed to take.

"How are you?" she asked.

"I've had better days," I deadpanned.

"I'm sure," she said.

Any hope my old friend was checking in on me was quickly erased.

"The board of LA Publishing had a meeting and decided to terminate you," she said.

"Yeah. OK. That makes sense," I said. It was the best news I'd heard all day.

"Do you know who your lawyer is going to be? We may need to contact them," she said.

"Molly, I don't care about the magazine. I care about what's going on with this situation and my family. I'm getting a criminal lawyer, not a civil one," I said.

"OK, well we're going to put your stuff into a box. You can pick it up tomorrow at 7 p.m. We'll need your keys, the company debit card, and any gift cards you still have."

"OK, I'll see you then," I said.

* * *

The next day, I met my lawyer, David Van Dyke, an acquaintance of my father, for the first time. He was probably twelve years older than me, hair unkempt, but brilliant. He reminded me of myself that way, but clearly he made better decisions which led us to opposite sides of the conference room table. Melissa and my father came to the meeting.

"The first thing we need to establish is if this is a litigation game or if it's a sentencing game," said David.

"It's sentencing," I said. It would have been stupid to try and bring this case to court. I knew I was guilty, and I knew they had the evidence.

"You first need to understand this is going to be a long process. It's March 21, 2014. We want this to last as long as possible. The longer the better. We're going to build a great resume here. We're going to show the judge that here you are a pillar of the community, and you just made a horrible mistake.

There are reasons you made that mistake, and you are going to do everything in your power to fix things and not reoffend," said David.

He said we should cross our fingers the case didn't go federal because mandatory minimum sentencing meant I would do at least five years of prison time. If the charge stayed what it was on a state level, one Class C count of Possession of Underage Sexually Explicit Material, I could be looking at anything from just probation to a year in prison.

"So we're not looking at anything like ten years?" asked Melissa.

"Oh no, no. As long as it stays state and as long as they don't add a ton of charges at the indictment, but like they say, you can indict a ham sandwich. A grand jury is going to indict you. But as long as it stays state, we're going to ask for a long probation with Draconian conditions, and we're going to try to get out of this without jail time."

The first part of building my resume was very necessary, getting back on my medication as quickly as possible. I visited my doctor the same day who prescribed a new cocktail of bipolar meds, and added Ativan, a strong anti-anxiety drug. I was also given the name of Jennifer Wood, a therapist with Blue Willow Counseling in Lewiston. I'd never seen a woman for counseling before but needed someone immediately, so I decided to go with her.

David thought that it was a good idea I seek treatment for alcoholism at an out-of-state rehabilitation facility. I didn't think I really needed it because I didn't believe I was an alcoholic, but thought if it would look good to a judge, I'd go pretend to be somebody with a problem. It would be easy to come out of the program a success and cured with a certificate twenty-eight days later.

I asked David if I should worry about the magazine, and he told me since I held such a small piece of ownership that I could just walk away. Ironically, when we left the meeting, Molly texted Melissa to ask how to get in touch with me. She told Molly to leave us alone, and I'd be by to get my stuff at 7.

David said if he were me, he'd still try to hold the film festival, but I could walk away from that too. With the S-Corp status and lack of assets, there was really no way for anybody to come after me. It was Friday afternoon, and I figured I'd give it the weekend to see if I could save the festival on Monday when things had settled a bit.

Unfortunately, it was a slow news cycle. I was one of the top two or three news stories on most TV newscasts all weekend and in the *Sun Journal*. More unfortunate is that the only "official" information anybody had was from the State Police press release which said almost nothing and had incorrect information, like I had no access to my children. The police assumed what my bail conditions would be and were wrong. Google and the Internet has made it possible for this error to be part of the folklore of this story forever, despite it never being an actual fact.

That night, when I went to get my things at the office, a police officer was waiting at the front door to hand over my box of belongings. I didn't get everything, but then again, they didn't get all my gift cards. I guess we'll call it even. Had I been handling things on their end, I would have let whoever it was come upstairs and get their stuff. Maybe packing it and having the police there is a better way of doing it, but it's impersonal and just lame in my opinion. After everything we'd all been through, having a police officer meet me at the door was insulting, but at least allowed for no awkward interaction.

Molly called Melissa's phone on Saturday, and I agreed to take the call when she said it was about the film festival. The newspaper that morning listed a bunch of filmmakers who bailed, and it was becoming clear that I couldn't have any connection to a festival that was supposed to start in less than two weeks.

"If there was a group of us who wanted to hold the film festival, would you let us and sign a waiver saying that you wouldn't sue us?" asked Molly.

I didn't need to know anything else.

"No, I wouldn't," I said, knowing it would be a shadow of what I had planned and would just drag my name through the media mud again.

"OK, I just wanted to check," she said.

A day or two later, there were news stories that a group including Molly, Sandy, and Chip Morrison were trying to save the festival, but they concluded they couldn't. Sandy was quoted as saying it was because I was the only one with knowledge of the festival's finances and Chip said people didn't want to be associated with a festival with my name. I found it ironic that some of my former film festival partners were so quick to point out to anybody who would listen that LAFF was a for-profit venture, yet they stayed extremely silent about the matter when they had a piece of the pie. It was never non-profit, and more ironically, all said and done, they did better financially from it than me.

Ramsey Tripp, director of *The Peloton Project*, called me on Sunday and first asked how I was feeling and was genuinely concerned. I don't know exactly how he got the number, but he was one of the only people who wasn't all about business and I didn't feel was judging me.

He asked if there was anything he could do to help put on the film festival, and I told him I was going to cancel it since people were bailing. My name was obviously poison, and while you can give the "innocent until proven guilty" rap, it doesn't matter in a case like this. He asked if I'd be willing to hand it over to him and let him try to save it. Since I knew he was a good person at the core, I thought it was the best possible solution. I mentioned thinking it could be some kind of fund raiser for the Franco Center, but I didn't know what that meant exactly. I just wanted the concept to go to the right hands.

I met with Ramsey and Dick Martin, the creative director of the Franco on Monday morning. I told them I couldn't talk about the allegations but had my side of the story which would come out in due time. It was the response David Van Dyke told me to provide people. They treated me so decently that it gave me hope others would in the future. Ramsey said he and Laura Davis wanted to spearhead an effort for a new festival. He said they were inviting others, some who were volunteers on the festival I was doing, and some who were my former partners to help, if I was willing to let it go.

I told Ramsey he could have it because I trusted his judgment and that he should just watch people carefully. That night, the ABC affiliate actually broke into its 5 p.m. broadcast to air a live news conference from the Franco that had Ramsey, Chip, Laura, Sandy, and a couple other people saying that a film festival called Emerge was going to be held in June.

From that point forward, any time a news article or story was aired about the Emerge festival, my name was included along with the words "Child Pornography." I'm sure Laura and Ramsey thought it was overkill as much as I did. They should have been allowed to push forward those first six months without my name constantly interjected into every story.

Chapter 22

My last sip of alcohol was at 11:30 p.m. on March 31, 2014, Pacific Standard Time. It was in the front seat of my brother Patrick's car at a liquor store in Laguna Beach, California. He picked me up at LAX with his fiancée, Nancy. I was told I needed to blow over .08 to have insurance cover the rehab facility that accepted me. It was such horrible coverage I wasn't taking any chances. I wanted to be far away from Maine, but near someone I knew and needed nice weather. Laguna Beach fit the bill. The drink was, appropriately, Red Bull and tequila.

After eight days, I was transferred to the rehab's Palm Springs facility ninety minutes away for my specific alcoholic needs. Ironically, I arrived there just as Coachella was taking place a couple of miles away. Imagine how many hundreds of rehabs there are in America and how many square miles there are in the country. What are the odds that I end up in a facility five miles from where I was going to be with my daughter on that same day? I had a television in my room and local news in Palm Springs had plenty of stories from Coachella. I know it was some sort of penance from the universe.

My sober date is April 1, 2014. I have not had a drink since. My bail conditions and my probation conditions (this book was written while I was on probation) won't allow it. The next day I could legally have a drink is July 29, 2019. It will be the day that the legal part of this ordeal, minus my lifetime on the sex offender registry is over. I will not be celebrating with champagne.

It took about five days for me to be willing to open my mind to the idea I was an alcoholic. Once that happened, it wasn't a long leap before I could fully embrace the disease. I've had it since I started getting my hands on alcohol regularly at fifteen or sixteen. I don't drink like most other people. I wish I learned that before I was thirty-eight.

*   *   *

While I was trying to understand my alcoholism in Palm Springs, Melissa forwarded me a letter from the LA Publishing Board of Directors. It said they had a prospective buyer for the company and demanded that I sign the enclosed document selling my shares for $1. They put together a list of grievances which would be forgotten if I signed, going as far as to rehash the fact I "stole" $400 to pay for heating oil years earlier.

I don't know if this was a scare tactic they came up with on their own, but I know they were aware I was in rehab. The *Sun Journal* ran a story letting everyone know I was seeking treatment because my initial court appearance was delayed. My guess is that they thought their letter would just be ignored and they'd move forward. I've got to believe it was nothing they showed Mike Malloy or Marc Roy. Those guys were too smart for something this amateurish and petty. I didn't take David's advice to just let the magazine go. If they were indeed looking at an offer, I was entitled to a piece of it.

I wrote back and said that I might sign, but I needed to know a few things and forwarded a list of questions about the transition.

As I fully expected, I never heard anything back and never signed anything selling my shares. From what I have gathered, certain assets were sold to a company that wanted to publish another magazine in exchange for assuming specific parts of our debt. I never got the full story.

That magazine, called *Current*, was run by a couple of hip amateurs who created something they wanted to read, and it closed quickly. I don't know if they ever recognized their magazine didn't reflect the real Lewiston and Auburn. It was not a mirror. It reflected something that didn't exist. It also covered Brunswick.

I think we proved a high-quality monthly magazine with good content could work in Central Maine. It just needs a better business infrastructure than I had the capacity to provide.

If I could do it again, though, I have to admit I wouldn't. While the community has some opportunity and is relatively safe, I wish I grew up and raised my family elsewhere. There is a parochialism here that is entrenched and will not change easily, at least not in my lifetime. Despite the PR and marketing to make people think otherwise, this is a community with a vast majority who are not open to new people, new things, and new ideas.

When parents and grandparents lament their children and grandchildren leave the area, it's because opportunity and a non-insular way of thinking happens outside of Androscoggin County. Despite the best efforts of a decent group of well-meaning people—we were among them at the magazine—you're just not going to successfully fight generations of this way of majority thinking. That kind of thinking doesn't foster the vibrant lifestyle a publication like *Lewiston Auburn Magazine* promotes. Businesses that cater to that lifestyle either won't locate here or when they do, fail. People would rather support big-box restaurants than the independent guys. Considering the population, the arts scene is anemic. There is no place to see a movie that isn't a major Hollywood film other than Netflix. That's not going to change anytime soon.

As I was writing this book, a referendum was held to determine if Lewiston and Auburn should merge into one city. It was crushed. The big charge of those opposing was that it was being pushed through by the "elite." This is Lewiston and Auburn, Maine. Elite means having graduated from college and owning a business. It's kind of sad.

The film festival as a proper company also closed with a relative whimper. About a year later, I cleaned out my garage at home of all of the signs, banners, and DVDs from years past. I sold the DVD players on Craigslist for $20 each. I really wish I would have been arrested after the festival in 2014. I think it would have been successful. These days, my parents still use pint glasses and pens with the magazine name on them. I have too many T-shirts promoting the film festival, but there's very little to remind me of either venture in my daily life. It's OK because it doesn't feel like that was my life. It was a life I let get away from me.

* * *

My twenty-eight days in rehab turned into sixty-seven days. It was transformatively awesome. Just before I left for California, my therapist, Jennifer, who I have continued to see since the week I was arrested, told me "Don't just play along. Give it a chance." I'm so glad I followed that advice. I walked out with the foundation to become a different, better person. I've worked on that person every day since.

While there, Patrick visited weekly, and I spent five days living with him and Nancy before I flew home. My relationship with him was made deeper by that experience than it ever would have been otherwise.

I saw a sexual behavioral specialist, Stephen Wolfson, off-campus, in Palm Springs, to begin to deal with some of the issues that were triggered during those last several months before my arrest. He was the one who first suggested a PTSD diagnosis. Those issues were linked to the trauma from my babysitter's home. He helped unlock and facilitate a lot of memories. I continued that work with Jennifer for months upon returning. Both helped me understand PTSD isn't a bullshit military-only diagnosis as I'd thought it was for years. Remembering that trauma, and how it related to me in the present, was not an easy process. I never could have imagined PTSD had a role in the downfall. Looking back, I see it popping up throughout life and am attuned to when it happens now.

Stephen and Jennifer both helped me understand how I developed my survival skills and how I felt they were put in jeopardy during my descent to rock bottom, triggering the PTSD. I didn't help matters by not taking my medication, almost never sleeping, and drinking all the time. Both used the term "the perfect storm," and it's what everybody has called the confluence of events that happened prior to my arrest.

When I returned home from California, I had a rough adjustment but decided to go back to work and try to live life normally while the legal system played things out. I took a job at call center in Saco which allowed me to be anonymous. Since I wasn't convicted of anything yet, I didn't have to admit to anything on the application.

The police eventually found the folder of my screen captures from the Omegle sessions. David told me of the twenty-five or so that I had, police believed three were underage. Along with plenty of delays already happening, this slowed the case down to a crawl. Two of these females, thankfully, were not underage. One however was. She was fourteen. And I was shocked.

There was a picture of her in the discovery files. As I previously mentioned, I had no recollection of her whatsoever, and I don't think most people would guess she was fourteen. Even in my most messed-up state, if a girl told me she was fourteen, I would have kept on clicking away to the next person. I know I would have. Nonetheless, that's not an excuse. What I did was wrong. It was disgusting. The fact there was a time in my life where I let my mental and intellectual health falter to the point where it was permissibly OK that it was even a gray area screams about how sick I was.

But, the discovery of the screen captures deeply complicated what was a simple possession case. Now, I was actually creating the pornography since I was making the captures myself. Because I wasn't telling the victim about it, it was considered exploitation. When I was finally indicted almost a year after being arrested, I had two Class B charges of sexual exploitation of a minor, five Class C charges of possession of sexually explicit material, and five Class D charges of possession of sexually explicit material. Worst case scenario was forty-five years in state prison, and that was if the charges didn't go federal, which they still could at any moment.

When my next court date arrived, as instructed, I entered a not guilty plea to all twelve counts and was once again the top news story, but thankfully the call center workforce is not one that follows TV news. I drove to Saco and acted like nothing happened.

During the months between the initial plea and whatever deal we would be able to work out, I was looking for contact information for Donato online when I stumbled upon an obituary for Corey. He had died two months earlier, and nobody had contacted me about it, which still stings. I don't think I would have had the courage to face all of those people I knew at a memorial service, but it still hurts my feelings nobody tried to contact Melissa to let her know what happened.

It took another six months, but eventually, the charges were reduced to one count of exploitation and two charges of possession, connected to the screen captures folder. Everything involving my downloading of folders was dropped. It all had to do with that one girl and the two screen captures I created of her.

Under state law, the minimum the District Attorney could offer was five years. That was his only offer, and he never sought more. The judge's hands were also tied for the most part. Technically there weren't mandatory minimums because there was a provision in state statute that said the judge could suspend some or all of a sentence if "extraordinary circumstances" were discovered. David pitched to the DA that I plead guilty, but before sentencing, I go off to a sex addiction rehab, then return for a pre-sentence investigation which would give the judge evidence to support a lesser sentence, almost as if a trial took place. The DA had no problem with this arrangement.

So, on May 14, 2015, I walked into court and plead guilty to the three remaining charges. Uttering the word "guilty" in court in front of a judge for such a major crime is a heavy thing to handle.

A few weeks later, I left for seven weeks at Santé Center for Healing outside of Dallas, Texas. It was very different, but just as transformational as my time in California. The depths to which I learned about myself and the connection I made to other sex addicts, alcoholics, drug addicts, and people with eating disorders was deeper than I've made with any group in my life. It was painful and scary to leave.

Rehab is hard to explain. On paper, you wouldn't think putting 25-40 very broken people together in an intense situation around-the-clock would yield positive results—but it does. I've heard the comparison to soldiers in a foxhole in that you bond very hard over this one time and place because nobody else knows what you went through as a group. It also makes trying to be close to your fellow rehab attendees on the outside after the fact almost impossible. Despite trying, I never remained close with rehab friends.

Melissa and the kids put up with a long and hard adjustment period upon my return from both rehabs. You come back ready to be a new person, but you come back to the same people in the same place where things went bad and they don't understand what you've been through. There are also plenty of naysayers. It's tough. I can see why many fail and fall back into their old behaviors. Thankfully, I didn't and that is mostly because of the support of my family, continuing to seek therapy, and taking my medication as prescribed.

The pre-sentence investigation took place in August 2015. That report was handled by the guy who was going to be my probation officer, Jason Taylor. He suggested two years of probation for my crimes. That report, along with all of the other personality and risk assessment testing I'd done, letters from both rehabs, advice from medical professionals I'd seen, certificates of completion from the rehabs, and a video deposition by Wolfson, the sex therapist, was sent to Justice Joyce Wheeler to help decide my case. Since she was only in Androscoggin County once a month, her schedule was tough. In early December, we learned that my sentencing would be January 15, 2016.

* * *

I had a terrific Christmas. With the assistance of my friend Brian, who I tried to launch my first magazine with a dozen years earlier, I'd started freelance writing again. He hooked me up with a few jobs. I was able to save some money and went to the mall with Melissa to do the Christmas shopping for the kids for the first time in years.

The result was a genuine feeling of doing something nice for the right reasons that happens now because of all of the rehab and therapy. It feels damn good. And while so many people were running from me, thinking I was evil, having a friend like Brian return to say, "Hey, we all make mistakes, this doesn't mean you're a bad person" was one of the most important things to ever happen in my life.

One quality, close friend can easily replace the hundreds of strangers I used to court and who now opt to crucify me on social media. It's taken a long time to realize it, but I can now see their praise was as uninformed as their scorn. We live in a time where people like to give you their expert opinion, no matter how little they actually understand. Rehab and therapy have given me the tools so that no matter if it's negative or positive, I don't get invested in what people who don't know me think.

Brian could choose to remember me as an arrogant prick taking his sick wife's money while trying to run *METRO* in 2003, but has let it go. He's 100 times healthier too, having addressed his demons. It's amazing how much two people in recovery can help each other, and he's been one of those pieces of support that I wonder if I would have been as successful if I'd gone without.

After my time in Texas, I asked Melissa to extend an olive branch to Marc Roy, and thankfully he reciprocated. Marc stopped by my parents' house a day or two after I was arrested to see if I was doing OK and dropped a message to Melissa saying I was free to contact him if I ever wanted to talk. I wasn't ready for a long time.

We got together a half-dozen times before I went to jail and I knew there were people in his life who thought he was making the wrong choice continuing a friendship that started when we were both thirteen-years-old.

I made sure to let Marc know that I didn't take his friendship for granted and that the sad excuse for a human being he had dealt with in the last year or two of the magazine had done a lot of work in the stretch that I avoided seeing him.

I wrote letters to a few people, most notably Dan & Sandy, Donato & Belinda, and Peter Rinck & Laura Davis. In each instance, I apologized for disappointing them with my actions and thanked them for everything they had done for me. I sat through a lot of 12-step meetings, and while I don't subscribe to everything they espouse, the idea of not only an amends letter, but a letter of appreciation is one that I like. I wasn't expecting responses so I wasn't disappointed when nobody contacted me.

Sandy texted Melissa right around the time of my sentencing telling her that she could do better than me. It frustrated Melissa, and she didn't tell me about it for a long time. I shrugged it off since I have learned through this experience I can't control the resentments of others. Sandy and I fed off each other's energy, and while it wasn't always positive, I still miss her friendship very much.

Paul ended up in Vermont as Kate got the better job she was looking for. I've never talked to him since he took the check for the film festival. Part of me thinks we could put everything behind us in five minutes and part of me thinks he'd never let things go. Much like the universe threw us back together at my brother's first wedding after not seeing each other for years, I'll let it work its magic again if it's supposed to be that way.

I lost track of what happened to Molly until after I got out of jail. I recently saw an article about a marketing company she works for. I miss putting on a show with her, be it one of our awards dinners for LAFF, or serving as celebrity chefs or something equally goofy at a fundraiser, singing karaoke duets at our Christmas parties, or simply talking to a small group of people. We were a great vaudeville act with a limited shelf life as a publishing team. I think even if finances had been spectacular, we wouldn't have worked together much longer than we did. A long-term personal friendship would never have been maintained.

When I found out Corey died, it had been a year since I talked to him. I honestly don't know if I ever would have spoken to him again had he lived. Getting in touch with me was not easy after my arrest. I not only deactivated my Facebook account, I defriended everybody on it. Melissa deactivated my cell phone number. I ignored my e-mail accounts and left for rehab quickly. I may as well have died, and in many ways, that person did. I think that was for the better.

* * *

I stood before the judge on January 15, 2016, ready to hear my fate, twenty-two months after being arrested, but already knowing I was a different, much healthier person who was ready to be vigilant in making sure his health was the top priority for the rest of his days. It will always be a project, and I will always have to watch diligently for missteps, but most people who knew me before the arrest, but also saw me just before sentencing, said they saw a different guy. I still had the same personality, but it now came with compassion, empathy, and calmness.

I knew whatever sentence I got, I'd be able to handle it, worrying more about Melissa, the kids, and my parents. I was going to get what I deserved. They weren't.

I explained to the judge what happened to me and took full responsibility for my crime, explaining that I was not going to rationalize nor minimize what I did. I gave her my multi-tiered plan to not reoffend including not drinking, a regimented medicine schedule, not running another company, and not falling back into a routine of watching online porn.

When the time came for Justice Wheeler to rule, it was clear she was debating between nine months in county jail and three years in state prison. I got the nine months. Knowing the alternative was a strong possibility, Melissa and my father, who were in the courtroom and testified on my behalf, were happy. David was thrilled with the outcome, and while I hope it's the only time I ever have to use his services, he was a godsend.

The sentence itself was eight years, with all but nine months suspended, and three years of probation, along with lifetime registry on the sex offender list.

Did I get enough time? Too much? Too little? The judge made her decision, and I decided to accept it. I don't argue that I should have got more or less nor do I care about positions others take. It is what it is. Get elected to the Legislature and change the laws if you think it should be more or less.

Unfortunately, social media allows a certain kind of person—many of whom have the most to hide—to scream the loudest without putting anything into perspective. It's like the senator who fights for anti-gay laws, yet gets nailed in an airport bathroom getting hand jobs from a male prostitute. I'm learning in the last few years, those who point fingers and yell the most have the greatest amount to hide.

I don't think what I did makes me evil. I was sick. I think somebody who knowingly sells heroin to a fourteen-year-old is worse, but you don't get as good a headline with that story. As a politician, suggesting the state put the heroin dealer on a list for the rest of their life doesn't get the votes that supporting a sex offender registry does. I think if I qualify to be on a watch list, anybody who abuses or neglects a child in any way also deserves to be there, but I'll fight that battle another day.

I met so many people in rehab and jail who made dumb mistakes. I met very few truly evil people. Most people just aren't getting the mental health attention they need. I don't minimize or rationalize their crimes any more or less than I do mine. We all made heinous errors in judgment for different reasons. But in most cases, they were exactly that: Mistakes. Some are minor. Some are major. Some deserve long prison terms. That doesn't mean they are bad people. There are plenty of bad people who never spend a day in jail. I don't think your character is necessarily tied to your relationship with the correctional system.

I had a one-week stay before I had to report to jail. Thankfully, I was able to enjoy time with Melissa, Kaden, Katrielle, and my parents. I also spent time with Brian and Marc. It was telling that two friends I had a dozen years earlier would be the two I knew I could count on to be there when I got out of jail. Nobody I'd acquired as a "friend" during the magazine or film festival years would be waiting to get coffee with me upon release.

While I thought the media coverage was almost always fair, it was my old friend Mark Laflamme who penned the only article that ever humanized me, the day after I was sentenced. He talked about waiting for me to angrily deny all charges when they first came out, but that day never came.

In the column, he mentioned that he and I had met a couple times the week before I was arrested because I was trying to convince him to do a Q&A with the magazine for our next issue. I don't remember meeting with him once, but I don't doubt it happened. There's a lot I don't remember. I have a feeling most of it I don't want to remember.

Melissa dropped me off at 8:30 a.m. on Friday, January 22, 2016, at Androscoggin County Jail. The first thing I did was look out the tiny window in the pod I was placed in with a dozen other men. There was Auburn City Hall. There was Rinck Advertising. There was Marc's old office. There was my bank. I could almost see Gritty's and the building that was the magazine's last office. Thankfully a tree blocked that view.

I used to rule that world, I thought. In nine months, I'm going to be grateful just to be a part of it.

Epilogue

I was released after serving six months and six days, on Melissa's birthday, July 28, 2016. Between "good time" and a job cleaning the pod, almost three months were knocked off my sentence.

What ifs plagued me for a long time after the arrest. What If I could go back to my brother Patrick's wedding rehearsal dinner in Virginia, and Paul was not there? Would any of this have happened? It's hard to say. What if I went back and gave Melissa and my kids the love and attention they deserved during the first two years of the magazine's existence? Would I have made the same mistakes? Maybe. Maybe not. What if I had hired a bookkeeper from Day One? What if I hadn't started the Lewiston Auburn Film Festival? What if? What if? What if?

Until I got deep into therapy, only after hundreds of hours of one-on-one and group sessions was I able to answer the "What If" that plagued me the most: What if I can't forgive myself and move on? The ironic answer was to stop trying to hopelessly figure out the What Ifs. As many have said, mine was a "perfect storm" formula of bad decisions and personal demons coming home to roost at the same time. My energy is better spent making sure it doesn't happen again.

When I was in the midst of my sickness, I didn't sleep well. I didn't eat well. I did nothing well. Had I continued on that road, even without the illegal pornography, I don't think I would be alive now. I didn't take care of myself and my health, especially my mental health, deteriorating to a point that I wasn't making in-character, rational decisions. The police intervention probably saved my life. Now, I sleep just fine. It took several years and almost full-time attention to fix the deep, infected open wound. Now, it's a nasty scar. It's a scar I see and beat myself up a little bit for daily. But as for slumber, once I was caught, I immediately began to sleep well.

I was barely alive and am thankful in many ways March 20, 2014, took place to shake me out of where I was. I entered jail a mentally and physically healthier person than I've ever been. Between the rehabs, therapists, other professionals I worked with and personal work I've done, I've had the luxury of deeply examining my life and health that most people never get. Today, I live with plenty of regret and shame, but I live with a clarity and sense of peace I never thought possible.

I left a trail of victims and not just the obvious ones—the females I took advantage of on the computer or my close family and friends. I've tried to make amends with them. I also caused pain for so many people, from readers, to filmmakers, to advertisers, to co-workers, to acquaintances. I'm truly sorry. After I was arrested, I put myself into exile because of deep, deep shame. It's still there, but it's time for me to at least apologize for hurting anybody—emotionally, monetarily, or any other way—because of my actions. I inflicted a lot of damage on a lot of people, and it did not, nor does not, go unnoticed. I'm sorry.

I'm going to continue to tell my story of addiction. I think hearing from somebody in my situation versus a clinical psychologist could have been a bit of a wake-up call before I went completely off the deep end. I've got to create something positive out of my experience and hopefully help a few people and cause there to be a few less victims in the world. I started a website to tell my story and hopefully be a source of hope for others at www. RecoveringPornAddict.com

There are always going to be those who hate me. I have reluctantly come to accept I can't manipulate them back into my good graces, nor should I try. Letting go of what they think of me has been freeing. And no matter what any detractors think, they should know it's not going to stop me from trying to make things right.

Acknowledgments

I've been writing about my life professionally for over twenty years now but never thought I'd write this kind of story. There are many people who deserve credit for what you're holding now.

First and foremost, my wife and children. They stuck by my side through the most trying section of my life, and I know I caused some of the most trying moments of theirs. I love you Melissa, Katrielle, and Kaden.

My parents deserve just as much credit. Their support of my recovery has saved my life in multiple ways. I will be forever in your debt, and I love you.

My brother Patrick, and his wife Nancy, stood by my side when I really needed it. I think this experience brought us closer together. Thank you for looking at an early draft of this book.

The two people I consider my closest friends, Brian and Marc, never let their friendship waver during my recovery, and were a huge part of regaining my health. Thank you both for the help you provided on this book. It would not be where it is today without either of you, and neither would I.

Thank you to all the people I shared a pod with at Androscoggin County Jail for letting me spend all my time relatively unbothered writing the first draft while I was incarcerated. I hope that whatever brought you there has been changed for the better.

My main therapy providers, Jennifer Wood and Scott Efland, continually encouraged me to tell my story. Their advice, guidance, and ability to recognize when to shut up and just let me babble has been key to my recovery.

Finally, John Paul Owles at Joshua Tree Publishing deserves a nod for being the first publisher to see beyond the many labels people have put on me and giving me the opportunity to share how I turned so many lives upside down. Other publishers were scared. You were not. Thank you.

About the Author

Joshua Shea is a freelance writer and former magazine publisher from Auburn, Maine.

Shea was born and raised in Lewiston, Maine, and started working in journalism at seventeen years old in 1993 for his hometown newspaper, *The Sun Journal*. Having caught the news bug, he worked his way up the ladder at various newspapers throughout New England over the next fourteen years serving as both a writer and editor along the way.

In late 2009, he launched *Lewiston Auburn Magazine*, the first lifestyle magazine of its kind in central Maine. A little more than a year later, he helped create the Lewiston Auburn Film Festival, also the first of its kind in central Maine. Shortly thereafter, he captured a spot on the Auburn City Council, where he served for two years.

Now several years into recovery, Shea works mainly as a ghostwriter for corporate clients. While he has written numerous books for others (or under a pen name), **The Addiction Nobody Talks About** is both his first memoir and long-form book published under his real name.

He has one wife, two children, two dogs, and four cats.

Shea operates **RecoveringPornAddict.com**, where he provides information about pornography addiction. You may contact him through that website.

ML 6/18